# Whi[illegible]
# M[illegible]lims Are
# Repenting,
# the West is
# Capitulating to
# the Radicals



Raphael Israeli

Strategic Book Publishing and Rights Co.

Strategic Book Publishing and Rights Co., LLC
USA
www.sbpra.net



ISBN: 978-1-68235-773-6

# Contents

# Apologia and Acknowledgments

The world is ablaze: a war in Ukraine without an exit in the horizon, fateful collateral Russian menaces on the adjoining Scandinavia, the Baltics and the Balkans, and the danger of a mammoth nuclear disaster amidst the fighting; Iran going nuclear with no one to arrest her imperial ambitions in Middle Eastern locations controlled by radical Islam; famine spreading like an epidemic in Ethiopia and other poor lands in the customary pattern of the rich getting richer and the poor making more children and then taunting the West for failing to feed them, while in neighboring Somalia, the Shabab launch yet another terrorist onslaught against tourist, and at the same time that Iran uses its Islamic Jihad and Hizbullah proxies to kindle fire in the Middle East; Western Europe starved for energy and shackled by her enslavement to Russian supplies, and the loss of its will to stand up and fight back; Afghanistan, with its 40 million hostages, half of them oppressed and enslaved women under the Taliban regime; unrest in more countries than there are peaceful ones, some of them, like in the Sahara, Nigeria, Mali, Libya, Lebanon, Yemen, Somalia, Pakistan and Kashmir, the Arabian Peninsula and the Middle East, due to the grip of radical Islam which has been watching in the aisles for such chaotic world to develop in order to restore its lost strongholds in ISIS, al-Al-Qa'ida and Boko Haram territory so as to make new headway when possible; some of the turbulent Muslim communities in the West, which are determined to reject Western values and impose their own, as demonstrated by the dismal failure of the multi-decade American (and Western) effort to impose their model of rule in Iraq and Afghanistan; and the current retreat of the US (and the helplessness of weakened and disoriented Europe) from the world scene which accepts, by failing to counter and deter the Russian expansionism in Europe, the Chinese provocative stance in the Orient, and the Iranian ambitions of Tehran in the Middle East, backed by nuclear and ballistic incapacitation, all ideal conditions for radical Muslims' growth, cannot help but facilitate the fulfillment of their dreams and blueprint.

Beginning in the 2000s, many Muslim moderates, first those writing from the safety of the West and having internalized the meaning of tolerance and coexistence the Western way, such as Boualem Sansal, the audacious Algerian intellectual, who dared to launch onslaughts on Islamic radicalism[1] and who became a famous French writer[2] in his own right; and then, gradually, courageous Muslims in the moderate Muslim countries which leaned toward the West and elected to do away with extreme religious fanaticism[3], as evidenced in the Abrahamic Pacts between Israel and the Gulf States (later accrued by Morocco)[4]; and finally even some hardcore Islamic regimes, like Saudi Arabia and Sudan showing signs of mollifying, mainly due to American influence or pressure, or due to local strategic or economic developments. Remain, however the

[1] Boualem Salsal, *Gouverner au nom d'Allah:Islamization et Soif de Pouvoir dans le Monde Arabe,* Gallimard, Paris, 2013.

[2] During the revived Salman Rushdie crisis, when this Indian Muslim writer was stabbed in New York during a public address, 33 years subsequent to the infamous *fatwa* that was issued against him for his *Satanic Verses*, by Ayatullah Khomeini shortly before his death in 1989, Salsal wrote: "La fatwa de l'Iran contre Salman Rushdie attente à toute l'humanité" (Iran's fatwa against Salman Rushdie amounts to a life attempt against all humanity) *Le Figaro*, 20 August, 2022.

[3] R. Israeli, *Paranoia, Inferiority Complex and Fanaticism: The Case of Islamic Attitudes Towards Jews,* Strategic Books, TX, 2018.

[4] See R. Israeli, *Glittering Stars in a Dark Landscape,* Strategic Books, TX, 2020.

intractable diehard Muslims, both Shi'ite and Sunnite, like Iran and Afghanistan respectively, which however castigated an shunned internationally, would always land back on their radical feet, and the transnational radical Muslim movements, like al-Qa'ida and ISIS, who inconvertibly resurge here and there, like phenixes when defeated, with new Chiefs in the style of Imams, Ayatullahs or Caliphs, when their predecessors are killed or otherwise removed from control. Two issues must be clarified in this context: Why are we talking of moderate vs radical Muslims and not of radical Islam or "Islamism"? And how these differentiate in their long term prospects? The long-held myth of two kinds of Islam: that of the well-meaning moderate majority and that of the violent radical "Islamism" must be deconstructed, for the Muslim Believers themselves do not recognize this distinction. There is one Islam, united under one *umma* which upholds and defends the five Pillars (*arkan*), the same and only Allah and His Messenger, the same Holy Book and Hadith, and the *shari'ah* emanating therefrom, with the four Schools (*madhahib*-Hanbalite, Malikite, Shafi'ite and Hanafite) inter-recognizing each other, and only the Shi'ites dissenting. The radical Muslims, who interact and usually accept other Muslims, only differ from the bulk in the degree and rapidity of the implementation of the tenets of their faith. Both share the ideal of the ultimate Islamic takeover of the world, but the moderates realize that it is unfeasible and have reconciled to the notion of equality between nations in international relations, while the diehards insist, against all odds, in defiance to others' convictions and notwithstanding all obstacles, to fight incessantly in Jihad (which is not one of the Five Pillars), like the Prophet in his time, regardless of the sacrifices, the ordeals and the setbacks he incurred, until triumphal Islam prevails. These two branches of behavioral (not theological) Islam occasionally accuse each other of being "un-Islamic" or even "anti-Islamic", but except for satisfying their passion for argument and debate, and show the world their opposition to the deeds of their rivals/competitors for public opinion, little is to be imputed to the essence of that debate. For the moderates, by dubbing the others "fanatics" and "un-Islamic", they tag themselves by inference as the "true Muslims" and reasonable "moderates"; for the radicals, it is a means to claim Islamic legitimacy, while accusing the others as incontrovertible "heretics" who "who have sold out" to Western values ("Westoxication"), thus deserving to be toppled and replaced by the "true Muslims".

Even the ultimate blueprint for the triumph of Islam (because it is not a question of compromise, reconciliation or accommodation with other creeds) is ideally shared, for the moderates remaining an apocalyptic dream for the end of times, when Islam triumphs universally, and in the meantime avoiding conflict with others and maintaining good neighborliness, while the radicals cannot wait to implement it here and now, violently if need be, using the good old way of Jihad, followed by the Prophet himself, to either spread Islam by *da'wa* (propaganda/missionary work- a proposition agreed by all Muslims), through immigration and penetration of others' territory (a strategy also followed by all Muslims), failing which, fighting asymmetrical wars, as venerated Sheikh Yussuf Qaradawi counsels, and radical movements (ISIS, al-Qa'ida, Hizbullah, Hamas, Islamic Jihad, Boko Haram, Shabaab, Laskar-e-Tayibah and others) and radical regimes (Iran, Afghanistan, and at times Libya, Sudan, Yemen and Somalia), practice. Radical movements also govern the great advantage over radical states, of acting outside national territories and not in their name or within their jurisdiction, so they cannot be held responsible in the world system of nation states which is prevailing internationally. Therefore, these movements have developed appropriate plans for their confrontation with the West, which they are confident they can defeat (like they did to Soviet Communism in Afghanistan in the 1980s and Western Capitalism in Iraq and Afghanistan in the 2000s) by their persistent Jihadi struggle which excels in operation without contaminating itself with the burden of responsibility and the chastisement of reprisal. The masses are usually supportive of these unnamed popular efforts to beat the West, especially when they register success, which is imputed to Allah's direct assistance to the Islamic cause. The particulars of this blueprint, which have been culled from various radical Muslim writings and declarations, and from the rapid pace of conquest and expansion of Islam when it sprang out of Arabia in the 7th Century, and in no time had come to encompass much of the civilized medieval world, have been elaborated upon elsewhere[5].

This volume, like all my previous work of the last half century, has been facilitated by my home base at the Truman Institute for the Advancement of Peace at Hebrew University in Jerusalem, to which I am immensely grateful. But the responsibility for all the errors of style or interpretation that may have befallen this text, remain exclusively mine.

Jerusalem, Summer and Fall, 2022

[5] See R. Israeli, *Islamikaze: Manifestations of Islamic Martyrology*, Frank Cass, London, 2003, pp. 443-447. The concept of Islamikaze (the combination of Islam and Kamikaze (the Japanese pilots of the Pacific War in the 1940s, who sacrificed themselves by crushing their planes on American warships), are one of the lethal weapons chosen by some Islamic radical movements (that are dubbed in the West "suicide bombers"), to fight their enemies without leaving any trace of their "nationality" or claiming any other national or territorial affiliation, so as to evade retaliation.

# Introduction

## *The State of Islam in the Tri-Polar World*

In the Summer of 2014, a previously marginal organization that few had heard about, headed by an obscure self-declared cleric-warrior that no one had paid attention to, suddenly erupted into public consciousness, first in the Middle East, then in the rest of the world, when it began to make amazingly successful inroads into vast parts of chaotic Syria and Iraq, and then as it launched deadly attacks on non-Muslims that came under its jurisdiction, and began to execute Westerners who happened to venture into the territories under its control. Only then, did world public opinion realize that that was a Sunni Muslim gathering of fanatics, led by cleric Baghdadi and self-named "*Da'ish*" (ISIS- the Islamic State of Iraq and Syria), which was intent on spreading its rule by the force of conquest in those critical areas of the Middle East. That movement, which made stunningly rapid gains in those areas of the Arab world, and in so doing attracted volunteer youth from the Muslim world as well as from the West (as well as Israel), soon came up with the assertion that it was aiming at establishing a caliphate, harking back to the ideal mode of government that had been prevailing in the post-Prophetic Islamic world (after AD 632, when the Prophet died) and until the fall of the Ottoman Empire at the end of W W I (1914-8). One became necessarily intrigued by the many questions that were raised, seeking to understand what made that petty Muslim cleric to aspire so high as to wish to declare himself a Caliph ? Who were his followers, what was the secret of his sweeping success, and what were his chances to succeed?

For any keen observer of the Muslim world the comparison was compelling to the rise of the Taliban in Afghanistan in the 1990's, where taking advantage of the chaotic situation generated by the lasting civil war and the devastation it inflicted, a local cleric, Mullah Omar, followed at first by his *madrasah* students (Taliban) in the religious center of Qandahar, took control of that city and then of all of Afghanistan. There too, thousands of volunteers had flocked from most Islamic countries, financed by Saudi Arabia and trained by the CIA, who were seeking to defeat the Soviet power which had invaded the country on Xmas Day of 1979, arguably "upon the invitation of its government". After the Soviets were routed and retreated (1989), a civil war had erupted between the warrying factions for the control of the country, which only added more destruction and disunity to that unfortunate land of conflict and dissent. The emergence of the Taliban on the scene was the main factor which reunited the country, imposed a similitude of government, enforced "peace" and order under a very strict puritanical regime (1996-2001), until the American incursion in 2001, in the wake of the September 11 attack on the US by al-Qa'ida, which was given refuge by the Taliban, removed it from power (but not from existence). There are so many parallels between the two situations, notably the American intervention, aided by some of its NATO allies, in both, that it is tempting to probe the similarities and the differences between the two, and perhaps try to draw some lessons from the American fiasco in both cases. The major differences between the conditions in which these wars were being, or have been lost by the Americans, are already clear nonetheless: The Americans were attracted to Afghanistan in order to defeat the Soviets there at the height of the Cold War, and then they were compelled by the September 11 (2001) events to turn against Afghanistan and Iraq and to try to install a Western style democracy there. While seeming initially successful, they ultimately proved that they could operate only in the respective capitals of those countries (Kabul and Baghdad),and even that under American guns, but the deep countryside in both countries remained outside the American pale, and was adamant to stay under harsh Islamic rule, which after a decade or two defeated the Americans and their allies and forced them to retreat in disgrace. In Iraq and in Afghanistan, where they had invested thousands of lives and hundreds of billions of dollars, in two decades of fighting and reconstruction, and in a genuine attempt to let Western democracy take root, the half-hearted or openly hostile response of most of the conservative Muslim population, except the liberated women and a handful of genuine human rights reformers, which was directed not only against the self-appointed Western liberators, who were treated as invaders, but also to their and their agents' attempts to impose the new order, ended up in dismal failure.

Already in the late 1980s and 1990s, both worldwide and within local Islamic communities, did not stop stunning the incredulous and increasingly suspicious world public opinion who watched, with a mixture of fear, doubt, uncertainty, awe, and hope, such a parade of successive happenings in the world of Islam that were revolutionizing our universe, but of which the powers- that- be seemed helpless to change the course. While in the West the great concerns were focused on the dwindling of the Cold War, the Gulf wars and the primacy of the United States in the emerging unipolar world, on the other side of the ideological aisle, there were the two giant Communist civilizations: the Soviet and the Chinese, which were undergoing shattering processes of change, each in its own style and pace. In the Soviet Union, Mikhail Gorbachev, the general secretary of his powerful Communist Party, who had experienced several confrontations with President Ronald Reagan over the Star

War and who had also signaled his intention for opening up to the West and to liberalized reforms, was elected president (May 25, 1989). He launched his *glasnost* (transparency) policy, which meant a relative freedom of the citizenry to speak their minds, allowing Western media to be present in Soviet cities and talk to frustrated and critical Soviet citizens. But the economy was lagging behind, since *perestroika* (restructuring) would begin only later and would take time. In the meantime, the *konsum* government stores presented empty shelves, though the dissatisfied citizens could now complain freely to the Western media in Gorky Park and other central venues where the populace experienced want high inflation and no consumer goods to have. That signaled that the Communist economic system, which rested on a thin layer of a veneer of appearances, had started to crack. A bitter humor began to develop, claiming that what New York and Moscow had in common was that in both nothing could be bought for rubles. Neither did the humiliating withdrawal of the Soviets from Afghanistan in that year help to enhance the Soviet dwindling prestige. The taste of freedom, accompanied by the feeling in Eastern Europe that the Soviet superpower could and would no longer interfere by force in its satellite countries as it had done in Hungary (1956) and Czechoslovakia (1968), began to cause those satellites to dare to peel away, like the layers of an onion, from the visibly weakened carcass of what was once the Soviet Empire: first the outer layer of members of the Warsaw Pact (Poland, East Germany, Romania, Hungary, Bulgaria, and Czechoslovakia) and Outer Mongolia, then the second layer of the fifteen "federated" members of the Soviet Union: the Baltics (Estonia, Lithuania, and Latvia), Moldova, the five Muslim republics of Central Asia (Kazakhstan, Kyrgyzstan, Uzbekistan, Turkmenistan, and Tajikistan), the Caucasus (Armenia, Georgia, and Azerbaijan), and finally Belarus and the Ukraine, the latter still experiencing in our days the lingering effects emanating from the shattering of that vast empire into pieces. Russia, the extant body of what was the Soviet Union, remains a weakened, though still threatening, grumpy neighbor trying to rebuild its lost stature and prestige. To top it all, on November 11, 1989, the Berlin Wall fell, and the process of unification of Germany on the one hand and of dismantling the Cold War structure on the other began. For the Islamic world, the net gain was the addition to the world of Islam of six new countries, the five of Central Asia and oil rich Azerbaijan, the Caspian Sea strategic neighbor of Iran.

By contrast, China, with the diminutive but dominant Deng Xiaoping at the helm in the post-Mao era, learned from the Russian fiasco and preceded restructuring to transparency; namely, it eliminated economic socialism, allowed private property, and encouraged capitalist development, but maintained a heavy fist on political liberties by continuing to champion the "dictatorship of the proletariat," which held the monopoly on power in the hands of the Communist Party. Unlike the Soviets, who had layers to shed and were forced by their satellites to do so, the Chinese, who had not been defeated or humiliated in any foreign venture, continued to profess from time immemorial the concept of a unitarian state, in which power stemmed from one center. There are cultural "autonomies" in various parts of China, but no idea of federation has ever crossed their minds. The Tibetans and the Uighurs in Xinjiang understood that, much as they would have liked to secede and accede to some sort of semi-independence, the Chinese system would not allow it. Therefore, economic reform and development was the only legitimate channel of change to which all the people of China could aspire. That pattern has indeed made China a world powerhouse of economic growth, manufacturing, technology, innovation, trade, and financing and has arguably produced such a level of contentment and national pride among the populace that major civilian unrest has been averted so far. The September–October 2014 unrest in Hong Kong, due to Beijing's announced intent to interfere in the promised democratic system ("one state, two systems") when the former British colony reverted to Chinese control in 1997, may signal a change of that orientation, that was reinforced and confirmed in the Presidency for life of Xi Jingping and his BAR (Belt and Road) concept of his international relations, which also meant the transcendence of China as a world power from merely in economics into the political and military spheres. In November of 1989, Deng Xiaoping, the progenitor of the Second Chinese Revolution, which put China back on the capitalistic road of prosperity, resigned the leadership of his country and passed the helm to the younger generation of leaders. He is remembered as the man whose two figurative slogans had turned his country around. The first was that "it was not important whether the cat was black or white, as long as it caught mice." That put to rest the old debate that had been launched by Mao and celebrated during the Cultural Revolution (1966–76), giving precedence to the ideologues (the party commissars who served at all levels of society and the military) over the experts (the professionals, engineers, and managers who had the talent and the skill to obtain rational results from the available resources. The second slogan was "When you open windows some mosquitoes might get in," which showed an understanding toward the problems of unemployment (breaking the "iron rice bowl" principle), urbanization, inflation, massive migration to the urban centers in search of work, the unprecedented growing gap between the new tycoons (it was no longer shameful to get rich) and the poor rural population, and the visible differences in the pace and depth of development between the booming coastal areas and the backward interior. The Islamic world "discovered" in the wake of China's opening to the world, another new territory of oppressed Islam- the Uighurs- who had been hidden in the mysteriously remote vast Xinjiang Province, which found itself in the immediate neighborhood of the newly liberated Islamic countries of Central Asia, which revived its own Islamic sentiment and activity.

In the Islamic world at large, the great events of those years centered on the towering figure of Ayatollah (the Sign of God) Ruhollah (the Spirit of God) Khomeini, the founding father of the Islamic Revolution in Iran and the great innovator of Shi'ite doctrine. In contrast with the four prevailing schools of law in the Sunna, which encompass about 90 percent of the 1.5 billion Muslims in the world and whose laws are fixed and immutable since their savior had been the Prophet Muhammad, the Seal of the Prophets, and no one after him was expected to reveal himself to humanity, the Shi'ites live in permanent expectation of the revelation of the Hidden Imam. This means that if in the Sunna the ideal utopia has already happened in the past, from which we can only keep distancing ourselves as the years and centuries revolve, in the Shi'a hope is placed in the return of the Hidden Imam in some indefinite future, in order to produce universal prosperity, justice, and happiness for all humanity. The great luminaries of the Sunna usually counsel their followers to submit to the incumbent rule under which they live, even if it is not satisfactory to their religious taste, for a bad ruler is always superior to chaos, for in disorder no Islamic tenets can be operated. The Shi'ite scholars, on the contrary, have always been rebellious, especially when they were not in power. This restlessness, which has always been tinged with messianic and utopian elements, has lent to the Shi'a the characteristics that we today identify in Muslim restlessness and unrest. Therefore, the Islamic Revolution that we witnessed in 1978–79 in Iran, which was intended for exportation—indicating its universal and messianic import—must be seen as the precursor of the Islamist uprising, because it professed the exact goal that the current Muslim rebellions and radical revolts proclaim today: to remove the present illegitimate tyrant and establish in his stead a just Islamic order (like the Islamic parties in Turkey, Egypt, Morocco, Tunisia, Syria, Yemen, Somalia and others that all have this element of *revival* and *justice* in their very names), which will precipitate the coming of the

Imam Mahdi (the Guided Imam, the corresponding term in the Sunna to the Hidden Imam in the Shi'a). The fact that this dream has not yet come to pass does not reflect negatively on the missed and unfulfilled utopia; quite the contrary: the longer the waiting, the more acute its sense of urgency and imminence. There were many attempts made by Sunnite doctors of the Holy Law to invite the Shi'a to join the Islamic consensus by turning it into a fifth school of law, with the intent of unifying all currents of Islam and putting an end to its internal debates. But the Shi'a always rejected the preconditions of the union, for had it joined the consensus, it would have had to renounce during the Friday prayer the denunciation of the first three caliphs for having usurped the caliphate from Ali, the sole heir of the Prophet who deserved it, according to Shi'ite belief. It is evident that the Shi'ites would not accept that position, since Ali and his descendants were the central figures in their narrative of Islamic history, and their acceptance of Ali as fourth in the apostolic succession of the Prophet would mean admission and recognition that Ali was not wronged, and therefore there was no harm to redress. Conversely, the entire Shi'ite martyrology is founded on the suffering inflicted upon Ali and his children by the two people they loathe most— the first Umayyad caliph, Mu'awiyah, and his son-successor, Yazid—who have become in Iran the paradigm of oppression and injustice for having murdered Ali and his sons together with their retinues. The Sunna, on the contrary, will not accept the Shi'ites' hatred of the three first "righteous" (*Rashidun*) caliphs as usurpers, disrespecting and cursing them accordingly. The Shi'ites would not renounce the special status of Ali in Islam as the cousin of the Prophet and his son-in-law, while in the eyes of the Sunnites all four first caliphs deserve the title of righteous, are equal in status, and are all second only to the Prophet, who was the most perfect of all humans, designated by Allah as his last messenger. When Ayatollah Khomeini declared his Islamic Revolution in Tehran in 1979, he tried to gather the Sunnite–Shi'ite rift under the umbrella of the world Islamic revolution that he was professing, as he intended to spread it to the entire world and sweep in its path all Muslim peoples. He thought that his revolution would overshadow all the theological differences that looked insignificant in his eyes, compared to the great unifying themes of revolutionary Islam. He indeed had some success—when he harnessed non-Shi'ite Syria, Shi'ite Hezbollah in Lebanon, Palestinian Sunnite radicals, and Sunnite Sudan to his purposes—and turned Tehran into an international center of terror that attracted other fanatic movements, including Sunnite Hamas, and Islamic Jihad.

Ayatollah Khomeini also changed the doctrine of the Shi'a. He had begun to develop his revolutionary ideas under the shah's Iran, and acted audaciously and creatively when one considers his élan, his out-of-the-box thinking, and the far-reaching political consequences that ensued. The first thoughts that Khomeini started to develop cost him, inter alia, fifteen years (1963–78) of exile in Najaf, Iraq, one of the holy places of the Shi'a because it was the site where Ali, the first imam is buried. It was there that Khomeini brought to completion and published his *Islamic Revolution,* in which he outlined his positions and plan of action, a sort of *Mein Kampf* that he was to implement step-by-step. He was then compelled to leave Iraq by Saddam, who had sealed an agreement with the shah on the border between the two countries in the middle of the mighty Shatt al-Arab, where the Tigris and the Euphrates converge before they pour into the Persian/Arab Gulf. His main thought that would have appealed to the Muslim crowds today would have been the need to eradicate the bad rulers and to install in their stead Islamic regimes under Shari'a law. Khomeini's Iran was the first to do that, by an Islamic revolution in which the clergy played a crucial part, followed by the Taliban in Afghanistan in the 1990s, and then by Iraq, which, under American tutelage, applied that same principle through a Western-style democracy, which brought the oppressed Shi'ite majority under Saddam to power, much to the chagrin of the Sunnite Arab Gulf states which feared

Iran's Shi'ite power, until the new menace of ISIS appeared on the country's horizon in the 2010s and undid those efforts. Khomeini's doctrine was revolutionary from yet other aspects, because it provided the ideological infrastructure and underpinnings for a new model of rule in which the clergy were actively involved. For him, because the ayatollahs are the supreme sources of knowledge, wisdom, and inspiration, it is only logical that they should also be the rulers—somewhat similar to the prince who is also a philosopher in Greek and Western philosophy. Khomeini developed two concepts that anchored his suggested revolutionary change: *marja' taqlid* (the reference for emulation), which meant that the supreme head of the clergy (*ayatollah uzma*), being also the supreme spiritual power, ought to be the reference that all aspire to emulate, a modern variety of the supreme model of the Prophet that is current in the Sunna; and second—*wilayat al-faqih* (the rule of the jurist), which signified that the wise and knowledgeable cleric ought not only to counsel and guide,but also to rule in practice. These two principles turned the passive state of expectation of the return of the Imam Mahdi, who would bring salvation, into an aggressive initiative to precipitate such a momentous event.

To those familiar with modern Jewish history, this could be comparable to the revolutionary doctrine developed in the 1920s and 1930s by Chief Rabbi Kook in Palestine, whereby it was not enough for Rabbinical Jewry to sit and wait in the Diaspora for the coming of the Messiah to provide redemption, but it had become necessary to rise and practice Zionism by settlement on the land, nation-building, development, and social and political action as an avenue for getting there. Khomeini probably viewed these two concepts as personified in him as a result of his scholarship, his lifelong struggle against the tyranny of the shah, and his spiritual qualities, which made him a *mujtahid* who is thus qualified to continue his innovative *ijtihad* and express the will of the Hidden Imam pending his return. Unlike the Sunna, for whom the gates of *ijtihad* had closed since the passing of the great luminaries, the founders of the four schools of law, by the tenth century, the Shi'ite *mujtahid* had undertaken the task of innovative legislation, through which his verdicts ought to be the law. Hence it was only natural that membership to parliament in Iran was to be assigned to mullahs, who understand the matter of religious legislation and the will of the Hidden Imam. Khomeini wrote that only the mullahs were able to get people out into the streets and motivate them not only to die for Islam, but also to beg that they should be allowed to sacrifice themselves for Islam. When one watches today (2022) the vivid validity of the anti-Salman Rushdie *fatwa* which had been delivered by Khomeini 33 years earlier (in 1989), when a Muslim of Iranian origin tried to stab to death the same Rushdie who had exiled himself to the US in order to escape the Khomeini verdict, one can understand the power and the resolution that characterize Islamic fanatics' determination. Two more famous writers who became victims of this terror found refuge in the US: The Italian Oriana Fallaci who was menaced in her own country for criticizing radical Islam, and Aa'yan Hirshi Ali, the Somalian Muslim refugee who became a member of the Dutch Parliament, but was compelled to run for her life to hide in New York, due to the inability of her adoptive country, just like the impotence of Fallaci's European country, to protect a safe existence to their citizens in the face of Muslim mounting aggression there, though no authoritative fatwa by a prominent Muslim jurist was pronounced against them.

In the present reality where Human Rights as a concept and a policy that most nations pretend to respect and wish to be viewed as such, most moderate Muslims parrot the Western principles of the American and French Revolutions, though in practice most of them fail to implement them[6] and cover up their misdeeds in

[6] R. Israeli, *Human Rights and Human Development in Arab and Islamic Lands*, Strategic Books, TX, 2022.

flowery but duplicitous "Constitutions", which spell out all the proper words of liberalism and freedom, but lend different significance to them[7] in their attempt to bend them to suit the authoritarian regimes of Islam, instead of daring to reform their own undemocratic tradition along Western constitutional ways. However, Americans and Europeans, in their supreme effort to accommodate Muslim countries, after themselves manifestly exhibiting their own failure to democratize the Islamic world, have on the contrary pushed the radical Muslims to the arms of the authoritarian Superpowers, to which resemble much, both in the style of their regimes and in their common hostility to the West, thus provoking an internationally complex, impermeable and intractable world order. In effect, believing that if they meant well, then the entire span of humanity would behave likewise, Westerners did not relent on their delusions, like most recently under the Obama Administration (2008-16) and his followers about the "significant common ground linking America and the Muslim world, which offered a real promise to his mind that working together ["engaging"] with other leading international players [ specifically Muslims] to improve the human condition across the world in general, including the Muslim world, was possible and vital". Improving the human condition is what America's ideals have been all about, for the eternal notions of the American Constitution, that "life, liberty and the pursuit of happiness" are not just hollow words; they embody the ideals that lay at the foundation of America's aspirations, not only for itself but for citizens around the world. Thus, they embraced the idea that human development has broad and highly relevant significance for humanity in general and for the functioning of harmonious international relations. Human development is a concept that embraces

[7] R. Israeli, *Duplicitous Constitutions in Arab and Islamic Lands*, Lambert Academic Press, Dusseldorf, 2022-3.

enhancing the quality of life for the whole world; it encompasses the key dimensions of economics, health, education, human and civil rights, democracy and freedom, all protected by an independent judiciary, and sustained by a high quality of life. But in practice, if America ever had any "common ground" with the Islamic world, it was based on economic and strategic interests (mainly petroleum and military positions during the Cold War, and mainly strategic common grounds presently, as its dependence on foreign oil has dramatically plummeted), never on shared values of democracy, freedom and human rights that radical Islam, and even less radical Westernized Muslim individuals have declared as alien and "hated" in and by their societies. And when the US tried at an exorbitant human and material price to enforce those ideas in Afghanistan and Iraq, it finally realized that its dismal failure to enforce and promote them reflected precisely the lack of such a common ground.

Numerous have been the manifestations of this alienation between the Western world of Human Rights as described above, and the Muslim interpretation and application of its ideas, as amply sampled in the above text. On 9 and 10 November, 1998, the Office of the High Commissioner for Human Rights at the UN, under Mary Robinson, in cooperation with the Islamic Cooperation Conference (OIC), organized at the UN Office in Geneva a seminar, entitled: "Enriching the Universality of Human Rights, Islamic Perspectives on the Universal Declaration of Human Rights", to mark the 50th Anniversary of the Universal Declaration of Human Rights, ostensibly "to promote respect among peoples and a better understanding of the significance of cultural and religious backgrounds in the context of the Universal Declaration. It was said that twenty experts in Islamic Law and Human Rights were selected by the Hight Commissioner, in consultation with the OIC, though no final resolutions or conclusions were expected from that august gathering, due to its "academic character". Thus, all the High Commissioner could conclude was that "it had opened a channel of communication and indicated her intention of publishing the proceedings of the seminar", which was finally done in a shortened version owing to "lack of resources".[8] Mary Robinson, like President Obama, highlighted the Greatness of Islam and its immense contribution to the dialogue between civilizations and to the building based on respect of human rights of the global civilization based on respect for human rights…We all know "the greatness of Islam and its civilizations and its immense contribution to the richness of human experience…through the profound belief and of the Muslim religious theology…It has shown itself to be universal in nature and has the dignity of the human person, tolerance and equity at the core of the message… It was in this context that I was happy to accept the invitation of the Foreign Minister of Islamic Republic of Iran to facilitate a process of preparing Islamic commentaries on the Universal Declaration, and today's seminar is a key element in that process.[9]"

The three themes that were discussed (rather "preached" by the Muslim participants), were the principle of non-discrimination, civil and political rights, and economic, social and economic rights in Islam. But, due to Robinson's commitment to preserve the "scholarly objective" nature of the speeches, the discussion was limited only to the invited experts (all Muslims). In her ignorance of Islam and her extreme desire to please and avoid controversy within the rules of political correctness, she defied the totally contradictory statements of those experts and rendered a disservice to the cause of human rights by legitimizing the revolting Islamic version of "human rights" as a worthy topic of discussion on the international stage. Did she not hear, or understand, the repeated statements of Iranian officials, including at the UN, of their wish to wipe Israel

[8] UN Document-.HR/IP/SEM/1999/1 (Part I), 15 March, 1999.
[9] Ibid.

from map? Did she not see the murderous horrors that the radicals of al-Qaida committed all across the world? Did not she identify the cruelty and oppression that many Islamic regimes were practicing against their own civilians while she was praising its greatness, tolerance and contributions to humanity? Was she ignorant of her next door neighbor to her UN Palace in Geneva Bat Ye'or's numerous books on the enslaved Christians and Jews under Islam[10]? If she had persisted in her job until 2022 she would have had to resign in disgrace when she took cognizance of the new specific studies of human rights in Islam.[11]

The other attempt of the Obama Administration at engagement with a Muslim power was done when it thought that an agreed deal with Iran, to limit and supervise its nuclearization program, would contain, or at least slow down its pace, has proven futile, unwittingly aided by President Trump's (2016-20) determination to scuttle that deal altogether and better rely on harsh, and growingly harsher, economic sanctions. Both of them ignored or simply were ignorant of the ideological foundations of the regime of the Ayatullahs which hates, despises and is committed to resist any Westernization ("Westoxication" in their parlance) or reform which would obviate or weaken their "Death to America(and Israel)" slogan which seemed to endure as the most solid and consistent base of their rule. Both strategies were a priori doomed to failure due to the Shi'ite doctrine of the Hidden Imam which governs that regime, and came to its most brutal expression during the eight years of President Ahmadinejad, who came to see and present it not only as an apocalyptic vision or traditional belief in the end of times when the Hidden Imam will appear and bring justice and plenty to all humanity, but as an imminent divine program of action to be

---

[10] *The Dhimmi, the Decline of Eastern Christianity under Islam, Eurabia, Islam and Dhimmitude* are only a few samples.

[11] Israeli,Raphael *The Rebellion of the Dhimmis; Human Rights and Human development in Islam,* both published by Strategic Books, TX, in 2022.

implemented under our very eyes. As a former Mayor of Tehran, that president, who had no clerical pretentions himself, seemed to be in constant expectation of fulfilling that prophecy in his own days, as the "pangs of the Messiah" indicated to his deluding mind, namely that the more pressing and worsening earthly conditions in the world, the nearer the realization of that day of relief and redemption for the Shi'ite world. According to that logic, bad or disastrous events were the surest signs of imminent messianic days, hence the vanity of the logic behind the great powers' balance of power, which was at the base of MAD (Mutually Assured Destruction) which alone prevented a new world war, each power being deterred from attacking or threatening the other by reason of their mutual capacity to annihilate the other in case of a nuclear conflict. Therefore, under the spell of that theory, owning nuclear power or being threatened by it, far from deterring the Ayatullahs in Tehran, on the contrary augmented their creed in the imminence of apocalyptic days, which under that scheme would invalidate MAD and make it obsolete and unnecessary. He and his coreligionists were firm in their belief that it was precisely that threat of annihilation which augured the return if the Imam, i.e. that the worse was the best, the darkest was the most promising.

The recent rise of China to the rank of a world power, first economically but then also militarily; first regionally in the Pacific Rim and then also in the Middle East and Africa; and also gradually in its worldwide Belt and Road project, and especially due to its rapprochement to Russia by reason of its rising tensions with the US and association with Putin's war against Ukraine (winter 2022), which results in his confrontation with NATO and the West in general, a tectonic change has been in the making in the international relations and the inter-faith tensions, pitting Islam not only against Christianity and Judaism, as described above; but also imposing on it to rethink its attitudes, positions and choices no longer between the Capitalist and Christian West and the formerly

Communist and Orthodox East, but also towards Eastern Asia and its dominant powers of the Confucian tradition: China, Japan, Korea, Vietnam and its economic "tigers" of Taiwan and Singapore, in which neither Christianity nor Islam have been preponderant and where the historical burden of *dhimmitude* had never counted. According to a recent account of the American Foreign Policy Council[12], the great changes threatening East Asia, both domestic and external, where the world center of gravity has been shifting in recent decades, including World Islam, whose two thirds of its numbers are Asia, will probably also affect the world balance of power, in various locations, not only due to the rapidly deteriorating relations between the Super powers in the wake of the Ukraine War but also by reason of the rise of Germany once again as a military power on the one hand and China's impressive show of force in the Pacific as well as in space on the other.

In the heyday of the Cold War, the two world blocs were pitted against each other: the West, with the United States, Western Europe, and several regional alliances, arrayed against the Soviet Bloc, with its on-again, off-again Communist allies, including China, Yugoslavia, Albania, Vietnam and North Korea. The members of the Warsaw Pact countered the West on a standstill deterrence governed by MAD (mutually assured destruction) that was based on mutual nuclear threats of extermination many times over. But already in the 1950s Tito's Yugoslavia took its separate path toward a more humane Communism, and the Sino-Soviet rift was occasioned by a more doctrinaire Chinese separatism that did not accept the Americano-Soviet path of coexistence amid the Cold War. That meant that each of the three powers could not converse with the other two, and this in fact turned the world into a tripolar competition, though admittedly China was the less competitive and

---

[12] Eisenman (ed.), China Reform Monitor 1496, February 23, 2022, Washington DC.

the less potent of the three. The collapse of Communism, which had momentarily allowed the world system to be dominated by the United States, has caused since 1989 the emergence of the tripolar world once again, with Russia, under Vladimir Putin, reasserting its place as a world power and China, with the engine of its spectacular economic success, emerging as a third leg in this new tripod of the world order. All three now converse with each other and even engage in diplomacy concerning several world problems, but the potential for rivalry and even for confrontation between them continues to increase. The tripolar world is being constructed not only as a consequence of the 1989 watershed in the world of Islam, [13] but is also dramatically influenced by it. Except for the Crimea and Ukraine crisis, which erupted in 2014 and scarred the US–Russia collaborative efforts, until it escalated into the Ukraine War in February 2022, most of the other topics of disagreement between those two powers have either emanated from the radicalized Islamic world of post-1989 or remained linked to it in the long run. China's rifts with the West in the United Nations and other diplomatic arenas, while generally supportive of the Russians because of their common pro-Arab/Islamic policies, have strictly toed the line of their particular interests, especially in the economic and energy domains. While each component of the power tripod has its own axe to grind, there is no doubt that they all looked for areas of convergence with each other, for it is always easier, cheaper, and more expedient to achieve a goal by agreement rather than under duress and amid controversy where the contending parties may have to sustain the payment of high prices. For example, Russia, who has consistently supported the Assad regime in Syria in order to defend its own naval bases in the Latakia area, has deployed tremendous efforts to prevail on their client to dismantle its chemical weapons

---

[13] R. Israeli, *Years of Upheaval: Axial Changes in Islam in 1989,* Transaction, NJ, 2016.

arsenal under the threat of American military intervention, rather than see Assad and his regime crumble and be taken over by the rebels. The most powerful of those rebels are radical Muslims from various denominations who are not likely to embrace Russia as an ally should they gain the upper hand. The Russians prefer to keep Assad in power rather than line up with his enemies. On the other hand, other Muslim radicals who are fighting on Assad's side, such as the Iranians and their Hezbollah clients, certainly feel blessed by Russia's support of them, as a superpower umbrella ensures the continued flow of arms from Russia and its unflinching diplomatic backing in international fora.

Two icons had been sustaining the structure of this world order: the consensual myths of the awe from the "international Community" and the fear of disturbing the "sacrosanct stability" lest the maintenance of the world balance be jeopardized. And both tenets were violated in the Ronald Reagan era (1981-9) as the Soviet power dwindled, and he dubbed it the "evil Empire" and urged it to tear down the Berlin Wall. For he realized that the Communist power, which had tied together Eastern Europe as a vassal of Moscow, was no longer worth of maintenance, and he launched the "Star War" which finally exhausted the Communist regimes which could not sustain it economically and were bankrupted. The distinction finally dawned on the West that the "stability" that the communist regimes and their peers in the authoritarian Islamic world, were negative and unsustainable, therefore called for their destruction, and that only free democracies provided a model of positive stability worth pursuing. In this situation of fragmentation and then break between the two major blocs, the entire idea of "international community", which was maintained by the prevailing equilibrium between East and West and saw to it that most nations shunned any international or transnational move that may upset the existing balance as reflecting a "silent" international consensus not to be disturbed (like altering international borders as they were set, agreed and accepted post W W II). With the newly established distinction between good and bad stability, the one worth encouraging and the other necessary to undermine, as the illusory stability was dismantled, "the international Community" was also dissolved, for the world returned to its fragmented self-interested blocs which sought each to fulfill its interest, each pitted against all the rest, and alliances started to coalesce and pulverize with the motion of a hand or the blink of one eye (the American Secretary of State under the Biden Administration is advisedly Blinken): Russia goes against Ukraine, once its closest ally and the cradle of its own civilization, bitter rivals US and Iran recording a historical return to the broken (in 2018) of the Nuclear Agreement of 2015; Gulf state who had acted in unison with the Palestinians for 70 years (that was a "negative stability"), opened their air space for Israeli air-traffic and for amiable relations. Old Turkish intimacy with Israel in the 1990s turned into enmity with the rise of Erdogan and his Islamic Party in the 2000s, and back again when new strategic and economic interests erupted. One can no longer find traces of the famous "international community", whose putative "common will" judgement was feared.

The Ukraine War seems to have brought that gradual deterioration to its summum as it overturned all when the bare nerves of the Powers' most existential interests came into the open. Due to its energy constraints, China has also backed Iran on the Syrian front and resisted any attempt to condemn it or impose sanctions against it, in spite of the ongoing massacres that were committed against the Syrians by their government and vice versa. Worse, in its desperate attempts to lay its hand on future sources of energy wherever it can find them, China has even allied with the fugitive war criminal former President Omar al-Bashir of Sudan, who was indicted by the International Court in the Hague for the massacres in Darfur, in return for the rights to search for petroleum there. Also, in the context of energy thirst and strategic pursuits, China has adopted a reverse policy of fighting radical Islam in its own territory in the rebellious northwestern province of Xinjiang, where the Uighur population has been in effervescence since the 1980s. This is an example to what length China, like other powers, is prepared to go in dealing with post-1989 Islam, for the sake of advancing its perceived national interests. The Uighur unrest has also provoked China to improve its relations with long-term rival India, which has also suffered from Islam both domestically and in the adjoining controversial territory of Kashmir, in spite of its traditional alliance with Muslim Pakistan, which has also been under the sway of Taliban and Lashkar-e-Taiba, both radical Muslim movements. The Chinese rapprochement to Russia even prior to the Ukraine War was probably also motivated by the enormous nearby Russian resources in petroleum and gas of Siberia. The Western boycott of Russia in the wake of the war could only strengthen the hand of China as an alternative customer.

Until the Ukraine crisis of 2014, the United States and Russia, under weak and hesitant Obama and militant and vindictive Putin, respectively, had gone into a pattern of dealing with their most urgent frictions in Europe and the Middle East by discussing them peacefully, if not resolving them. All this while the United States has been disengaging from its expensive wars in Iraq and Afghanistan, from the Arab-Israeli conflict, and from the Arab Spring that turned Islamic Winter, while also turning its attention to the Pacific Rim, specifically to China, Korea, and the local conflicts in the South and East China Sea. But as long as the Middle East kept burning and the Arab Spring raging, the Russians were welcome junior partners to the US in various peace processes as long as they were perceived as weak, and they could be therefore made members of the inanimate "Quartet," that club of impotent powers that has achieved nothing so far, and when any achievement appeared on the horizon, it was the Americans alone who negotiated it and dealt with it. For the other participants it was merely geared to maintain an eye set on the "political and diplomatic horizon," realizing full well that the "horizon" referred to an "imaginary line that ran farther away every time one seemed to reach it". But Russia, which has been entrenched in Iran and its proxy Syria, has been trying to reopen the doors of other Arab countries by posing itself as an alternative to disappointing America, which seemed to be resolved to abandon involvement in the Middle East. Indeed, after the United States relinquished its old ally, Hosni Mubarak of Egypt, and supported the Muslim Brothers instead, those who unseated him elected one of theirs, President Mursi; and then President Sisi who overturned Mursi, was chastised by having part of the American aid to Egypt suspended, so Egypt turned to Russia for compensation. The Saudis, who were furious at the United States both for abandoning Mubarak and embracing Mursi, and for the United States' failure to rein in the frantic Iranian effort to nuclearize, also began to talk with the Russians to create some compensating counterbalance. But even in that forum of P5+1, in which the three-polar super powers are supposed to collaborate on the Iranian nuclear program, a clear dichotomy is noticeable: the four Western participants are trying, more or less genuinely, to arrest Iran's race to the bomb, while Russia and China are being more lenient and protective toward it. The apparent abandonment by the US of Israel in that context, has forced her and the Arab Gulf countries which are most threatened by Iran, to draw together and form an alliance.

The War in Ukraine has perhaps altered all that too, with Biden's US reorientation toward the Far East, and shift towards NATO and Europe which could not be publicly resisted by Russia, who may have even regarded that change of emphasis as relieving her from the US rivalry in the Middle East. But China's considerations are different. She has been considering the American presence in the West Pacific as a penetration into her sphere of influence and a direct threat to her, something like 1930s Japan, who had resented far-away America as an impediment to her building the Asian

Co-Prosperity Sphere, which she thought belonged exclusively to her by right and nature. Japan has in the meantime turned from rival to ally of the United States, and China from ally of the United States, when under Japanese occupation, into a rival that now contends for hegemony, out of her natural desire to translate her vast economic power into a political and strategic advantage. The stakes are high: not only does she have a vital interest in defending the islands in the South and East China Sea, which are also claimed by Japan, Korea, Vietnam, Taiwan, and the Philippines, but she also can revive and sustain her old revendications of Taiwan now that she is also military capable of substantiating them.

First and foremost among those claims is Taiwan, the American supported dissident province that since the rise of Communist China in 1949 has posited a direct challenge to Beijing under the title of the Republic of China, based in Taipei and claiming sovereignty over the entire Chinese subcontinent. During the Cold War, the Taiwan Straits had been one of the most dangerous places in the world, with the American Seventh Fleet poised to defend the nationalist regime, which had placed its military outposts right on the islands of Quemoy and Matsu in the bay facing the Chinese mainland. But since President Nixon's visit to China in 1972 and the establishment of diplomatic relations with Beijing in 1979, the United States has relaxed its tight embargo on the China coast, and the relationship between the two countries has gradually improved, always at the expense of Taiwan. Sino-American relations have grown considerably, with the Chinese economy booming at the breakneck pace of approximately 10 percent a year in average for the past thirty years, and the American economy shrinking to the crisis ebb of 2008. That reversed the economic balance of power in the world: no longer was poor and backward China dependent on the United States' wealth and generosity to feed its own people, but it was the United States in crisis who needed the Chinese economy to wean itself out of the crisis. This reversed dependency inevitably raised the prestige of China in the world as a vast economic system, and correspondingly weakened the United States' stature. There were four major consequences to the reversal: one, the Chinese gamut of choices was noticeably diversified; two, the United States' options were narrowed; three, China has begun to upgrade its military stature to bring it to par with her economic and diplomatic successes; and four, China embarked on a more vigorous campaign to reinforce its grip on Xinjiang in view of its strategic and energy-wealthy resources.

Since China's first attempts to reach out to Israel for military and farming technology in the 1980s, which were kept under wraps due to China's fears of damaging its vast relations with the Muslim world, things have evolved. Israel's expert technical abilities in those two domains, which permitted China to upgrade its weaponry and agricultural output without undertaking any unbearable expenses that she did not have, have opened new opportunities for both parties to meet each other's needs without compromising much. China has continued to support the PLO and established diplomatic and commercial relations with almost the entire gamut of Muslim countries, while at the same time cultivating secret contacts and an advanced technical collaboration with Israel; in other words, Israel was for China a desirable concubine with whom a relationship was maintained as long as it was discreet. Israel, which unlike other Western nations, did not attach any strings to her aid program, found it expedient to impact Chinese military, economic, and agricultural development, pending the establishment of diplomatic relations sometime in the future. That happened in 1992, and within a few years the two countries' scope of collaboration had surpassed the thirty-year-long Sino-Arab trade relationship. By 1992, China had begun to understand that relations with Israel did not necessarily preclude good relationships with the Arabs or other Muslims. Twenty years after those relations were erected and despite the extraordinary intimacy they have achieved over the years until the AWACS crisis erupted[14], none of the Arab and Muslim countries have rescinded their relations with China. Moreover, China's unquenchable thirst for more sources of energy has produced an unusually close relationship between Beijing and Tehran and caused further Chinese inroads in East Africa, where sizeable Muslim populations dwell, including Darfur (Sudan), South Sudan, Ethiopia, Tanzania, Kenya, and others. Israel's accessibility to China was allowed because it was too small and too insignificant to impose human rights respect, as America and some Western powers had done for a time.

While Chinese relations around the world continue to prosper, the United States' failure in some Muslim states, notably Iraq and Afghanistan; its abandonment of its trusted clients in Muslim countries such as Tunisia, Egypt, and Yemen; and especially its helplessness in the face of the Iranians' race to the bomb, which it will end up accepting, have generated a vast estrangement of the United States among its most important allies in the Muslim world—Saudi Arabia and the Gulf states—and have raised some doubts in other countries, such as Jordan and Morocco, on the United States' ability to stand beside her allies when the chips are down. Some extremist movements, such as the Muslim Brothers, al-Qa'ida, and Islamic Jihad, have derided Muslim governments who have relied on the United States, comparing its inconsistent conduct with the firm and steady commitment of Russia to its allies, such as Syria, come what may. Concerning the issue of China's upgrading its military capacities in order to assert its dominion in the oceans that surround it, several contradictions have emerged, as in the best tradition of Maoist ideology. On the one hand, it was Israel that ran to the succor of China since February 1979's rout of its forces on the Vietnamese border by enabling China to upgrade

[14] Galia Lavi, "Interview with Y. Schihor: American Interests Affect the Changes in Israel-China Relations", *Special Report of INSS* (Israeli Institute of Strategic Studies), Tel-Aviv University, Aug.8, 2022.

its military equipment without incurring unbearable and unaffordable outlays in foreign currency, and keeping the affair under wraps in order not to raise the wrath of the Muslim world. On the other hand, exactly when Sino-Israeli relations were reaching the climax of intimacy in the mid-1990s, the Falcon/ AWACS crisis came about, which forced Israel to cancel the deal and pay damages to the frustrated Chinese for violating the contract with them, thus threatening the very relations between the two countries, which had been slowly, secretly, and painstakingly built over the previous decade. It became evident that when the United States and China were put on the scale, US-dependent Israel had no choice but to conform to the US line, after it was threatened by its closest friends in Congress that they could not countenance that deal, which was based on Boeing platforms stuffed with Israeli electronics and would have yielded the most advanced early-warning systems to the Chinese in the Pacific, thus posing a threat to American national security there. As regards the embarrassing internal problem of the Uighurs which has caused international outrage against China, and especially in parts of Islamic world, the Chinese concept of a unitary state ruled from one center, reinforced by the modern notions of sovereignty and effective rule, and by its strategic and economic importance, has rendered Xinjiang every bit an integral part of the Chinese homeland as every other province of China, including Tibet. Even the fact that the latest transmutation of the Turkic Uighurs had made some of them zealous Muslims, did not convince the Chinese to categorize them on that basis, since the only differentiation between peoples they knew was ethnic, not religious. So, as there were Hui Muslims in China proper, there were Uighur, Kazakh, Dungan, Kyrgyz, and other minority groups who believed in Islam in East Turkestan. But unlike the cultural autonomy promised to its minorities by the People's Republic, the Chinese state not only oppressed any sign of religious, linguistic, or ethnic autonomy but—due to Xinjiang's strategic importance—it intensified the settlement of Han youth in the province to dilute Uighur aspirations and frustrate their newfound nationalistic enthusiasm. The Uighurs then realized that not only could they not follow the example of their nearby compatriots (Kazakh, Kyrgyz, Tajik), who had been released from the Soviet yoke and become independent, but they were now bound to see their limited autonomy shrinking further in Beijing's attempt to choke separatism. The Uighurs were now outnumbered by the Han in their own province and many of them had been settled throughout China, to the point that they felt strangers in their own country, and their youth were being encouraged to seek work in Chinese big cities. Thus, dilution worked both ways, but the Uighur presence throughout China would also facilitate their subversive antigovernment acts, as the 2013–14 bombings in Beijing and Kunming attested, and as the Chechnians in Russia had caused much trouble in Moscow when it attempted to crush their quest for independence.

In this light (or rather obscurity) the current Uighur problem should be regarded as an international issue between the Han majority and the Uighur minority and not simply as a Chinese domestic issue. For, in spite of the lack of any chance for the Uighurs to achieve any sort of separation, or even a meaningful autonomy, their enthusiasm for self-determination did not wane. Second, there is evidence that the rebels received some aid, and not only spiritual, from other Muslims who regarded their struggle as an extension of the universal Islamic aspiration to assert itself and of the impact of the success of Islam in Afghanistan and of the independent Central Asian states. Indeed, Uighur riots have been triggered not only by Chinese oppression but also by the atmosphere of Islamic victory, first against godless Soviet Communism in Afghanistan and then against oppressive Western imperialism in Iraq and Afghanistan, and now against the rising second Communist superpower that has been trying to overwhelm them. The rebels certainly understood that, like their Tibetan counterparts, they stood no chance at bringing China to its knees. Their incapacity to posit a real challenge to China would nonetheless continue to kindle their hopeless enthusiasm, encouraged by the Uighur diasporas in the West and by Islamic bodies like al-Qa'ida and ISIS. The Uighur crisis in China rapidly overflowed into a wide array of Chinese interests, both with the Islamic world and the wider world in general, as part of those axial years of the 1990's Islamic successes and beyond. The Uighur protest escalated from a minor incident in Guangdong in 2007 to a demonstration of 3,000 Uighurs, including many high school and college students, in Xinjiang that summer. The riots turned violent, and the events reverberated throughout the world media as "breaking news," in spite of the Chinese information firewall that attempted to contain it, then to minimize it, and finally to justify it by explaining their circumstances. And though more Han people were victims of these events than Uighurs, the latter were inevitably conceived as the oppressed underdogs and treated by world media accordingly. Exiled Uighurs around the world, not only within China itself, propagated the outcry of the oppressed, magnifying it in the larger context of demands for an advanced autonomy, and even independence, occasionally conjuring up the Tibetan plight, which had garnered sympathy and criticism of the Han majority a year earlier. This context was also convenient for the comparison between Rebiya Kadeer, the exiled leader of the Muslim Uighurs and president of the World Uighur Congress, and the moribund though popular Dalai Lama[15].

China's plight in the face of the danger of increasing world Muslim protest in the future against her Xinjiang policy was dramatized by its apologetic response to the "Maghribi Al-Qaida" (AQIM) threat to take revenge on China for the death of 46 Muslim Uighurs in Urumqi. No mention was made in that threat, as in its threats

[15] Jane Macartney, "Rebiya Kadeer Accused of Being behind Uighur Violence in East Turkestan," *The Times,* July 7, 2009.

against Israel or the United States, of the 136 Han Chinese who had perished in those riots, or of the offenses the Muslims had themselves committed to generate the confrontations that brought about those fatalities. Threats were also made of retaliation against the large numbers of Chinese employed in Saudi Arabia and other parts of the Middle East and North Africa[16].It urged "to chop off their heads in their work places or in their homes, to tell them that the time of enslaving Muslims had gone." This was the first time that any al-Qa'ida group had threatened China and its interests so directly and so boldly. In fact, in June 2009, the al-Qa'ida branch in North Africa (AQIM) was reported to have ambushed an Algerian security team that protected a Chinese construction project and killed as many as twenty-four guards. It has also been noted that increased chatter on the Internet among active jihadists indicated that information was sought about Chinese interests in the Muslim world for targeting purposes, claiming to avenge the perceived injustices in Xinjiang.[17]

In this maze of international relations, where everyone is involved with everyone else and ideologies stand in opposition to immediate economic or political interests, the Israeli-Arab relations have also been changing rapidly, with Israel still leaning heavily on American support, but at the same time maintaining a dialogue with Russia, despite the latter's raising so much indignation worldwide for its onslaught against Ukraine. It also preserves its solid relations with China and India, both of which have resented American and NATO's intervention on the Ukraine's side of the war. Israel has also recently widened its alliance with pro-Western Sunni Arabs in Egypt and the Gulf, as well as revived its contacts with Turkey which, while a member of NATO and a permanent aspirant for joining the EU, has until recently strongly supported the Muslim

---

[16] In Algeria alone there were some 50,000 Chinese workers.

[17] See Malcolm Moore, *Daily Telegraph,* July 14, 2009. See also Jane Macartney, *Times Online,* July 14, 2009.

Brothers ideologically in conformity with Erdogan's lifelong firm religious convictions that have not certainly changed overnight. Iran's nuclearization, which for Israel and its new Arab allies is the main existential issue which brings them together and preoccupies them as their top priority, is not viewed by the US and NATO members as their main concern, and they are eager to relegate it to the second plan, the first one being Europe's security for the EU members and their energy needs, and perhaps third for the US after China (and the Pacific Rim in general), and then Russia's rivalry and the fate of the Ukraine. According to the analysis of former Israeli Intelligence general, Yossi Kuperwasser[18], if Iran decides to enrich its current stock of uranium into a military grade, within four months it could have enough for four nuclear devices. So, while in the prolonged Vienna round of nuclear negotiations (2021-2), the U.S. could have pressured Iran to renounce the dangerous advances it has made to produce nuclear weapons, and demanded a much better agreement through a combination of sanctions and a credible threat to use force, there are indications that the U.S. has surrendered to Iranian demands on relieving sanctions, due to its apparent new concentration focused on conflicts with Russia and China. The consolidation of Iran's position is not seen as a threat significant enough for the US administration to mobilize to thwart it. At the same time, however, while American leaders declare their commitment to preventing Iran from acquiring nuclear weapons, and they delude themselves that a return to the agreement will contribute to this, in practice, the new envisaged arrangement paves a safe path for Iran to becoming a nuclear power. Thus, if the agreement does go into effect, Israel will have to advance a covert campaign to thwart Iran's nuclear program. If, in the immediate term, Iran will slightly back away from the nuclear

---

[18] *Yossi* Kuperwasser, *The Jerusalem Issue Brief, Vol. 22, No. 5, March 21, 2022,* the Jerusalem Center for Public Affairs

threshold, Israel must use this additional time to develop the ability to thwart Iran's nuclear program. This in itself, while solidifying its links with the Sunni Arabs, might create tensions with the US that Israeli can ill-afford.

In spite of the widening base of Israel's expedient relationship with the Arab Sunnis, backed by the West, the rapprochement is rarely felt among the Arab populations, since many of them are still deeply haunted by the conspiracy theories that had been pumped into their heads for four generations since the birth of Israel, about its evil nature which merits its complete annihilation, and about its perceived support by the Christian West, which Muslims believe is historically doomed to lose its hegemony to the resurging Islam. The Islamic mistreatment of the *dhimmi*s has been revived by resurgent Islam, and nourishing the anti-Israel and anti-Western sentiment, both clerical and nationalist, political and popular, to the point of openly defying the Arab governments who have yielded to the *Realpolitik* of crafting a Middle Eastern alliance of interests between Israeli Jews and Arab and Turkish Sunnite Muslims, to stand fast against the Shi'ite Muslims of the Persians and their allies in Syria, Lebanon and Yemen. By simply scanning through the press and broadcasts, not to speak of the sermons in mosques throughout the Islamic world, both Sunnite and Shi'ite, one wonders whether the promise of peace that the growing pro-Western and pro-Israel alliances that the Abraham alliances have inspired, just like the previous peace treaties that Israel had signed decades ago with Egypt (1979) and Jordan (1994), stand any chance of piercing through the opaque Islamic wall.

# Chapter One

## *Repenting Moderate Muslims Coming Back to Reason*

Years prior to the stunning breakthrough effected in 2020 by the Arab Gulf states, with American encouragement, courageous Arab and Muslim individual intellectuals, who either lived in the West or in the rare Muslim countries which tolerated a limited and controlled dissent, an occasional daring article appeared in the media criticizing the Arab traditional consensus against the US and Israel.[19] Especially viewed against the background of the hefty volume of hatred, poison and lies poured daily on Jews, Zionism and Israel in the Islamic media[20], the enlightened, even sympathetic sentiments exhibited by those "glittering stars" seemed quite extraordinary, especially when we bear in mind the very harsh chastisement some of those daring dissidents incurred in Arab and Islamic lands. The open breakthrough unfolded in 2016, when a series of extremely favorable articles appeared in the Saudi media[21], the most negative and harsh towards Israel hitherto. They could not have been published without permission from the authorities (political but religiously inspired), probably triggered by American pressure and MBS (Muhammad Ben Salman), the apparent heir to the old Sultan and

---

[19] R. Israeli, *Glittering Stars in a Dark Landscape,* Strategic Books, TX, 2021

[20] R. Israeli, *Hatred, Lies and Violence in the Islamic World,* Transaction, NJ, 2013

[21] R. Israeli, *Paranoia, Inferiority Complex and Fanaticism*, Strategic Books, TX, 2018.

the instigator of some major reforms in the Kingdom, aimed at opening it up to the world, though tinged with some very "undemocratic" deeds bordering on the criminal. Though the Prince still hesitates to repent totally on his country's previous fanatic hostility towards the Jews and Israel, there is little doubt that it is only thanks to his passive consent that Saudi Arabia's skies have opened to Israeli flights and the rapidly building up relations between Israel and some Gulf States have been made possible.

As has been expected throughout world history, there is always a gap, more or less wide, between the ambitions and aims of a nation as well as its individual members on the one hand, and the actual achievements they attain in real life. But in the case of Zionism, this abused adage is double-edged: it can be considered negatively due to the centennial systematic frustration of all attempts of Zionism to attain recognition from the Arabs of its rights for resettling on its ancient land; but it must also be regarded positively when assessed on the merit of its legendary growth, development in population and economy, and in scientific, medical, technological, and especially hi-tech achievements, which launched it from a poor, almost desolate, besieged and menaced country, deprived of means of survival, within the space of two generations, into a well-to-do and advanced start-up nation. Moreover, its actual attainments have indeed by far surpassed anything the fathers of Zionism had ever imagined or striven to achieve. But if economically, technologically and even institutionally the new country of Israel has done truly well, despite its constant war situation and domestic challenges, and emerged as a modern democratic state despite its many unsolved problems; on the most crucial issue of its acceptance and recognition of its national and international legitimacy by its Arab neighbors in general, and its bordering countries in particular, a century was to elapse before a kind of so-called "peace arrangement" was formulated, with much left to be desired, and usually at great cost, and always threatening to break apart, so brittle it remained. Never had the achieved "peace" gain the characteristics of a sound and "normal" neighborliness like the one between Belgium and Holland or the US and Canada or Mexico. So much so that when in 2020 the American Administration under President Trump mediated a novel arrangement between Israel and certain Gulf States, which in any case had never been involved directly in hostilities previously, it was talked about and described as "normalization" (in Arabic *Tatbi'*), to contrast with the vehement Arab masses, in Jordan, Egypt and elsewhere, who insisted on their reluctance of *tatbi'* even decades after their countries had signed "peace" treaties with Israel. To lend credence to this general disgust from *tatbi'*, Palestinian notables who are permanently haggling against all the peace proposals since Oslo (1993), have threatened to "boycott" their few Arab kin who had dared to commit the crime of "normalization".

The ethno-nationalist bias in Islam against Western civilization, and especially against Israel, Zionism and Jews, which also connect to the Western regard to human rights in contrast with the Arabs' reservations about them, is only one aspect under which the Arabs wish to appear to act in order to avoid being scrutinized by the West under the seemingly "primitive" "religious war" cloak, so as to appear rather as "modern" "freedom fighters". But, in effect, like it or not, the Arab-Islamic contempt and hatred toward the West and the Jews, draw mainly from religious sources which have pushed the contradictions between them a notch up into intractability. For since the 1920s, the Mufti of Jerusalem, Haj Amin al-Husseini, had consecrated the struggle with the Jews in Palestine as an Islamic one notwithstanding his presentation to the world as a nationalist one in the context of the national awakening of new nations. Modern Arab nationalism, which was kindled upon the breakup of the Ottoman Empire, during W W I, has also founded one of its definitions of Arabism on the language basis, meaning that anyone who was an Arabic speaker was considered Arab, regardless of one's genuine ethnic descent. It is the commonality of the use of the Arabic language, together with its privileged status under the Ottomans and its holiness and the tongue of the Prophet, which consecrated it throughout Islam. So, Arab nationalism has become almost coterminous with Islamic rule, although the contradiction between them has been emerging more and more deliberately as radical Islamic revival gained more territories and populations as we shall see in the next chapter. Because while for Islam, Christianity and Judaism are at best mere revealed creeds, whose followers can be accepted by the Islamic overlords as *dhimmis,* namely "protected" people, adepts of an inferior and aberrant faith, as long as they submit to the Islamic superiority; all the rest, that is pagans and rebelling dhimmis who pretend to have attained sovereignty, independence and equality with Islam are simple "Infidels" whom Muslims are enjoined to fight and subjugate and make them "to pay the *Jizyah* out of hand", or be eliminated. Christians and Jews (namely Westerners) as nations, who defy the Word of Allah by declaring their very existence, simply do not exist, for the world is exclusively divided between Muslims and the Infidels who are in perpetual war with each other until the latter capitulate. The West can emancipate and modernize its laws, and write its human right rules, but the Holy Law of Islam, including its skewed view of human rights, is forever incrusted in stone as the Word of Allah in the Holy Book and therefore immutable. Only a courageous human-conceived and human-applied reform by an iconoclastic and fearless secular leader, the like of Ataturk in modern Turkey, and to a lesser extent of a Habib Bourguiba in Tunisia, and hopefully of young, energetic and visionary MBS, may perhaps perform this miracle, Islamdom has been waiting for.

In some way, even Human Rights and Human Development, which have become the commonly-declared and universally proclaimed hope for beating poverty, disease and ignorance, which widely affect the poor parts of the Islamic world, stand in counter-thesis to Islam, and the more radical-reactionary-restorative and conservative Islam, the less is its inclination to modernize and liberalize itself, and to admit that there can exist a self-operating human and humanitarian mind which can challenge or ignore the Word of Allah. The Muslim countries which have "normalized" with Israel, because of their enlightened or just "interested" leaders have declared so, simply act to the tune of their autocratic leaders who are inspired by modern and Western ideas of public opinion in the now defunct "International Community", which necessitate open politics, with some elements of human rights injected in them. But there is no telling when a charismatic cleric who rejects modernism and embraces re-Islamization as the panacea for his poor and oppressed people, might capture the imagination of his followers who do not understand human rights in any case, and reverse the trends as was done in 19th Century Sudan and Libya, by the Mahdi and the Sanusis, respectively, or the Muslims in 19th Century China who rebelled under the charisma of their Ma Hualong self-made Imam[22]. In such an event, which can unfold bloodlessly as in Egypt's Arab Spring (2012), led by the Muslim Brother, Muhammed Mursi, who proceeded to a scheme of rolling back some of the moderate and relatively liberal policies of Mubarak his predecessor. He could have succeeded had he not been tottered by his Chief of Staff, General Sisi, who acted firmly against the scourge of the Muslim world:either a Muslim-authoritarian- shari'a-oriented and Human Rights-blind ruler, who also chose confrontation with the West and Israel (like the Taliban in Afghanistan or Khomeini in Iran); or a military strongman, the type of 19th Century Muhammad Ali in Egypt, who modernized and allowed some leeway in civil rights, but at the prize of absolute rule and unlimited power. This will always require some ruler who also considers the benefits of collaborating with Israel and the West, as well worth

---

[22] R. Israeli, *Muslims in China: A Study of Cultural Confrontation*, Curzon Press, London, 1980.

"normalization" with them, pending the swing of the pendulum the other way. To bring to bear in the international arena these reversals that moderate Muslims are beginning to internalize, no less audacity and change of mentality are required in the Islamic world. In the poet's words: "There is nothing stable in the world; uproar is your only music."[23] There is an atavistic human quest for stability. The fear to lose what one has, the suspicion emanating from uncertainty, and the need for repetition of the known and the rehearsed are stronger than the curiosity to explore new avenues and more overwhelming than the daring it takes to change the familiar. Therefore, change and turmoil have been the domain of the outstanding few, while conservatism and stability are the region of the many. Not surprisingly, conservatism and stability have been safeguarded by those who could lose from change, whereas change has been the motivating force behind the have-nots, revolutionaries, and progressives who can only gain from change. In politics, national and international, the catchword is *stability*; namely, regardless of the nature of a domestic regime and of the uneasy coexistence between various powers on the international arena, everyone craves stability. In other words, better to have a stable evil government somewhere than to have a more benevolent administration collapse every now and then unpredictably, throwing the country into instability and chaos. With a stable regime, one asserts, one could do business and rely on continuity, expectancy, and accountability; with a chaotic system one is afraid and reluctant to deal, lest investments be wiped out, alliances collapse, regional security be compromised, and trade halted. But one has to pause for a moment to ask whether stability is always desirable, possible, or even necessary; and whether change, especially if it is for the better, is not preferable even when it generates chaos, disorder, and unpredictability, at least in the transition phase. Hence, instead of taking stability as a paradigmatic axiom

[23] John Keats, *Letters*, January 1818.

and as a prerequisite for peace and prosperity that one has to pursue at any cost and under all circumstances, one ought to differentiate between desirable and undesirable stability; there is a stability one ought to encourage and another that one must undo—a good stability and a bad one.

These cultural and religious reservations notwithstanding, most of the Islamic world has become attracted over the years to the Western advantageous way of life, and most of it, in the Middle East and the Far East, the latter becoming the center of gravity of the Muslim world population of over 1,5 billion, has embraced modernization which is most cases meant Westernization. Moreover, due to the opening of the world to unprecedented commercial and cultural interaction, mixtures of populations have been effected, more by massive Muslim populations streaming to the West than the other way around. In consequence, no European country has preserved its character, uniformity, cultural, religious and linguistic homogeneity, to the point of the European countries cultivating, for a time, the concept of multi-culturalism, namely tolerating many cultures dwelling together in one country. That experience took time to explode in the face of many nations who woke up, belatedly, to the diluting and then dwindling which led to the toning-down, then to disappearance from the scene, of the local cultures. That was especially remarkable in the largely populated countries if Europe (Germany, France and England), which had absorbed millions of Muslim immigrants in their midst. But the mixture with alien populations and the creation of multi-cultural societies was a *fait accompli,* which has been regarded quite differently by the migrants and the populations which absorbed them. For most of the migrants (legal or otherwise), the opportunity to find a job and achieve a better life was achieved; but a more or less noticeable portion of them, usually the more religiously committed, created local Muslim oppositions to the established native leaderships which strove for integration, and instituted instead a mood and trend of separation and isolation, which also viewed their immigration to foreign lands which they supported and encouraged as a sort of "Cultural Jihad", aimed at Islamizing Europe in the long run. For the native European population, one part (the multi-culturalist) regarded it as a blessed reinforcement to the diminishing European population due to its low birthrate; the other part, as an invasion of their country by aliens who are changing its character by importing into it "strange" and not always positive patterns of conduct or desirable ambiences for living. Hence the growing bifurcation in the West, as well as in the lands of Islam, between moderate Muslims, many of whom are repenting for past frictions with the West and Israel, and radical Muslims who see themselves as the standard bearers of the revival of Islam, of its expansion, by conquest or immigration, of tottering existing pro-Western regimes in their lands' and countering, violently if need be, any attempt to repent on past Muslim behavior towards the West and Israel, or to take up measures to mend it.

Prior to the momentous events of World War Two, which tore countries apart, caused untold death and destruction worldwide, and turned accepted norms and conventional wisdom upside down, the world's cultures, religions, ethnic and linguistic groups were centered on their local, national or regional turf, within clear boundaries, except when war or forced colonization brought a culture to encroach upon another's territory. But after that horrendous war, new patterns of population movements were conceived, by force or under agreements, by design or plying to humanitarian conditions, under one pretext or another, which generated admixtures of populations, religions, customs, languages, thereby creating new frictions, instability, suspicions, fears and clashes between civilizations, climaxing in acts of terrorism that the world has failed to devise ways to combat effectively. One has to take cognizance, however, that some of the colonized nations before the war had had their part in promoting their own self-confidence and sense of superiority over others, attitudes that had caused them to mistreat different cultures and minority groups within their borders, or to evince their hostility toward them by invading and subjugating them to their rule beyond their own borders. That was in fact the nature of all major Empires, where the ruler, be it Mongol, Abbasid, Ottoman, Russian, British or French, imposed its own rules over the subjected populations. The result in all cases was the imposition of the hegemonic power's culture, language, often religion and mores, over the occupied populations. Very often, the subject peoples chose to adopt the ways of the rulers and learned how to acculturate into the hegemonic culture (in the Western colonies that was called "Westernization" or "modernization", and in Islamdom "Islamization"). Christian missionaries who came on the footsteps of their colonizing authorities usually elected to characterize their mission as *civilisatrice* that leads to "salvation", via the "Gospel of Christ", and the like.

What happened after World War II, and the turmoil it caused in the world, was not only the massive movements of independence in the colonized world, but also a reverse tendency of the colonized nations to migrate *en masse* to the lands of their previous occupiers. The reasons, or pretexts were not missing: the Western manpower having been depleted during the War on the one hand, and the immense needs of rehabilitation and reconstruction having never been so pressing and acute, on the other, that the easy answer was to import a "provisional workforce" (in German they called it the *Gastarbeiter*, the term "guest workers" pointing to their temporary status. On the importers' end, it was convenient and fast to rely on their previous colonies to recruit the requisite foreign manpower, due to the supposedly linguistic and cultural heritage that the colonizers had left behind: the British in India and Pakistan, and the Middle East, the Dutch in Indonesia, the French in North Africa; the Germans elected the Turks, their allies from World War One, who though ignorant of German culture and language, were the most emotionally approachable for temporary work, which would ultimately be followed by their repatriation to their countries of origin. At first, in the 1950s and 1960s, most workers arrived on their own, conscious of their provisional status, and they were well content to dispatch home the proceedings of their labor and to visit occasionally their families back home during work vacations. But life necessities proved stronger than the intentions of the host nations and the rhetoric of the politicians. Soon, people began to either bring in their families or to intermarry with local women and start their own families, and many of them produced a second and third generation, which was now fluent in the languages of the adoptive countries, and whose expectations and demands kept growing: education for their children, family reunions with their relatives left behind, local citizenship in order to obtain also civil rights, and social and religious services to fit their needs. The individuals who had migrated to the West to find work and improve their standard of living, and were Muslim for the most part, became by the 1980s and 1990s solidly organized according to countries of origin, linguistic or ethnic groups, or religious congregations of various denominations, although mostly hailing from Islam.

Most of the immigrants had by now attained a critical mass (over 10% in France, maybe 7% in Germany and Britain, and an average of 5-6% in most of the rest of Europe, somewhat less than that in southern Europe (3% in Spain and Italy), and even less in the Balkans and Eastern Europe, which perceived the Islamic "peril" earlier than the others, and have taken energetic measures to counter it, much to the chagrin of their more liberal partners in the EU, by blocking Muslim immigration almost totally. The promoted fear from that "menace" emanated from the history of the Islamic invasions of Europe: in the 8th Century Islam had invaded Europe from the southwest, occupied the Iberian Peninsula and advanced into southern France, until arrested by Charles Martel in Poitiers in 732; as they were finally expelled from there in the 15th Century, the second attempt was launched by the Ottoman Empire from the opposite direction of the southeast, when they occupied the Balkans and ultimately advanced to the gates of Vienna, whence they were repulsed and started their retreat. The latest "invasion", it has been argued, is being made by "peaceful" means, through mass immigration, to which the West must ply due to its standards of civil and human rights and commitment to absorb "political refugees" running away from cruel and undemocratic regimes, which also happen to be located mostly in Islamic countries in Africa, Asia and the Middle East. The greatest practitioners of this policy in the West naively sang the praise of what they dubbed "multi-culturalism", being unaware of its long haul subversive effects, or simply choosing to ignore them. The end result has been that no western country has kept its original character, demographic homogeneity, prevailing Christian religion, or even its predominating national language. When one strolls in the streets of Stockholm, Hamburg, Geneva or Rome, Paris or Nice, London or Birmingham, one observes a landscape never seen in the past: a confusing mixture of peoples, looks, languages and modes of behavior, which necessarily dilute the local culture to the point of making it unrecognizable. In other words, one can no longer go to Sweden, Britain or Switzerland to delight in their environment, ambience, heritage and culture, for those values and assets have been vanishing in their original form. This new developing admixture has been blessed by UN idealists, and also by some naïve Western leaders, before they woke up to its dangers, as "serving the cause of peace and understanding between nations and individual humans"; and by the migrating people of the Third World, who lust for an unlimited open door in the more advanced and freer West. But its greatest drawback has been its unilateralism: it is only the Islamic world which falls upon the West and alters it to its tune, while the reverse simply does not happen, for the Islamic world remains almost in its original purity without outside interference, as though colonization had reversed course, and it was now the turn of Islam to impose a temporary multi-culturalism on Western lands in preparation for taking it over as a first step towards achieving dominance, that is Islamization, of the universe.

In countries of immigration, like the US, Canada and Australia, the situation is not much better. There was for centuries a predominant Waspish element in those lands, but then the various waves of immigrants have been changing their character to the point that talking about an American culture, or a Canadian culture or an Australian culture has become laughable, for such things do not exist anymore in their original sense. In the US, one century and a half after the civil war, which was fought on the noble issue of repealing slavery, but caused the breakup of the country apart into a deadly civil war, and caused hundreds of thousands of dead and wounded, clashes between White and Black have persisted as a daily affair, with tensions mounting, bitterness and resentment increasing, and no solution in sight. To a great extent, the Islamic element in the inter-cultural frictions throughout the West has become similar to the Black issue in America[24], in exacerbating the moods as if to prove the unfeasibility of multi-culturalism. In Canada, the French separatist movement for a "free Quebec" persists, and the continued influx of immigrants, inter alia from Muslim countries, continues to build up a Muslim community which has already been colored with extremism and has recorded some attempted acts of violence and terrorism. In Australia, the mixture of races and cultures, which had evolved so far peacefully for the most part, has united most Aussies against the occasional manifestations of terrorism on the part of Muslim immigrants who have elected to preserve their Islamic values over the still dominant Anglo-Saxon culture[25].

---

[24] R. Israeli, *Black Upon White: American Racism and Black Dignity,* Strategic Books, Tx, 2020.

[25] R. Israeli, *Muslim Minorities in Modern States*, Transaction, NJ 2009.

To illustrate the destructive effects of the blind "multi-culturalism", adopted since the 1980s, which culminated in dotting the map of Europe with a growing number of caches of weapons, terrorist gangs and committed Muslim ideologues, we shall procure here some case studies of the countries that have mostly suffered from its consequences, notably Britain. All of them, backed by others, like Germany and the EU institutions, have elected to call those terrorists "criminals" in order to differentiate them, as it were, from the vast masses of "peaceful Muslims" who were moving to the European continent, ignoring the fact that almost wherever a settled Muslim community of immigrants grew, it was bound to fall, sooner or later, under the spell of militant preachers who would end up inciting rebelliousness and terrorism; and that those who engaged in terror were not "criminals" in the traditional Western sense. For criminals break the law for material gain: money or other assets, while Muslim terrorists do not aspire for any material benefit, and are on the contrary putting their lives on the line, for ideological/religious reasons and purposes. Thus, as long as European and American leaders and scholars were reluctant to call a spade a spade, and refrained from dubbing those culprits what they were-, namely Muslim terrorists, multi-culturalism continued to dig in and terrorism went on unchecked. But when peoples woke up to the threat that has transformed their lives and they started to vote for politicians who recognized the truth, it was almost too late to turn back the clock.

The first observation anyone makes who happens to render a sporadic visit to any country where multi-culturalism is experienced, is the salient variety of the populations one runs across in the streets of cities: light complexions and dark ones, civil clothing of the most updated fashions, for men and women, along with traditional dress, with robes for men and veils for women. In these cities, stands for fast food with the familiar and luring tastes and fragrances, coexist along with foreign odors and some alien tastes, that are sometimes very distasteful, not due to their intrinsically disgusting nature but to their unfamiliarity with the place where they are emitted. In short, when things seem to be out of place, people get disoriented, local residents accustomed to certain landscapes, faces, colors, tastes and smells, sounds and languages, are no longer sure where they have landed or where they have ventured. Exception is made, of course, in countries like Brazil, where material and temporal multi culturalism had been at the foundation of the country from its inception. In other parts of South America, the descendants of the Inca, Aztec, Maya and other local civilizations, are still marked by their particular physical traits and cultural and economic marginalization. But wherever Muslim minorities are involved in multi-culturalism, their added religious components are bound to emerge and cause disruptions. One is tempted by the phenomenon of the massive resistance to the "conspiracy" of world globalization, for instance during the E-7 and E20 conferences, where the violent demonstrations tend to encompass parts of the immigrants into the Western countries, to conclude that multi-culturalism is only one manifestation of the world globalization, which endeavors to mix economies into one system that is remote- controlled by the big corporations. According to this theory, globalizatiion also strives to control the peoples of the world by mixing them together into one spineless mass of nationless crowds that are not bound by patriotism, ideology, culture or language, but are only committed to a single world system. This is precisely the crack where Muslim minorities penetrate Western democracies, taking advantage of their liberties and civil rights, to undermine them from within. For while they ostensibly support a world government, and in the process disrupt the system in the countries of multi-culturalism where they found shelter, many of them are determined and persuaded that the future belongs to Islam and that the waning of Christian Europe and the West in general, heralds the emergence of the Muslim world and its taking control of universal dominion.

Certainly, many practitioners and promoters of "multi -cultural-ism" use that terminology, not due to its philosophical or moral or humanitarian implications, like the presumption of a universal world where the human individual is more important than nations and states, and that all human creatures are equal and deserving of the same right to happiness and access to the goodies of life, but to serve what they consider as their long term interests. For example, many politicians who watch with an open eye the constantly decreasing reproduction rate in the West, which is due mainly to the pessimism with which prospective parents view the future and are therefore reluctant to marry, much less to engender children, realize that unless they import human reinforcement from the outside, they would face in one generation an acute shortage in manpower to replace workers in the factories, take care of the aging populations, and to strengthen the productive part of society which alone can manufacture enough wealth to sustain the rest. This seems a very positive mode of thinking, not very characteristic of governments in Western liberal democracies, who usually sacrifice the rational planning for the long haul for the immediate interest of appeasing enough minds to win the next elections. But when solutions are chosen for the rising problems of the day or of the future, they do not have necessarily to opt for the massive import of destitute Muslim refugees who may be potentially inimical to the Western nature of the shelter country and its people, but they could be much more cautious, gradual and digestible. By multiculturalism one usually means a social pluralism in which one ethnic, religious or linguistic group does not predominate over the others, no group is required to waive its character in order to accommodate he others, and no dominant ethos, historical, cultural or otherwise is permitted to marginalize the others. This is perhaps possible in immigrant societies, like the US, Canada and Australia, where the national, cultural and demographic character of the land has been in a state of flux since the inception of those countries, to the tune of the incoming immigrants. But even then, those countries had chosen their basic foundational character as Waspish, Western, democratic, Christian and Anglophonic, and all newcomers know that they have to abide by those rules and adapt to them if they want to acculturate to their host societies. So did Latinos, and Jews who immigrated to those countries, and to a great extent also the Asian immigrants of Indian, Japanese, Korean, Vietnamese or Chinese origin. The only problematic element which has wrecked that peaceful evolutionary pattern, by which immigrant societies have been absorbing their new comers without any need for multi culturalism, has been the Islamic one. Due to its refusal to melt into this sort of society where its distinctive character would be diluted and then lost, except for their religion that they could keep as a faith of the individual, and to its readiness to use force and violence to enforce its distinctiveness, it has differentiated itself from all other minorities, who also refused to melt and disappear but also reconciled to the idea that assimilation was unstoppable in the long run and that they had no other recourse than accept it, which they were supposed to have done implicitly the day they had relocated to their new land.

Multiculturalism as a political philosophy involves ideologies and policies which vary widely, ranging from the advocacy of equal respect to the various cultures in a society, to policies of promoting the maintenance of cultural diversity, to policies in which people of various ethnic and religious groups are addressed by the authorities as defined by the group to which they belong. Multiculturalism that promotes maintaining the distinctiveness of multiple cultures is often contrasted to other settlement policies such as social integration, cultural assimilation and racial segregation. Multiculturalism has been described as a "salad bowl" and "cultural mosaic". Two different and seemingly inconsistent strategies have developed through different government policies and strategies. The first focuses on interaction and communication between different cultures; this approach is also often known as interculturalism. The second centers on diversity and cultural uniqueness which can sometimes result in intercultural competition over jobs, among other things, and may lead to ethnic or politico-religious conflict. Controversy surrounding the issue of cultural isolation includes the ghettoization of a culture within a nation and the protection of the cultural attributes of an area or nation. Proponents of government policies often claim that artificial, government- guided protections also contribute to global cultural diversity. The second approach to multiculturalist policy making maintains that they avoid presenting any specific ethnic, religious, or cultural community values as central. It has been referred to as a cocktail of cultures, languages and art forms in which "everything becomes everything else". Thus, the pro-multi-culturalist movement in the West (and Japan for that matter) finds its rationalizations in the pressing needs to fill in its depleting demographic reserves, due to the negative procreation that generates a negative population growth; in the future needs for labor manpower; in the necessary influx of young people to replace the constantly aging local populations; and in the need for the West to maintain an amiable relationship with the Muslim world where those migrants might originate. Some governments in place also vouch for increased influx of immigrants into their territory, not only to prove that their policies of multiculturalism have worked, but to expand their political base by incorporating the supposedly grateful immigrants into their political parties and ensure their continued hold on power. Governments in liberal democracies usually act like fire brigades which have to extinguish fires at every turn to keep their populace satisfied and be voted in in the next elections, and they ignore the grim future that awaits their countries two or three decades hence, when they are no longer in power. Only totalitarian regimes are assured of the longevity of their hold on power, therefore they can plan for the long haul, and they devise their five-year plans in consequence. It is a fact that the less democratically inclined regimes in Europe, as one travels eastward, where until recently doctrinaire regimes had predominated, the less proclivity to adopt multi-culturalism and the more restrictions on Muslim immigration into their borders.

But the Muslim immigrants, who are allowed into the West under the liberal-democratic governments who promote multi-culturalism, view things slightly differently: they endeavor, first and foremost, to increase their numbers by encouraging more immigration in order to reach the irreversible critical mass, and more conversion to Islam of the Westerners who are lured and fascinated by the successes of Islam in Europe, and they often read into the future more intelligently than their host countries.. Secondly, they demand, in the name of the civil rights they acquire in their asylum countries that *Shari'a* laws and Muslim customs (like forced marriages, honor killings) be made to apply by their hosts, the fact that their numbers in jails in the West by far surpass their rate in the population notwithstanding. Thirdly, they prevail upon their adoptive countries direct their foreign policies to their tune, for example, on their negative attitude towards the US, their policy in the Middle East and in favor of the Palestinians, and in shackling the West in any future conflict with or inside any Muslim country. They attain those goals by congregating in certain voting constituencies and making sure that no member of Parliament in their voting zone could be elected unless he or she supported more Muslim immigration, and favored their political and international agenda, even against the stated government policy. Reinforcing communal cohesion so as to become a political force to be reckoned with, they often self-impose isolation of Muslims in their own neighborhoods where they find themselves as a prevailing migrating minority, beginning with Muslims in China since the 8th Century, to the Muslim villages and townships in Israel, the *cites* around Paris and the Muslim quarters in Detroit and London. Secondly, an independent Islamic educational system is devised around the globe, through the lavish establishment of mosques, schools and Islamic centers throughout the Western world, taking advantage of their liberty to do so under the liberal regimes of the West, notwithstanding the continued persecution of Christian minorities in Islamdom and the banning of the Christian Mission in many Muslim countries, most of all Saudi Arabia, which does not even permit non-Muslims into its borders. The renowned educational system that the Turkish Fethullah Gulen built in the US is only one spectacular example of this quiet and subtle, but steady, subversive and effective penetration into Western society in order to transform it. In multiculturalism as a term, there is much ambiguity since it can serve many social and political causes, and it is not merely used to promote cultural pluralism in countries which, due to political and historical circumstances, found themselves grappling with a plurality of ethnic or cultural groups. Multi- culturalism is not always a choice made voluntarily by countries and people, who usually elect uniformity, homogeneity and familiarity of their citizenry, which can more easily allow a social contract and avoid social and political frictions between various parts of the population. However, rare are the countries where there are no minorities, and their omnipresence everywhere, when aggrandized by their numbers, who are unwilling to yield to the predominant culture, or by a religion whose followers reject any form of government that is not their own, brings us to the collision course. Watch the case of Yugoslavia which after Tito's death which broke up into its components. But there the ethno- religious groups were also territorial and that facilitated their secession into Orthodox Serbia, Catholic Croatia and the Muslim majority Bosnia, and enabled Muslim Kosovo to break up from Serbia. Other authoritarian countries, like Syria, Iraq, Libya, also broke up into their ethnic, tribal and religious components when the leaders who held them together passed away or were weakened by the "Arab Spring" that was launched in 2010/11 and has not died out completely six years later.

That was the situation when domestic historical conditions had shaped the regimes of multi-cultural countries. But the problem of multi culturalism is more often visible when applied to aboriginal ethnic groups, like the Indians of the Americas, the aborigines of Australia and New Zealand, or to foreign groups who immigrated to the countries in question and maintained their distinctiveness. The Palestinians, including Israeli Arabs, for example, regard themselves as natives of their land and they rebel against the imposed Jewish government upon them. But they should perhaps refrain from embracing the above precedents and parallels, which have kept the native aborigine population marginalized and impoverished. Besides, while the other natives in other countries were *in toto* taken over by those who colonized them, Israeli Arabs are only a small part of the Palestinian people which dwells elsewhere and strives for its own sovereignty. Foreign immigrants have usually done well when they accepted the dominant cultures they knew they would be acculturating into when they immigrated, save for Muslims who, due to their identification with the universal Muslim community, the *Umma,* have had more difficulties than other minority groups to adapt to the new cultural background and acculturate to it. Different is the situation when a culturally different territory is amalgamated with another country or culture, like Hungarian-inhabited Transylvania and Voivodina which were integrated into Romania and Serbia, respectively, or the Arab areas of the Galilee and the Negev which became part of Israel. There, multi culturalism always runs the risk of escalating into *irridenta* and endless political clashes like those occasioned by the German Danzig Corridor in Poland and the Sudeten in Czechoslovakia on the eve of W W II, or the Russian minorities in the Ukraine and the Baltics today. Academics and political armchair strategists can theorize at ease about the morality, fairness and desirability or multiculturalism, or its interculturalist version, but only people who have experienced its related misfortunes, either from the minority aspects which has existed in bitterness, sense of discrimination and wish to disengage, or from the majority angle which is replete with suspicions, fear, terror and estrangement in its own land, can deliver a worthy judgment of their condition and the possibilities of remedying it. Therefore, there is no much use to the various anthropological and sociological theories, nor is there any point to rely on this or that political philosophy to unravel the complications caused by these unfortunate situations, especially when they are intertwined with economic interests and political power. The gamut of definitions and interpretations has so widened as to encompass ethnic, religious and linguistic minorities, but also minority nations, indigenous peoples and even the disabled. Most of all, the academic debates have been focusing on whether multiculturalism is the best way to deal with immigrants and refugees, be they gradually and legally invited in, sorted out and absorbed according to state organized blueprints, or fleeing from zones of combat and flocking across borders uninvited, capitalizing on Western democratic societies customs and moralities which compel them to absorb refugees, rescue people in danger and extend immediate humanitarian aid to them. But these humanitarian measures, which are unique to the West, do not specify what happens next. Are they unlimited in time, space and volume, or only provided the numbers of absorbed incomers, and the length of time of their accommodation in the host countries accord with the economic capacity of the host country, the size of its population and the ethnic and religious feasibility of receiving and absorbing the newcomers without causing disruptions to the fiber of the existing societies; are the latter obliged to absorb them, under what conditions and for how long ?. For example, populations running away into enemy countries, or from hostile cultures and religions with regard to the absorbing countries, can the shelter countries be expected to take them in, are the latter obliged to absorb them and for how long? Should the Allies in W W II, for example, have been requested to absorb German of

Japanese refugees running away from those Axis regimes? These are some of the dilemmas many western countries have been tackling these days once the idea of multiculturalism has proved abysmally inadequate to resolve them.

# Chapter Two

## *Radical Muslims Seeking Predominance*

The part of the Islamic world that refuses to submit to the seduction of Western multi-culturalism, and strives, most of all to Islamize their own regime at home, does not content itself with openly rejecting Western ideas, and is adamant on confronting the West in an asymmetrical war due to its own weaknesses, has therefore launched a worldwide plan to reverse the peaceful advances of the repentant moderate Muslims by struggling against them openly by all the means available to them:

a. Nourishing ideologically and supporting materially the Muslim radical movements worldwide (Muslim Brothers, al-Qa'ida, ISIS, Hamas, Hizbullah etc.) which strive to topple the moderate governments in Islamdom and take-over the rule;

b. To turn the migration into the West from a search for economic opportunity into a quiet and peaceful Jihad that would eventually Islamize the West;

c. In the meantime, diffuse Islam by *da'wa* (propaganda/mission) in the lands of the Infidel, inter alia through dissident Islamic institutions (mosques, Islamic centers, schools);

d. To precipitate these processes, launch deadly terrorist attacks in all major cities of Europe and the US, in order to drive fear (*irhab* in Qur'anic parlance) in order to encourage them to convert into Islam or obey its domination.

e. They reject, lock stock and barrel Western ideology which they regard as "Westoxication", refuse any negotiation, compromise, dealing or reconciliation with Israel and the West, and vow a battle to the finish to dominate them.
f. While rejecting the West and belittling, even despising, its culture and its technological advances, they line up outside its consulates worldwide to gain visas to facilitation its permeation so as to undermine it from within; and they use cars, microphones, Internet, all Western innovations to beat the West in its own game.

An overarching consideration lay at the base of this thinking in the minds of the radicals, that is their foundational Muslim rejection of non-Muslim rule. The question of Jihadi Islam, that wide, amorphous and unpredictable coalition of radical Islamic movements and countries, which can strike anywhere directly, via their ISIS, al Qa'ida, Hamas, Hizbullah, and Islamic Jihad branches on Israel's borders, or anywhere around the globe, has been widening and deepening as more and more erstwhile relatively moderate Islamic countries, like pre-Erdogan Turkey, and pre-Khomeini Iran, have shifted towards radicalism and turned their old alliances with the West and Israel into a virulent anti-Western and anti-Israeli stance. Worse, as the numbers of anti-Western Muslim countries and movements keep making inroads, and occasionally waning out, their worldwide presence in all parts of the globe causes the state of siege around the West (and Israel) to feel tighter and the chances of accommodation between these clashing civilizations ever slimmer. While great powers and advanced countries can wield enough wherewithal and weave appropriate alliances to defend themselves and their allies and overcome the threats, even when occasioning overseas incursions, small and vulnerable countries like Holland and Israel, whose populations are limited and fear of being inundated by immigrating and multiplying Muslim populations, feel and behave differently. Their means are also limited, and their very existence hangs on a patron state or an organization like the US, NATO and the EU, that they perceive the emergence of radical Islam in their neighborhood, and the menace it poses to their existence as very concrete, immediate and overwhelming. In this state of affairs, movements of Muslim terrorists who have shown their mettle in sowing destruction and death, loom larger than life and their threat has grown very real and imminent. Above all, the doctrine of *Islamikaze,* erroneously called in the West "suicide bombing", and by other Muslims *istishhad* (martyrdom), which means active self-sacrifice for the Islamic cause, not as passive or accidental victims, that had been sanctified by the Muslim Brothers since the 1930's and 1940s, against the British in Egypt and Palestine, and against the Jews and the British in Mandatory Palestine and Israel. It was taken up by the Hizbullah in Lebanon, first against US and Israeli presence there in the 1980s, and has become of universal usage by all Muslim terrorist movements, after they had repeatedly warned the West about their contempt to life, because as martyrs their real eternal life is assured in Paradise, in contrast with the Western approach which sanctified life. As the Israeli presence in southern Lebanon wore on, those operations were intensified until they became the routine trademark of the violent encounters between the Hizbullah and Israel, and between Islamic radicals and the West in general. Unlike the Shi'ite martyrs who emulated the martyrdom of Hussein in Karbala, and have acted passively with the goal of self-inflicting pain and suffering, the modern *Islamikaze* have shifted their doctrine into an active one that inflicts death and destruction on the enemy, even at the cost of their own lives. The long succession of *fatwas* delivered to justify these acts, has indeed provided the rationalization for the mostly Sunnite *Islamikaze* groups to launch their deadly and massive attacks on Israel and the West. It is quite amazing indeed to watch the Sunnite radical groups adopt the Shi'ite ways, not only by embracing the Iranian and Hizbullah Shi'ite *modus operandi*, something that has been evinced in the collaboration of Iran and Hizbullah with the Sunnite Hamas and Islamic Jihad, but also by creating their own version of the supreme sacrifice and suffering. Indeed, in the battlefield of terrorism in the Path of Allah, we have seen 19 adepts of al-Qa'ida committing collective acts of *Islamikaze* within one hour of each other on American soil on September 11 (2001). Al-Qa'ida and ISIS fighters in Afghanistan, Iraq and Syria, have defied death in the face of American and Syrian air power, as do Hamas and Islamic Jihad operatives in Gaza, or the Muslim terrorists of *Lashkar-e -Tayiba* in Kashmir or in India proper, or the *Boko Haram* in Nigeria. They slay their own compatriots with the same senseless and blind zeal as they do when they attack foreigners. This universalization of Sunni Muslim terrorism also carries with it a growing daring in the operations, to the extent of its banalization in view of its frequency, diffusion and beastly cruelty. Not only the massive attack of September 11, but especially the almost daily attacks on Israel and its civilians during the 1990s and 2000s by the Hamas, the Islamic Jihad and even PLO-related Palestinians, and the recurrent acts of terror throughout the Western world, from the US to Australia, have rendered these harrowing acts routine to the point that they became "part of life", as if they were God-ordained and impervious to human preventive initiative. So much so, that the Western world has had to adopt a new mode of life, with long lines in airports and at the entrance of stadiums and public building to provide some sense of security to the terrorized populations.

Even though Israel has become "accustomed" to the horrendous sights of Arabs and other Muslims celebrating over the spilled blood of their victims, when delirious and ecstatic Muslim crowds evince outlandish eruptions of jubilation following breaking news regarding "successful" attacks against Israel or the West, with no one in sight to rein them in, what unfolds in those orgies of joyous and vindictive hatred in the cities of the Muslim world where these radicals operate, is particularly hair-raising. While Israel and the West were mourning their dead in a somber dignity and internalized pain, the Muslim supporters of the murderers were distributing sweets, dancing in the streets amidst cries of "Allah Akbar !", as if to attribute to Allah their great "feats" of murder against their sworn enemies, as if they had been perpetrated by Allah's order and under His support. They then went again into the repetitive ritual of burning the flags of their enemies, or trampling them under their feet as if possessed by frenzy. Since the demonstrators are not for the most part the participants in the real murderous events themselves, who had often perished as martyrs (*shahids)* in the operation, they sometimes reenact the horror symbolically to share it with the public, praising Allah for His intercession on their behalf. In Nablus, during the Palestinian *Intifadah* that broke out in October 2000, a most disturbing exhibition was presented to the general Palestinian public in the city public square, which showed in inhuman detail the replicas of severed limbs and body pieces of Israelis who had perished in a blown-up restaurant of a passenger bus by a Hamas terrorist. It was only the reports by deeply disgusted foreign correspondents, and the protest of Israelis who did not want to relive that horror by seeing it replicated on the screens, which convinced the Palestinian Authority, which was committed under the Oslo Accords to put an end to terrorism, to move the exhibition indoors instead of closing it down and arresting its promoters. It is understood that by widening the scope of the viewers of those scenes among the public, to the point of rendering them a sort of street theatre, even if most viewers were not part of the radical Islamic movements, the organizers expected to elicit respect and esteem for the self-immolating heroes, and to encourage the new recruits of tomorrow who are bound to emulate them. In other words, unlike the inward-turning stories of the suffering enacted by the Shi'ites for the sake of commemoration, identification with the sanctified martyrs, and self-hardening in order to stand the excruciating trials to come, radical Muslims today elect to harden their crowds and cultivate their audiences by boasting about the gruesome suffering they inflicted upon the enemies of Allah.

Having learned to take seriously the radical Muslims' stated intentions of annihilation against Westerners and Israelis, due to their historical experiences under Islam as *dhimmis*[26], many Christians remaining as minorities in the occupied Christian territories by Muslims in the past,and many Eastern Christians today, had tasted the yoke of Muslim dominance. Many Arabs and Muslims are under a pressing psychological need to erase the humiliating "anomaly" which permitted Christians and Jews, the submitted *dhimmis* of yesteryear, who had lived for centuries at the mercy of Muslims, to emerge as sovereign nations which today predominate in the world, and stand up against them after they had even colonized them. The mistreatment of Christians and Jews under Islam, in the Middle East, North Africa and the Iberian Peninsula, has been a matter of some controversy. Scholars like Bernard Lewis, Marc Cohen, and Moshe Maoz, have taken the more lenient attitude towards the various Muslim regimes in history, pleading for understanding of the context of that era. Others, like Michael Curtis, Bat Ye'or and Andrew Bostom, and lately Dario Fernandez, have demonstrated and solidly documented the sorry story of the extermination of entire Christian and Jewish communities, or their forced conversion to Islam in the domains of Islamdom. Be it as it may, the humiliating effect of the *dhimmi* status of the Christians and Jews under Islam has been universally recognized as having generated a deep hatred and contempt towards Christianity as a universal rival, and towards the Jewish minorities throughout Islamdom, until the latter was converted to anti Zionism when Israel was born in 1948. During the years of Islamic conquest, expansion, and the ensuing annihilation of some of the existing Christian and Jew-

[26] See Bat Yeor, *The Dhimmis,* and R. Israeli, op. cit.

ish communities, occupation, coercion, forced conversion, and cruel subjugation of the non-Muslim communities which survived were practiced on a large scale. The general picture, however, was even much bigger and much more painful than the persecuted Christians and Jews themselves in their particular locations, for Islam went on a triumphalist journey to rule the world, as a divine vocation, and to convert its population to Islam, except for the followers of the monotheistic creeds, who were offered the "generous" choice between converting and being integrated into the dominant Muslim society, or keeping their faith under the *dhimmi* status and paying in return for their protection the poll tax, the *jizya,* which was levied in a debasing manner, to exhibit in public the inferior status of the non-Muslims and encourage them to convert.

The occupied territories where those people lived were dubbed *Dar al Islam*, the Abode of Islam, or *Pax Islamica*, while the rest of the world, was termed *Dar al Harb,* or the country of war, meaning that war was to be a perpetual tool in the hands of the Islamic rulers until and unless the entire world submitted to Islamic rule. For Muslims then, taking over others' territory was Allah sanctioned, by means of a holy war, that is *Jihad*, and anyone who did not submit to that divine edict was the enemy of Allah. Thus, unless Christians and Jews remained as *dhimmis* under the boot of Islam, their arrogant assumption of building their own independent states, and beating Islam in almost all confrontations with it since the beginning of modern times, was an aberration of history and of the Path that Allah had prescribed for the world. Since the Crusades, which were in fact a Christian attempt to recover the territories they had lost to Islamic conquest and expansion, and up until shortly prior to the end of the last Muslim Caliphate, namely the Ottoman sultanate, in the WW I, the West was often on the defensive from Islam. However, already in the 18th Century it started to conquer and colonize the Muslim world and bend it to its will, and even imposed the Capitulations regime on the weakening Caliphate. The mounting power of the Western democracies has since reversed the situation and put the West on top of the world, an affront that Muslims cannot forgive or forget. But, while most of the Islamic world has been aware of its weaknesses and backwardness, and realizes how much it depends on Western powers, the radical Muslim movements among it, led by charismatic people like Osama Bin Laden and his followers, have taken the requisite initiative and mobilized all their temerity and religious zeal worldwide to reverse the situation. They endeavored to revive the spirit of Jihad, defy the hegemony of the West and launch an all-out unconventional war against it to beat it into submission. They realized that if they cannot raise their own level to catch up with the West, they must defeat it in order to erase the humiliation that afflicts their present state. The modern Western world has become accustomed to discuss openly and debate publicly the rationality and justification of their policies, domestic and international. But Muslims and some of their supporters in the West, while using the same vocabularies in order to make themselves understood to the West, remain replete with misnomers to an extent that old notions have been confused with new ones, words lose their significance and expressions of political correctness have handily replaced accuracy. Words have come to be used to mean different things, to the point that we find it increasingly awkward to transmit certain messages, and find that we have to create new phrases and coin alternative words in order to avoid misunderstandings. Cases in point have been the widespread usage of "Islamist" (to distinguish from Muslim) as if there were two separate doctrines of Islam, one to serve the moderate "peaceful" Muslims, and the other to express the Jihadi tendencies of the radicals; and "suicide bomber" where there is no suicide, not even the semblance of a suicide in the thinking of those terrorist killers. For Muslims, there is one Islam, Jihad is not only the domain of the radicals, and the "suicide bombers" are martyrdom fighters for the cause of Islam, whom this author has suggested to dub *Islamikaze,* the combination of Islam and *kamikaze*, the notorious Japanese pilots of the Pacific War, who like their Muslim counterparts were prepared to sacrifice themselves (not to kill themselves) for the Emperor (or the Muslim Allah) in the process of killing their enemies[27].If, as some claim, there were a certain percentage of Muslims who are "radical", "fundamentalist" or simply "Islamists", while the majority is Muslim of the good brand, which politicians like Bush and Blair simply, but wrongly, called "peace-loving", then how come that we see vast crowds, which seem to represent the local Muslim majorities, in every place where Muslims burst out in violence, be it in Cairo, Gaza, Quetta, Teheran, Kabul as during the Cartoon Affair in Europe in 2006? What happens to those supposedly peace-loving majorities who are not supposedly represented by the violent crowds? And when Muslim columnists, including Western-educated and degree-holders, write in the mainstream journals of the Muslim world, including in "moderate" and "pro-Western" countries, like Egypt, Saudi Arabia or Jordan, genocidal wishes and virulent recriminations against the West and Israel, and expressions of joy after September 11 or when every time a bus or a restaurant blow up in the West or in Israel, with dozens of victims, are those celebrating frenzied people representative of "radicals" or of "Islamist" individuals? Then, where is the difference between peace-loving Muslims and so-called "Islamists"? While there are theological differences of nuance between Sunnites and Shi'ites, and within the Sunnites between the four Schools of law (*madhahib),* for instance between the puritanical Wahhabis of the Hanbali cult and the more lenient Hanafites on matters of *Shari'a* law, there appears to be unanimity among them with regard to Jihad wars and the contempt and hostility towards the West, because they all draw from the same medieval Abu Yussuf and Ibn

---

[27] See R. Israeli, *Islamikaze: Manifestations of Islamic Martyrology*, Frank Cass, London, ☒ 2003; and R. Israeli "Islamikaze and their Significance", in *Terrorism and Political Violence*, Frank Cass, London, Fall 1997, pp. 96-121.

Taymiyya and the more modern Hassan al-Banna, Sayyid Qut'b or Mawdudi. Understandably, not every Muslim would observe to the letter the strictest prescriptions of those scholars, but at the same time no sweeping, authoritative alternative doctrine to them has emerged to challenge them, let alone replace them.

Those referred to as "Islamists" call and regard themselves simply as plain Muslims, who are perhaps more zealous than others and wish to fulfill Muslim goals here and now. But are they so distinguishable from other Muslims that they deserve to be treated as if they were different Muslims or as if they had invented a different Islam? All religious Muslims venerate the great masters of contemporary Islam like Hasan al-Banna, Sayyid Qut'b, Mawdudi and Qaradawi, even if they are not categorized as "radicals". The latter relate to the masses of common Muslims the way activists or militants in a political party refer to the rank and file of sympathizers who only vote when the day comes, but are not involved in any day to day politics. But we do not distinguish between "radical" and "common" party members in politics. Yes, they differ, in both cases, as far as the degree of commitment, activity and observation of details are concerned, but we cannot set them apart ideologically, and they continue to belong to the same core of belief and conviction. For if there were a "liberal" or "moderate" tendency in Islam, it would be evinced, first of all, by theologians of Islam who would stand up courageously and battle against the ideas and theses of the "Islamists". However, while truly moderate and daring individuals of Muslim descent (and sometimes conviction) do exist, principally in the safety of the West, we cannot discern any significant trend of moderation and "peace-loving" inclination which rallies behind it masses of Muslims. So, what is erroneously dubbed "moderate" or "non-Islamist" Islam, is actually the silent majority who is, unfortunately, are more likely than not to follow the outbursts of jubilation when the West and Israel are harmed, to watch approvingly anti-Western and anti-Semitic series on television which depict

American or Israelis as blood-drinkers, world -conspirers and children-killers, and to avidly absorb genocidal statements by their leaders and clerics and reiterate their belief in the same non-sensical slogans and conspiracy theories that are circulated in their media. One year after September 11, Dan Rather of CBS News undertook a worldwide survey of Muslim (not "Islamist") reactions to those horrific events. From a sample of 8 Muslim countries, between Morocco and Pakistan, where he polled the literate population in remote villages in each one of those countries, the overwhelming majority of the populace, which was not "radical", spelled out their conviction that the horror was "of course" perpetrated by the Jews, the *Mossad*, the CIA, or in collaboration of the two, and such delusive fairy-tales.

Did the Palestinians suddenly become "Islamists" when the radical Hamas won elections among them in 2005? No, they remained as Muslim as they were before the elections. They burst into unabashed joy when September 11 happened, much to Arafat's embarrassment who sent his security forces to disband those "radical" children to avoid further disgrace. Why did they do that? Because they were indoctrinated by their school textbooks, which assured them of the imminent victory of Islam against the "corrupt and tyrannical" West. They burst forth in jubilation when Israeli and Western families were shown torn into pieces, and they re-enacted harrowing scenes of explosions against Israel, showing cardboard buses or restaurants burning and limbs of children flying around, with huge crowds of children, passers-by, shop-keepers, students and policemen clapping hands and rejoicing. Even their universities and school plays staged such re-enactments. Could all those be "Islamist"? No, in their eyes, Israelis and the West are perceived as the enemies of Islam (not of "Islamists"), therefore one should rejoice at their defeat, and because they are not defeated often enough for the Muslims' taste, no Muslim can skip the delight of re-playing that defeat and savoring it in slow motion. Another question is why America and Israel are particularly targeted and their national flags usually accompany each other, when a Muslim frenzy of burning and destroying burst forth in any part of the globe? The answer is two-fold: first both of those countries stand out as the consummate representatives of strength, modernity, prosperity and success, something which only brings out the impotence and backwardness of the Islamic world. That is the source of "humiliation" that the aggravated Muslims reiterate so often and so intensely, for only the existence of that successful world permits Muslims to grasp what they missed, and they get truly humiliated by the hopelessness of their lagging behind. Secondly, their dream to remedy the situation by creating a *Pax Islamica* to encompass the entire universe, has been scuttled principally by Israel in its immediate vicinity and by America worldwide, for the US is the only power able and willing to stand up to them and obstruct their goal of establishing a world caliphate. That double frustration has been shared by Muslims in general, regardless of whether one categorizes them as "Islamists" or otherwise.

After September 11 a talk show was held by *al-Jazeerah* network (representing what is known as "moderate" and "peace-loving" Islam) where the question was posed to the panelists and the viewers about whether Bin Laden was a terrorist or a hero. The only moderate panelist, a Tunisian, was mocked and humiliated by his co-panelists and by the moderator of the show for daring to dissent from the otherwise unanimous opinion which crowned Bin Laden as a national hero. Viewers who called or emailed from the entire Islamic world, were almost unanimous in the same consensus. That was not a poll among "Islamists", but among the rank and file of Muslims, most of whom were supposedly the educated owners of PC computers. Yet, their reaction was "Islamist" in substance. So, where is the distinction? Yes, there are *Islamikaze*) activists who are ready to blow themselves up for the cause of Islam, in the process killing westerners and Jews. But they are only a handful, who are recruited, trained, financed, indoctrinated and dispatched by a vast infra-structure of Muslim states, organizations and individuals, and surrounded by the sympathy and admiration, often adulation, of the vast masses of the Muslim public and the mainstream press in countries that are clients of the US or signed peace with Israel. Who is then an "Islamist" among all those layers of activists and supporters, and who is the "moderate" and "peace-loving?". In the US and Europe, it was found that several Muslim intellectuals, leaders and clerics, who gained favor with the authorities and access to the highest echelons of power, for their supposed "moderation", and their openness to "dialogue", were later arrested for their illicit fund-raising for Muslim terrorist organizations, for incitement to terrorism or for suppressing women's rights; did they suddenly turn from "moderate" to "radical"? No, they were the same Muslims who were perceived previously as moderate when they acted or refrained from acting in a certain way, but became "Islamists" when they were caught red-handed engaging in subversive acts against their host countries. In both instances they acted as Muslims in the name of Islam; it is Western and Westernized Muslim scholars who attached to them those epithets which they themselves never recognized. Most Muslims who cite the relevant passages from their sources to justify their deeds, and they do it regularly and perennially, are also used to make blunt anti American and anti-Semitic and genocidal statements, and no amount of rhetorical maneuvering can mitigate that fact. It seems that the fictional distinction that is drawn in the West between Islam and "Islamists", which is usually made either by Western scholars and politicians or by Muslim moderates who live in the West, emanates more from an instinct of self-defense and survival than from a sober observation of reality. In Muslim countries themselves it is often hard to tell who is who, inasmuch as Palestinian, Saudi, Egyptian and Pakistani clerics who belong to the "moderate" establishment, often issue *fatwa*s and deliver sermons that are every bit as "extremist" as the "radical" ones. Even imported or home grown Muslim clerics in the West do not make any effort to distinguish or to distance themselves from "Islamists", because they themselves cannot tell the difference. Western scholars and politicians, who want to cater to Islam, for electoral or other worldly perks, on the one hand, but cannot ignore the rage of their own people against violent Islam, on the other hand, find shelter in that distinction which allows them to claim that the Islam they support or defend is "moderate", while the violence that their people condemn emanates solely from the "extremist Islamists". At the same time politicians and scholars critical of Islam need that distinction to shelter themselves from accusations of "racism" and Islamophobia, as if multi-ethnic and multi-racial Islam were a "race", or of anti-Muslim bias and hatred. Muslim scholars and public figures who live in the West resort to that distinction in order to avoid a blanket condemnation of Islam of which they are part, and to escape suspicions by their coreligionists that they "sold-out" to the West or that they committed an act of "treason" against their culture and religion. Many of them find it more expedient to claim that they are "secular Muslims", a notion that is unacceptable to Islam in all its nuances, and some of them convert to Christianity in order to feel free to lash out at their previous religion, though they know that they are handily offset by the much larger numbers of Westerners who convert to Islam.

Matters are further complicated and made less comprehensible to Western minds by the paranoia and conspiracy theories that are very widespread in the Muslim world, among "Islamists" and others alike, whether Muslims are modern and western-educated or traditionalist and obscurantist. Those theories that are rampant even among Muslims living in the West, would insist that world leaders who support Israel are Jewish (like Presidents Reagan and Bush), that the UN of all places, is the mastermind of the Jews who utilize it as the tool for their world dominion, and that the major violent acts that shook the world, like the world wars, the world revolutions and September 11, were all the fruit of Jewish creation and execution, with or without Western connivance and collaboration. Their minds are so permeated with these non-sensical theories that they become impervious to logical, rational debate that is open to argument, discussion and to persuasion. Therefore, the difficulty of dealing with Muslim minds consists not only of removing the mountains of pure delusion that choke their free thinking, but also of persuading them that the very attempt to counter-argue those futilities is not necessarily part of the world conspiracy that is being woven against them. It is possible to explain their imaginary picture of the world by their need to project on their enemies the conceptual and analytical shortcomings that bewitch them, but it is impossible to move them out of the illusory scenarios that they have constructed around themselves and then they cling to them with a tenacity that defies and contradicts Western standards of conduct. The result is that even when Muslims initiate and launch an act of violence, they accuse the West of it and dub it, or what led to it, as an act of "aggression" of which they are the victims and which calls for their retaliation. As long as the Muslim anti-Western and anti-Semitic discourse was internal, little attention was paid to it in the outside world. But since the end of the Afghanistan War (1979-89) which also signaled the end of the Cold War and the return of the *Mujahideen* to their Muslim home countries, tremendous energies were released by the *Afghanis* (i.e., the foreign battle-hardened veterans of the war in Afghanistan). Those energies have been channeled both domestically (Islamist activity in Algeria, Saudi Arabia, Sudan, Lebanon, Egypt, Jordan, Pakistan and Taliban Afghanistan), and internationally to wage a worldwide Jihad, led by Bin Laden's al-Qa'ida, and carried out simultaneously on Arab, American, African, Asian and European soil. The rising prices of oil in those days afforded some oil-producing Muslim countries and their rulers the possibility to finance the spread of Islam of the puritanical and violent brand in the West. They also absorbed some of the unemployed *Afghani Mujahideen,* while the others were turned loose and ended up in the battle fields of Iraq, Lebanon, Bosnia, Chechnya and Palestine, and then Iraq and Syria, or became mercenaries of violence in America and Europe. The Danish Cartoon Affair of 2006 proved a golden opportunity for Muslim regimes, which began to feel the heat of terrorism breathing down their necks, to re-direct the rage and fury of their masses outwardly against the West and Israel, regardless of whether we define them as radicals or moderates. For Western institutions were attacked in Libya, Egypt, Palestine, Syria and Lebanon, and the boycott of Danish products was launched by Saudi Arabia and other Gulf states which are usually considered "moderate" and "pro-Western". When one examines the spread of Islam into Europe one must take stock of all those considerations, and come to the conclusion that it is not enough to account for Muslim immigrants into the Old Continent and its transformation at their hands, but also go into the dialectic between European counter-measures after the major acts of terror that have occurred there and the Muslim worldview which regards those defensive measures as aggression, persecution, racism, and discrimination against the ever-docile and always "poor", helpless, innocent and "victimized" Muslims who had just come to seek work. When Britain or Germany idolized multi-culturalism as a way to "enrich" European culture, and celebrated the fake "difference" between moderate Islam of the mainstream and the violent few, the Muslims regarded that goodwill gesture by and large, as an attempt to dilute Islam in order to dominate and eliminate it. Only their unrestricted and violent activity in Europe, and the recognition of their own mores and norms, such as wearing the veil, forcing marriage on their women or pursuing "honor killings", would be acceptable to them as a fair and acceptable behavior of the host countries towards them. In other words, not satisfied with full equality of opportunity, freedom of speech and of religious cult, Muslims demand special privileges for themselves, like the prerogative to train terrorists or incite violence against other fellow-citizens, because in their skewed view of democratic society, only too much freedom and *laissez-faire*, even at the detriment of the host state and society, is enough freedom for them. When they burn down a Jewish synagogue in Berlin or Paris, they expect their adopted countries to accept that as a matter of course, and they are often aided in that belief by the local extreme-left or extreme-right, or church organizations that boost Muslim demands due to their common anti-Semitism or in order to appear as "progressive" multi-culturalists.

Reverting to the right terminology, calling a spade a spade, is not only our duty to scholarship, which recognizes no biases, no self-serving ideologies and no catering to political correctness, also re-establishes straight lines of communication between authors and readers and between scholars and their peers, and forces upon everyone in the field to play by the same rules. It is unthinkable, for example, that ideology-driven volunteers, who are ready to make the ultimate sacrifice for their convictions, should be denigrated as "suicide-bombers", however they may deserve denigration, or that anyone who lacks the courage to criticize any aspect of Islam should hide behind the spurious excuse of only bashing "Islamism", while Islam pure and simple remains untouchable and beyond reproach. One should also recognize that injecting massive doses of Islam into an already difficult dispute, has turned the Muslim- Western confrontation into a bloody and insoluble conflict. Listen to Bin Laden's and to Iran's and other Muslim radical threats toward the West and take them seriously, and do not dismiss them as pure rhetoric and boasting. Watch the senseless and cruel execution of Daniel Pearl in Karachi and others in the killing fields of ISIS or the terrorist acts done by al Qa'ida and others of their kin, and listen to the threats and attacks against Jews in Europe and on Israel's borders by Hamas and Hizbullah), and you will get a sense of this asymmetrical and uncompromising battle. Acting so, the dispute was pushed one notch up, because from the quantitative issue it used to be, involving territories, compensations and other measurable and negotiable assets, it grew into a qualitative problem dealt with in absolutes, in Allah-given terms, which are not subject to negotiation, let alone compromise and settlement. Anyone reading the Hamas Charter[28] or viewing the Hamas conduct on Israel's borders with Gaza, cannot have missed this trend since it was elected by Palestinians to guide their destiny. In short, westerners should realize that Islam, not Islamists, are their ideological rivals and potential enemies, and terrorist movements like the al Qa'ida and Taliban, the Hamas and Hizbullah are the long arms which resort to *Islamikaze* to sow terror in the west and discourage it from resisting this onslaught. Diluting the Islamic rivals by singling out Islamists among them, deprecating their death and terrorist contractors by calling them "suicide bombers" and denigrating their home grown idealist followers by dubbing them "criminals", not only does not address the problem of Islam in general, but lends to it legitimacy.

Basically, Muslims are required to live under Islamic rule, but it is a fact that Muslims have been moving in masses into foreign lands, and that the queues for immigration visas to non-Muslim countries keep growing incessantly. There is need, therefore, to reconcile between the desirable and the realistic. The desirable is rooted in the glory of Islam at its inception, when it spread like a brush fire all over the known world, either by conquest or by commerce or through the missionary work of the Sufi mystics. The political theory developed which divided all humanity into three kinds of people and the lands they inhabited into two categories. In the first place, there we the Muslims, the complete humans who had submitted *(Muslims)to* the Will of Allah, then came the people

[28] R. Israeli, The Charter of Allah: The Platform of the Islamic Resistance Movement" in Y. Alexander (ed.) *The 1988-89 Annual of Terrorism*, Martinus Nijhoff, 1990, The Netherlands, pp. 99-134.

of the Book (the Scriptuaries), mainly Christians and Jews, who possessed a divine revelation in a holy book, delivered to them by one of Allah's Messengers, Jesus and Moses, respectively. But since these people have distorted the original message, until it was updated, as it were, by the Seal of Messengers, the Prophet Muhammad, they are in an intermediate situation between the Muslims and the Pagans. They deserve to be protected people (*dhimmis),* provided they paid the poll tax (*jizya*) in recognition of the superiority of Islam and in submission to it as humiliated people. Pagans, the lowest category of people, were to either convert to Islam or perish during the occupation of their lands by Islam, or run away until Islam caught up with them in the next round of Islamic expansion. Thus, the domain under Islamic rule was called *Dar al-Islam,* or the House of Islam (*Pax Islamica*), regardless of the composition of the occupied population, for there can be a House of Islam with non-Muslim majority during the first phases of the Islamic expansion, until the pagans were killed or converted, and the Scriptuaries could either convert their religion and turn Muslims or resign to their minority and permanently humiliating status. Beyond the Domain of Islam lay *Dar al-Harb,* the Domain of War, namely the land yet to be taken over and Islamized.

Hence the preference and recommendation of Islam to its adepts to live under the House of Islam, for only there could the requirements of the faith be fulfilled without fear of coercion. It was recognized that Muslims could circulate under certain limitations and condition, during their trade travels or journeys for other purposes, but that sort of movement was temporary by nature. In more recent times, when Muslims began to settle in non-Muslim lands, they had to work out solutions to accommodate the contradiction between their Allah-ordained role as members of the ruling faith of the world and the actual reality where Islam was conquered, debased, beaten, humiliated and ruled by non-Muslims, as if "history had derailed from its set path of Islamic dominance. Therefore, while in their own lands that were occupied by Christians (Like Andalusia), Jews (Palestine) and Hindis (Kashmir)they could rebel and regard it as their right to recapture what they had lost, when they moved or found themselves inside non-Muslim ruled territory, they had either to reconcile to the debasing idea of living permanently under Unbelievers, which is an unbearable solution, or get out and moving back to Islamdom. For if they stayed, they would have to conclude that while the rule was held by the heathen, namely that they lived in the Dominion of War officially, the liberties of life and worship are such that they can accomplish the tasks of the Believers unscathed, and therefore they can constitute a sort of spiritual if not physical Muslim enclaves that they consider as enclaves of the House of Islam. This is the situation that permits Muslims to congregate massively in many European cities today where under multi-culturalism they could maintain their own neighborhoods, mores, dress, worship, ambience and even language undisturbed. In such countries, they can even attain the critical mass that prods them to make demands for more concessions to their faith, and their mosques and cultural centers become also lairs for political and religious activity, some acceptable to the host countries, but some reaching a degree of subversion, like violence and terrorism, as to become intolerable. When that balance is disturbed, then many Islamic groups, that are dubbed "radicals", "islamist" or "terrorist" in the West, "Jihadis" by the Muslims activists themselves, judge that their imagined House of Islam in their enclaves had turned into an inhospitable House of War, from which they either exit to go to fight elsewhere for Islam as itinerant Jihadis, or rebel locally against the host authorities, under the belief, hope or delusion at hat Allah will be on their side and ensure their ultimate victory. Others regard their very presence in the House of War, backed by more incoming waves of Muslims, legal or illegal, will augment their numbers to such an extent that they will come to predominate. In other words, the mass immigration of Muslims into the Western turf become in itself a sort of quiet Jihad, a peaceful substitute to occupation by force of arms, that will ultimately transform Europe into a real House of Islam.

If we wish to expand on the universal contexts in which the murderous behavior of the radical Muslim terrorists and their bellicose, fanatic and extreme cruelty which puts them beyond the human pale, we might mention, the excellent study by German political scientist Matthias Kuntzel[29], who spotted very curious similarities between the rising Muslim Brothers in the 1930s in Egypt and the Nazi nascent organization of that era, and go beyond into the symbols and other characteristics of these Muslim radicals and their Nazi contemporaries. Certainly, you need not to be contemporaneous with a mentor to inherit his ideology, as Lively and Abrams have demonstrated in the long apostolic chain of distorted minds, corrupt morality and deviant ideology which ended up in Nazism[30]. For example, the concept of Islamikaze that was analyzed above is very similar to the elite *Sturmabtleilung (*storm troops), the hard-hitting units who were used to fearlessly storm the enemies lines, which created a tremendous in the number of young dedicated volunteers, and were described by Robert Waite[31] as precursors of the Nazi SS and Gestapo, had many similarities to the cruelty, ruthlessness, dedication and perversion of Islamikaze of today, who hail not only from the rank and file of Palestinian PLO terrorists, but even more so from the more religiously fanatic Hamas and Islamic Jihad. Waite wrote:

Only a very special type of officer could be used. He must be unmarried, under 25 years of age, in excellent physical health…

---

[29] Matthias Kuntzel, *Jihad and Jew-hatred:Islamism, Nazism and the Roots of 9/11,* Telos Press, 2007.

[30] Scott Lively and Kevin Abrams: *The Pink Swastika:Homosexuality in the Nazi Party,* The Founders Corporation, Oregon, 1995.

[31] Robert Waite, *Vanguard of Nazism:: The Free Corps Movement in Post [W W I] War Germany, 1918-23,* Norton and Company, NY, 1969; and *The Psychopathic God Adolf Hitler*, Signet Books NY, 1977.

and above all he must possess in abundance that quality which German military writers call "ruthlessness". The result was that at the time of the armistice Germany was flooded with hundreds of capable, arrogant young commanders who found an excellent outlet for their talents in the Free Corps Movement [32].

The fact that those young people lived in an almost exclusively male conservative Islamic society, where pre-nuptial sexual activity is strictly forbidden and discredited, many of them tended to homosexuality. Their Nazi counterparts, where pederast homosexuality was rife, though they usually sought to keep it under wraps, was repeatedly documented[33] in post W W II Western research, and the public figures who were suspected of that vice were never ashamed, humiliated or repentant about it. But in the Arab and Islamic world, where homosexuality and pedophilia are a matter not only of religious prohibition, but also of personal, tribal and communal disgrace, since they throw a demeaning light on the manhood/machismo *(muruwa)* of the concerned people, the matter is not only concealed within families where it mostly recurs, but totally denied as inexistent, punished and confining its perpetrators and their victims to eternal humiliation, excommunication and even exile. Among the Arab community in Israel, some of those individuals (male and female, Muslim and Christian) who have been affected by this problem which is unforgivable in their milieu, have ran away to the Israeli-Jewish society, which is more tolerant of this phenomenon, to seek shelter and protection and even join Israeli political parties where they can rise to the level of Member of the Knesset, a level they could never attain in any Arab or Muslim country. And yet, they complain about Israeli democracy, which saved their very existence.

America and its allies' retreat from Iraq and Afghanistan in the

---

[32] Ibid, p. 27.

[33] Lively and Abrams, op. cit.

wake of their dismal failure to alter the latters' regimes, has been seen in the Muslim world not only as the defeat of Western ideas, first in Afghanistan against Soviet Communism and then in Iraq against American capitalism. Those long struggles had illustrated in their eyes the impotence of the dwindling and exhausted ideas against the might of the mounting Islam whose turn it is now to govern the world once again. That idea, which was contained in the Qur'anic verses that were incrusted in the inside circumference of the Dome of the Rock in Jerusalem (and repeated again in the makeshift mosque in which Muslims in Nazareth tried to flaunt their possession of the city in their aborted attempt to exhibit it in the open in the courtyard of the Basilica of Annunciation in 1995)[34], states very simply that: "Allah was neither born nor gave birth", thus totally deprecating the Christian Trinity and the idea that God had a son, for Allah was uncreated and eternal, which means a rejection of Christianity lock stock and barrel. And yet, no refutation of that doctrine emanates in modern times from Christianity, and the Pope still received the Muslim radical Imams who pronounce those words of blaspheme, visits those lands of Islam where these ideas persist, and under the guise of world fraternity and love, and tolerance of all opinions, it allows Muslim missionary work *(da'wa)* in Christian lands at a time when Christian mission is prohibited in most Muslim countries, and even the very existence of Christianity is forbidden in Saudi Arabia, which finances Islamic centers in most countries of the world. That kind of openness and tolerance is interpreted as submission and recognition of the upcoming universal rule of Islam.

[34] See R. Israeli, *Green Crescent Over Nazarerth: The Displacement of Christians by Muslims in the Holy Land,* Frank Cass, London, 2004.

# Chapter Three

## *The New Mood in Islam*

There is little doubt that the most earth-shattering event that has impacted the thought, politics, society, and conduct of the Muslim world in recent times has been the collapse of the Soviet Bloc, and with it of Communism as a competing alternative to Western capitalism. The ramifications of those developments were multifaceted among the Islamic countries. Internally, their old inborn Communist parties simply shrank into insignificance once it was shown that their promise had been a thin veneer of pretense, which waned away under the burden of its own inefficacy and helplessness in the face of the contemporary world's requirements. In view of its traditional dislike of the old Western rival, which had been reinforced by Muslim radical thinkers since Hassan al-Banna and Sayyid Qut'b, the great luminaries of the Muslim Brothers who had accused the Western colonizers of oppression, exploitation, and penchant for laxity in social behavior that corrupted the Muslim youth, it was no surprise that the West was shunned by the Islamic world, at least in theory. In those years, the Soviet Union, the loyal ally who had never failed its Muslim clients, seemed the alternative to counter the Western threat. Indeed, many promising young people in the Muslim world were invited or sent to Moscow to pursue their studies-cum-political indoctrination. They enrolled in professions like medicine and engineering or underwent other training courses that prepared them for community or political work in their countries. They learned Russian, and the elite among them took advanced degrees, such as PhDs in Marxist theory, Marxist economics, and Marxist history as viewed and analyzed from the Communist point of view. The case in point was Mahmoud Abbas, otherwise known as Abu Mazen, then a senior PLO official and after Yasser Arafat's death the president of the Palestinian Authority (PA). He chose a topic for his dissertation that suited both his dedication to fight Zionism and Israel and his host's propaganda line, which promoted anti-Semitism, masquerading as "anti-Zionism." His thesis, later published as a book, claimed a collaboration between Zionism and Nazism and diminished the Holocaust by cutting down the number of victims from six to less than one million. In other words, the import of those studies was not to discover historical truth but to serve the propaganda campaign of both his organization and his host's. The world has changed since, and Moscow reoriented itself toward a more correct relationship with the Jewish people, the Zionist movement and Israel, but Abu Mazen showed little propensity to "change his spots"[35]when upon his visit to Germany's Chancellor Olaf Scholz in August, 2022, he charged Israel of having "Committed 50 Holocausts to Palestinians", though no evidence was cited of the existence of death camps or crematoria, or other modes of mass annihilation were ever claimed to exist, except for the mass killing of Palestinians by Jordan in the "Black September", 1970 uprising against King Hussein, or during the Lebanese and Syrian onslaughts of Palestinian refugee camps during the civil wars there. What Abu Mazen neglected to mention was his predecessor in the leadership of the Palestinian movement, Haj Amin al-Husseini, who had collaborated with the Nazis and the Muslim Brothers during the 1930s and 1940s in the extermination of the Jews in the framework of the

---

[35] Allusion is made, of course to Jeremiah 13/23 where the skeptic question was asked: "Can the leopard change his spots?".

"final solution", the Germans committed to perpetrate it in Europe and the Muslims in the Middle East which was one of the targets of the Nazi conquests[36].

The Muslim students who dwelt in Moscow in the thousands, as part of the large body of invited cadres from all nonaligned nations, were not necessarily committed Communists but had a vested interest in training for careers without incurring any cost. They not only learned what was needed for their training but were also indoctrinated with the idea that the Soviet Paradise, which promoted exemplary models of economic and social development, was also the international hub of world peace and fraternity between nations. After the devastating Muslim defeat in the War of 1967 against Israel, it was the Soviet Union who helped rehabilitate the routed Muslim nations, replace their destroyed military equipment, and encourage native models of "socialism" that resembled the structure of the strict authoritarian and hierarchic Soviet Union itself, and of the Soviet Communist Party in their organization, centralism, and conduct. It seemed then that the Islamic world, save for the very conservative monarchical regimes of the Gulf, was comfortably placed in the bosom of the Soviets and well disposed to enjoy that position indefinitely. But 1967 also generated a countercurrent of religious revival throughout that Islamic world, especially following the October 1968 Cairo Islamic Conference, which convened chief clerics and scholars covering the entire span of the Muslim world, from Morocco to Indonesia[37]. In the painful soul-searching deliberations, which attempted to ponder the reasons for that unprecedented "glorious Muslim defeat" in modern times, they came to the conclusion that, while Islam had reached its climax close to the time of the Prophet and thereafter, when it was upright

[36] R. Israeli, *The Death Camps of Croatia: Visions and Revisions: 1941-5*, Transaction, NJ, 2013.

[37] D.F. Green, *Arab Theologians on Jews and Israel: The Fourth Conference of the Academy of Islamic Research*, Editions de l'Avenir, Geneva, 1974.

and ruled by the standards set by the Messenger of Allah, it was the Western corrupting influence on Islam that had caused its demise. The lesson was inescapable: only a return to Islam and its ancient norms could rescue it from oblivion. In other words, while Western utopia for progress and improvement lay sometime in the future and may be attained gradually by determined social, political, and intellectual measures; Islamic utopia was projected into the time of the Prophet in the past, and all that was needed was to strive to approximate the achievements of the Prophet's generation by studying and applying them in the real world. Hence the spread of many Salafi movements, connoting a return to the era of the *aslaf,* that is the ancients.

The Islamic movements, which emerged under various appellations, were not at ease with the Soviet alliance that had been thrust upon them as a matter of convenience. Therefore, as soon as the Soviet Union collapsed and the Communist parties in the Arab world withered away for want of commitment to the idea of Communism, a giant vacuum was created that needed to be filled urgently. In Israel, for example, one of the few places in the Middle East where a Communist Party was legal, an Islamic movement emerged where local politics had been previously dominated by the Communists (later converted to Rakah and then Hadash Parties that connoted "new democracy and equality"). So those who remained within the Communist Party and had brandished the names of Brezhnev and Ceausescu as the epitomes of ideal democracy, had to change their name, as other Communists in the rest of the world had done, as if they were beginning something new, and started lecturing Israel on democracy. The wedding of convenience between Islam and Communism had come to an end in any case. Russia, who inherited the Soviet Union, became a close ally to the least mainstream (i.e. Sunnite) Islamic regimes in the Islamic world, that is the Alawites of Syria, and the Shi'ites of Iran of Iran in an attempt to regain what it had lost on the way to rehabilitating the dissolved Empire. But the defeat of the Soviets in Afghanistan in 1989, which put an end to their ten-year, "Vietnam-like" venture, only precipitated Soviet prestige to its lowest ebb. For the world of Islam, the Soviet demise in Afghanistan meant more than that. It meant that Muslim *mujahideen* were able, by their primitive weaponry but with the aid of other Muslims, namely the Muslim volunteers who flocked in from the entire Islamic world, to beat one of the two superpowers and force her to retreat. The conclusion was swift and clear: the other superpower (the United States) could not be far behind, an assumption that was not off the mark in view of the upcoming retreat of the United States and the takeover by the Taliban in Afghanistan when foreign intervention ebbed in 2015 and drew to its end in 2021. Moreover, the very intervention of the Soviets on Christmas 1979 had been motivated by their fear, lest the Islamic upheaval that began with the Iranian Revolution one year earlier might seep into its five Islamic republics of Central Asia, which were adjacent to Iran (Tajikistan, Turkmenistan, Kyrgyzstan, Uzbekistan, and Kazakhstan), and to the Islamic Republic of the Caucasus—Azerbaijan—which borders Iran. The Soviets had hoped to stem that danger by demonstrating that the Iranian Revolution had been a paper tiger, but they eventually failed, much to the delight of Muslim radicals worldwide, who seized the opportunity to organize their forces and launch their onslaught on the West and the Jews.

The end result was that those six Muslim republics were freed from the Soviet yoke and became independent once the Soviet Federation crumbled. It was tempting for Muslims across the world to conclude that it was *their* mujahideen who were to be credited for that achievement and that thanks to other Muslims, not foreign powers, their brethren were liberated, increasing the number of Muslim countries to 57, almost one third of the world count in those days, when membership of the United Nations amounted to 180. The Muslim mood in the world was upbeat, not only due to the numbers of believers approaching the billion mark, billing their creed as "one quarter of humanity," but also boasting Muslim identity and promoting its international success. Indeed, the Organization of Islamic Cooperation (OIC), which had made its debut in 1968 as a result of the arson of the al-Aqsa Mosque in Jerusalem, when Muslims across the world rushed to falsely indict Israel of its premeditation, was a manifestation of that newfound pride. The first Rabat Summit Conference of Islamic countries in 1968, under the pretext that it was urgent to "come to the rescue of Jerusalem," was concluded with a unanimous decision to establish a Jerusalem Committee, headed by the host of the conference, King Hassan, who hastened to call the central square in Fez, the ancient Royal Capital (the Kyoto of Morocco),"the Jerusalem Plaza," to evince his loyalty to Islam, for he had been much maligned by many Muslim radicals for "selling off" to the United States, France, and Western values and for maintaining secret contact with the Israelis, all unforgivable sins in Islamic politics. Since 1968, membership in the OIC continued to grow in leaps and bounds, and in 1976 the incredible happened: Turkey, which under her civil governments jealously guarded her secular nature, and avoided any official involvement with religion, suddenly yielded to the public mood and agreed not only to join the OIC but also to host that year's conference in Istanbul. The symbolism could not be missed: what used to be the splendid capital of the Muslim Ottoman Empire and the seat of its glamorous Sultan, who was also the caliph of all Muslims, unexpectedly admitted to her Islamic past and present Islamic identity and joined that great association of modern Muslim states. Not since the disappearance of the Caliphate after World War One, when the Ottoman Empire was dismantled, had Muslims across the world experienced that feeling of great Muslim power converging together—as if the gathered heads of states of the Islamic world represented the corporate caliphate that was no more. Since the Istanbul encounter, the membership of OIC grew to include such countries as Uganda, who was not exactly Muslim but was ruled by a Muslim tyrant, Idi Amin Dada, and that was enough for him to draw his country into the fray. Naturally, since the rise to power of the Islamic Party of Tayyip Erdogan in Ankara in 2002, the feeling of exhilaration with growing Muslim power has heightened, as it did in the 1970s when Pakistan revealed its "Islamic bomb" and as the Muslim world is bound to boast again when Iran achieves its own. Admittedly, the Iranian Revolution of 1978 has caused unease in some quarters of the Sunnite majority, which fears the aggression of the Shi'ite Crescent, constituted by Iran, Iraq, Syria, and Lebanon, to the point that some Sunnite clerics have dubbed the Shi'ites as "worse than the Jews," a compliment not easily disbursed to a rival in the Islamic world. But, beyond these divisions, which pit Iran and its satellites against Saudi Arabia and its cohorts, there is agreement between the two parties that the victory of Islam takes no less precedence than the theological differences between Shi'a and Sunna, as long as Iranian power is kept at bay and does not threaten the relatively moderate Muslim countries like the Gulf States, Morocco, Tunisia and Jordan. For example, the acts of terror, which were invented originally by Shi'ites (and were wrongly dubbed "suicide bombings"), have become a favorite modus operandi of many Sunnite groups, such as Hamas, some PLO factions, such as the al-Aqsa Brigades, some terrorists in Iraq and in Afghanistan, and others. Hamas in Gaza has been relying on aid from Iran, and many Muslim terrorists convene for their annual meetings in Tehran, regardless of their Sunnite affiliation.

Those years that followed the Soviet debacle in Afghanistan also saw the rise of the Afghani phenomenon in the Islamic world. Tens of thousands of Muslim mujahideen had indeed been recruited by American encouragement and Saudi financing from all over the Islamic world to flock to Afghanistan and to fight against the hated Communist superpower until its capitulation. Those Moroccan, Saudi, Jordanian, Iraqi, Chechnyan, Bosnian, European, and other volunteers had gathered in Afghani camps financed by the CIA, and they kept the stream of reinforcements from drying up in that demanding ten-year fight against the Soviet Russians. But when dwindling Russia capitulated and the war was officially terminated, those Afghani outsiders returned home and began to pose a local problem for their governments. In 1989 and thereafter, those repatriated fighters, who had now become a roving international jihadist camp, ready to go where they were needed for the cause of Islam, soon became one major issue for their governments[38]. They went to Iraq to fight the Americans, returned to Afghanistan to face their former American allies who had assisted them against the Soviets, and then became the major component of the Syrian rebels against the Assad regime, al-Qa'ida, and the ISIS movement in Iraq and Syria. One of their founders and leaders, probably the most renowned and the most influential, was Osama bin Laden. Bin Laden contributed more than any Muslim at that time to debunk the myth that Muslim terrorism was due to poverty and disaffection. The South American favelas, those makeshift slums that surround all major cities in that continent, provide daily proof that material misery does not necessarily produce indiscriminate terrorism against innocent people. But bin Laden's personal wealth had attested to the contrary. He could have led an easy life, like his peers in Saudi Arabia, in the opulence of his palaces, but he elected to fight for his ideas in the mountains of Tora Bora in Afghanistan, pursued by American aircraft and Special Forces attempting to eliminate him for a decade or more before he was gunned down in his secret abode in the garrison city of Abbottabad in Pakistan in 2012. It also happens that the two most fundamentalist Muslim countries—Saudi Arabia and Iran—are also the richest, so that poverty could not have been the reason for their radicalism. While Iran

---

[38] R. Israeli, *Itinerant Jihadis:Arab and Muslim War Volunteers,* Strategic Books, TX, 2011.

continues to serve as the international hub of Muslim terrorism, it has been the massive participation of individual Saudi donors in the world jihadi effort that had first allowed thousands of Saudi volunteers to fight in Afghanistan against the Soviets, then for the 9/11 events to happen, and for the continued bloodletting in the Syrian civil war and in ISIS's onslaughts in Syria and Iraq. Under the Iranian nuclear threat, and the resulting discreet and half-hearted Saudi adhesion to the Abrahamic Treaty which brought moderate Arab countries to terms with Israel outwardly, and to adopt moderate policies domestically to protect their own regimes from the takeover by Islamic parties, as had happened in Egypt, Tunisia, Libya and Sudan, the changing mood in the mainstream world of Islam came to full bloom. Even radicalize Turkey under Erdogan, has shown signs of balancing out its enthusiastic support for Palestinian terrorism by a more compromising attitude towards Israel, taking account of its commitment to NATO which does not officially condone acts of terrorism in its areas of jurisdiction.

In Afghanistan Bin Laden had met the militant Muslim scholar Abdullah Azzam, of Palestinian origin, who devoted his latter years to posing the ideological fundaments of the universal jihad that radical Islam had launched against the United States and the Jews. He was, like others in his conviction, thoroughly influenced by the Imam's knowledge, his political and theological acumen, his total devotion to the cause of Islam, that he was swayed to the point of foregoing his family life and his initially positive economic activity, which had made him wealthy. Upon returning to Saudi Arabia as an "Afghani," who had been hardened by his battlefield experience as a *mujahid,* bin Laden became restless and fanatically determined to overthrow the corrupt and elitist royal regime under which he had grown in Riyadh. But soon he was singled out for the danger he posed to his peers in the kingdom, was stripped of his Saudi citizenship, which had caused much embarrassment to the relations between his country and the United States, and expelled from the country. He was on the road from then on, together with his nuclear family, on the lookout for a land of shelter that was Islamic enough to accept and protect him, poor enough to vie for the funds he could provide in return, and deserted and inaccessible enough for foreign powers to remain unable to locate him or to dislodge him from there. That land would serve as the physical base for his new organization, al-Qa'ida (literally, "the Base"), and as the metaphoric base of the world jihadi movement he was determined to found, lead, and fund by his own means.

The organization spoke about confronting "American arrogance" and world Jewry (not Israel or Zionism, as others who wish to dissimulate their anti-Semitism pretend), which were seen as close allies with Jews at the lead. They were accused of providing the ideological underpinnings for "controlling the world" under the well-known and widely diffused "world Jewish conspiracy", and other conspiracy theories that jihadi Islam, like Hamas and the Muslim Brothers, had liberally borrowed from the *Protocols of the Elders of Zion*. Powerful America, it was claimed, was the financial and military arm that was manipulated by world Jewry to achieve its goals. That was the reason that on September 11, al-Qa'ida attacked the Twin Towers and the Pentagon, the symbols of American economic and military power, and all over the Muslim world there was great jubilation. However, some Muslim quarters were so embarrassed by the scope of that horror that they tried to impute it to the CIA or Mossad, claiming that Jews were in any case involved in it. After he was ejected from his homeland, bin Laden sought and found shelter in Sudan, which in 1989 came under the rule of General Omar al-Bashir, who later became involved in the Darfur massacre and was indicted by the International Criminal Court for crimes against humanity. That poor country was hungry for bin Laden's foreign currency and was itself too involved in horrific mass murdering to resent bin Laden's terrorist schemes. For that reason, bin Laden settled there until the 1998 al-Qa'ida's terrorist acts against the American embassies in Kenya and Tanzania, resulting in hundreds of fatalities, both American and African, raised the wrath of the United States. The Clinton administration retaliated with a few bombings of the Sudan and threatened the host country with more unless bin Laden and his group were expelled from the country. In his search for a new asylum, bin Laden identified Afghanistan as such a target. Since 1996, the Taliban had taken over the rule in Kabul and established such a strict Islamic rule there under Mullah Omar as to make Saudi Arabia and Iran look like bastions of democracy and liberalism. The mullah was an unknown cleric who had gained spiritual control of his Taliban during the Afghani civil war. Once bin Laden was introduced to him in Kandahar, they became close friends, and the determined Afghani mullah guaranteed asylum to his guest, whatever the price he would have to pay.

The unipolar world of the 1990s and the dramatic fall of the Soviet Union were accompanied by vast economic troubles and deep social problems in the world. The rise of Islamic radicalism, which challenged Russia's hinterland and forced it to take harsh measures against its Muslims in Chechnya and the Caucasus, also helped shift world attention to a new vocabulary in the West that seemed to adapt to the idea that militant Islam was there to be reconciled, not to be fought, despite its many outrageous outbursts of violence against not only the West and Israel, but also against its own people. If we say, for example, that murdering Jews is the result of anti-Semitic hatred and contempt toward them, and that anti-Western violence is generated by a fanatic and intolerant Muslim creed, then how do we explain the mass killings of Muslims by Muslims, which account for the majority of fatalities in Islamic countries— Syrians against Syrians, Iraqis against Iraqis, Afghanis against Afghanis, black Muslims in Darfur by Muslim Janjaweed, and other mass killings in Algeria, Lebanon, Yemen, Pakistan, the Palestinian Hamas, and all the rest? The inescapable conclusion is that some trigger-happy Muslims, who are propelled by jihad, display their disregard for human life—which renders execution of others, capital punishment, hijacking, kidnapping, robbery, hostage-taking, beheading, mass murder, mutilation of the living and the dead, and torture—as an acceptable norm of conduct. Implementing Shari'a rules in domestic penal law, and even more so attempting to impose its standards on foreigners (like in the cases of Daniel Pearl in Pakistan, Salman Rushdie in England, and then in the US, the authors of the anti-Muhammad cartoons in Denmark, or the Christians of Nigeria by the Boko Haram), are the best indications of the low value of human lives in their eyes. When practiced against Jews, this view is rationalized in many ways—as "anti-Zionism," or vengeance for the "crimes against Palestinians," or "self-defense," or "reaction to Western arrogance and Islamophobia," to their "humiliation of Muslims," or "desecration of Muslim values," along with any other amount of trumped-up rationalizations. Underlying all those rationalizations is the burning desire by many Muslims to impose by force their ideals, values, and rules of conduct both on their own nationals, whom they view as apostates, thus deserving death, and certainly on their rivals, who are often considered as enemies of Islam and Allah and therefore are equally deserving of annihilation. No debates, negotiations, compromises, or arguments are possible with this "expression of the will of Allah," and therefore no perceived offense against or deviation from these rules is tolerable.

It is often claimed that this strict interpretation of Islam with its abuses, including a blatant anti-Semitism, is only the lot of "fanatic," "radical," "fundamentalist," or "Islamist" Muslims, usually quantified as some 15 percent of the 1.5 billion world Muslims, as if that were a different faith embracing different principles than those followed by the rank-and-file Muslims. In fact, even if that were true, we are talking about 200 million individuals, spread among all nations—from the Boko Haram in Nigeria to the Lashkar-e-Taiba in Pakistan—whose numbers are large enough to cause trouble for the entire world. In reality, all 1.5 billion Muslims belong to one creed, who uphold Sharia law to various degrees but champion the same tenets, though those who do not follow them to the letter are not adepts of another alternative faith known as "moderate Islam," which is sometimes dubbed by ignorant politicians as "a religion of peace" to distinguish from the violent and aggressive conduct of the "extremists." In reality, no such separate Islam exists, though there are certainly many truly moderate Muslims who have broken off from the bloody path of Sharia law, especially some of those dwelling in the West, who can from a safe distance criticize the recurring killings of "apostates," "traitors," the phenomenon of the Islamikaze bombers against Westerners and Israelis, the culture of death that is groomed in many Islamic lands, and indeed the unbridled anti-Semitic calumnies that are rife in their environments. But "moderate Muslims" have yet to produce an alternative doctrine and worldview that could rival official Islam or posit a creed and a set of rules to persuade Muslims to relinquish the Shari'a and embrace another way, thus excluding themselves from the community of the believers in the eyes of established Islam. Moderate Muslims often accuse the radicals, who are in fact Muslims who behave in accordance with the accepted rules of the Shari'a, of having "hijacked Islam" or distorted its real meanings, or misinterpreted it, and they in turn are condemned by their rivals for having abandoned the path of Allah or for having themselves been corrupted by Western ideologies. But, for better or for worse, it is the standards of the radicals that prevail in the Islamic world for the most part. One can watch the mass demonstrations in the streets of Gaza, Quetta, Casablanca, Durban, and Jakarta, or in the Muslim neighborhoods of Paris, London, Sydney, Amsterdam, and Toronto to realize how alive, universal, and popular are the Muslim mantras that are uttered, along with the rampages that are performed daily by men, women, and children, including leaders and clerics. Are they all Islamists? No, they are simply Muslims, and the common denominator that links them in their hatred of the West and the Jews is Islam, standard Islam, under the justification of the Sharia, which is promoted by their imams. While some moderate and courageous Muslim individuals will be there to save the honor of their faith when they raise their lone voices against the abuses perpetrated in the name of their creed, mainstream Muslims, including Westernized and modern professionals, intellectuals, and students, will also always be there to glorify in the executions of Westerners and Jews by Muslim terrorists, to write or broadcast in favor of the Islamikaze, and to distribute sweets in the streets to celebrate the deaths of Americans and Jews.The champions of the spurious distinction between the so-called Islamist minority and the peaceful Muslim majority—who became entrapped in their reluctance from a carpet condemnation of Islam lest they be accused of Islamophobia or racism (as if Islam were a race and not a multiracial and multicultural creed) if they are non-Muslims and of treason if they are—are also enslaved by another distinction of their own making, which has equally no leg to stand on. That is " Judeophobia," a parallel to Islamophobia, to separate from anti-Semitism, which is universally condemned in those circles and is no longer in vogue in the West, at least not in public. They explain to us that Islam has never been anti-Semitic, which proves their ignorance of Islamic sources, and that the current dislike of Jews is no more than Judeophobia, which has no historical roots and has been a modern, circumstantial, and fleeting phenomenon that does not warrant uncalled-for anxiety. If flagrant and constant anti-Semitism is reduced to temporary and passing Judeophobia, it would merely become a junior counterpart of Islamophobia, and a lesser evil, making it less objectionable and more acceptable, on par with Islamophobia, as a collateral phenomenon in modern society. Generally speaking, they would simplistically argue: how can Muslims, specifically the Arabs, themselves Semites, be anti-Semitic? It is exactly this war of words that has been engineered to obfuscate substance and increase the currency of Muslim terminology while at the same time depriving the Jews and their supporters from their traditional arsenal of words in the battle against anti-Semitism, which then needs to be clarified and understood. Could anyone explain in what way the Qur'anic condemnation of Jews as "descendants of pigs and monkeys"—which is routinely preached to all Muslims (not only "Islamists") by their clerics in the Islamic world and in the West—can be construed as merely Judeophobic and not anti-Semitic? Is this hallowed reference, which is as eternal as the Word of Allah, a circumstantial and fleeting pronouncement? To say so would be a blasphemy. It is used by Muslim clerics, as a matter of course, in such "moderate" and "pro-Western" countries as Saudi Arabia, Egypt, and Jordan, as a continuation of the traditional way to demonize and dehumanize Jews in order to facilitate their annihilation. What more would it take to call this a plain manifestation of violent anti-Semitism?

Words were created to transmit conventionally agreed-upon meanings. If each actor chose to lend to his words a different significance or to accuse others of distorting their meaning, then we would no longer be able to call a spade a spade or communicate with others on any issue. Anti-Semitism is the irrational hatred of the Jews, and it has been called so since the onset of modern research on this sinister issue in the nineteenth century. No amount of manipulations of words or creation of parallels to dilute that terminology will succeed, exactly as no coupling of the unique term *Holocaust* with Armenians, Darfurians, or Rwandans (incidentally, the first two massacres were perpetrated by Muslims) can blunt the poignancy of the Jewish Holocaust or rob it of its uniqueness. No wonder then that the most frequent manifestation of anti-Semitism these days, both among Muslims and among their European anti-Semitic allies, has been Holocaust denial, meaning that the devalued term has acquired a generic usage for all sorts of massacres: the hated Jews cannot even claim to have acceded to the "honor" of having been the unique victims of that calamity. The increased waves of recriminations of the Muslim world against the West and Israel during that axial era are also evident in the rise of Muslim parties in Turkey, Egypt, Jordan, Morocco, Sudan, and the Palestinian Authority. It has also found expression in the unbridled desire of the Iranians to go nuclear and in the thug-like rhetoric of its previous president Ahmadinejad against Western values and Jews, to the point of denying the Shoah in blatant terms, all indications of the spreading anti-Western antagonism in Islam. The zeal in the Islamic world has been directed not only against Israel and the West but aims primarily to sweep out of power their own Western-allied regimes, which are regarded as American stooges. As the major Egyptian paper *al-Ahram* put it, "Religious identity has replaced nationalist ideology,"[39] and that applies not only to Muslim countries but also amid Muslim minorities throughout their diasporas. This means that Muslim terrorism will continue to rise in both Europe and the Muslim world, hence the relevance of the present discourse as a precursor and follow-up to the saga of September 11 and its aftermath. One has to realize, nevertheless, the distortions of the basic characteristics of Islam by both scholars and politicians, who wish to depict a more benign and less menacing picture of the Islamic rise than it is. This is done through the two distinctions that we have mentioned above, which have become conventional wisdom among both critics and proponents of Islam. One is the artificial bifurcation between the so-called Islamists or radicals, who are the minority "bad guys" who spoil the lot by their violent deeds, lend a bad reputation to the majority of their coreligionists, and wage war against the West and Israel and the majority, which is arguably "peace-loving," shunning violence and having no quarrel with the West. The other artificial, and equally spurious, distinction wants us to believe that Judeophobia, which is an attenuated sort

[39] *Al-Ahram Weekly*, "Beyond the Vacuum," April 13–16, 2006.

of anti-Semitism posing as anti-Zionism and anti-Israel, has nothing to do with anti-Semitism; and that while Islam as a whole carries no traces of anti-Semitism, its present anti-Jewish manifestations are no more than a less lethal and vastly less threatening Judeophobia. It is clear that these "scientific" distinctions may have some empirical merit to them, but seem to have much more to do with political correctness—with a degree of sheepish dhimmi-like submissiveness or fear of being accused of racism—than with historical reality. It is an unconvincing argument that Muslims are merely anti-Israel and anti-Zionist and not anti-Semitic, when Jews in the Western Diasporas are habitually attacked by Muslims and have been historically mistreated, beaten, massacred, or forced to convert until compelled to leave the lands of Islam, apart from the fact that they were Jews. French Jews, British Jews, and Belgian Jews are all citizens of the countries in which they live and cannot influence the policies of the Israeli government even if they wished to do so. To attack them is totally gratuitous and is undeniably an expression of the innate anti-Semitism in Islamic thinking. The equivalent in Jewish attitudes would be for Jews to attack their fellow Muslim citizens in European countries every time a Muslim country defames, vilifies, demonizes (or indeed physically attacks) Jews in the media or school curricula, or subjects them to individual or collective economic boycotts, all of which actually happens on a sustained, daily basis in Muslim lands. If it were Jews who committed the attacks, that would be a case of Islamophobia, and the fact that it does not happen proves first that Islamophobia, at least on the part of Jews, is a figment of Muslims' imagination (bandied about precisely to combat the very notion of their pervasive anti-Semitism); and second that Jews, at least in the Diaspora, can distinguish between right and wrong and have never lost their sense of justice and civilized behavior, despite the relentless provocations of Muslims, and not only radicals, against them. When people are given the opportunity to express themselves freely in the Islamic world, such as in Algeria, Jordan, Egypt, Tunisia, and lately Palestine, it is almost invariably political Islam that gains votes, and since it is popular vote, it cannot be said to represent "radicals," exactly as it cannot be claimed that the more than 60 percent of Palestinians who voted for Hamas in 2006 were all Islamists. After September 11, a talk show was held by Al Jazeera network (representing what is known as moderate and peace-loving Islam), in which the question was posed to the panelists and their viewers about whether bin Laden was a terrorist or a hero. The only moderate panelist, a Tunisian, was mocked and humiliated by his co-panelists and by the moderator of the show for daring to dissent from the otherwise unanimous opinion that crowned bin Laden as a national hero. Viewers who called or emailed from around the entire Islamic world were almost unanimous in the consensus. That was not a poll among Islamists, but among the rank-and-file Muslims, most of whom were supposedly the educated owners of PC computers. Yet their reaction was Islamist in substance.

So where is the distinction between the supposed moderates and the alleged Islamists? Yes, there are Islamikaze activists who are ready to blow themselves up for the cause of Islam, in the process of killing Westerners and Jews. But they are only a handful who are recruited, trained, financed, indoctrinated, and dispatched by a vast infrastructure of Muslim states, organizations, and individuals and surrounded by the sympathy and admiration, often adulation, of the vast masses of the Muslim public and the mainstream press, and in countries that are clients of the United States or have signed peace with Israel. Who is then an Islamist among all those activists and supporters, and who is moderate and peace loving? In the United States and Europe, several Muslim intellectuals, leaders, and clerics, who gained favor with the authorities and access to the highest echelons of power for their supposed moderation and their openness to dialogue were later arrested for their illicit fund-raising for Muslim terrorist organizations, for incitement to terrorism, and for suppressing women's rights. Did those leaders suddenly turn from moderate to radical? No, they were the same Muslims who were perceived previously as moderate when they acted a certain way and who became Islamists when they were caught red-handed engaging in subversive acts. In both instances they acted as Muslims in the name of Islam. It was Western scholars and Westernized Muslims who attached those epithets of "moderate" and "Islamists," which the Muslims themselves never recognized. Similarly, clerics and other mainstream Muslims who dub the Jews "descendants of pigs and monkeys" based on a Quranic passage or cite the Hadith, which claims that on the Day of Judgment Jews will hide behind rocks and trees, but the rocks and trees will acquire the magic power of denouncing them and will invite the Muslims to come and kill them, are not exactly setting themselves apart from Islamists. All Muslims who cite those passages, and they all do regularly, are making blunt anti-Semitic and genocidal statements against the Jews, and no amount of rhetorical maneuvering can mitigate that fact.

Throughout the Muslim world, the legitimacy of Israel has been challenged, and the Holocaust is denied systematically, as evidenced by the popularity of such Holocaust deniers as Robert Faurisson, Roger Garaudy, or David Irving. Those countries also prohibited *Schindler's List* from their screens and condoned the violent declarations of the Iranian president on both scores. This is a common denominator among most Muslims, and just like the anti-Jewish stereotypes, nothing differentiates between radicals and moderates. That is the reason why we find Muslims contradicting themselves on the Shoah, denying it on the one hand and wishing Hitler had brought his annihilation plan to completion on the other; they also urge a "scholarly, free, and objective" research of the Holocaust, but only in order to prove that it never was. Similarly, the belief in and the spread of the *Protocols of the Elders of Zion,* the blood libel, the poisoning of wells by Jews, and conspiracy theories concerning the Jews are recurring themes in Palestinian (not only Hamas) as well as mainstream Egyptian, Jordanian, Saudi, Pakistani, and others' writings, systems of beliefs, and propaganda. Genocidal threats against the Jews have abounded not only in bin Laden's statements and in Ahmadinejad's delusions, but also in columns of Egyptian, Saudi, Palestinian, and other mainstream newspapers. Is this Judeophobia of the moderates or plain anti-Semitism of the Islamists? Words have a significance, and it is imperative to streamline our vocabulary; otherwise we are under the permanent threat of losing our ability to express what we mean or to comprehend what we are told. Matters are further complicated by the paranoia and conspiracy theories that are widespread in the Muslim world among Islamists and others, whether modern and Western-educated or traditionalist and obscurantist. Those theories that are rampant even among Muslims living in the West would insist that world leaders who support Israel are Jewish (like presidents Reagan and Bush), that the United Nations, of all places, is the mastermind of the Jews, who utilize it as the tool for their world dominion, and that the major violent acts that have shaken the world, such as the World Wars, world revolutions, and September 11, are all the fruit of Jewish imagination and execution. Their minds are so permeated with these nonsense theories that they have become impervious to logical, rational debate. Therefore, the difficulty of dealing with Muslim minds consists not only in removing the mountains of pure delusion that choke their thinking, but also in persuading them that the very attempt to counter those untruths is not necessarily part of the world conspiracy that is being woven against them. It is possible to explain their imaginary picture of the world by their need to project on their enemies the analytical shortcomings that bewitch them, but it is impossible to move them out of the illusory scenarios that they have constructed around themselves, and then they cling to them with a tenacity that defies and contradicts Western standards of logic. The result is that even when Muslims initiate and launch an act of violence, they accuse the West or Israel of an act of aggression against them, of which they are the victims and which requires their retaliation or vengeance.

Some insightful criticism of these upside down invention of history were published by Attorney Maurice Hirsch in the Palestinian Media Watch (PMW)[40], which shows how repetitive and adamant are these views among the Arabs:

According to the Palestinian Authority, Jews have no historical connection to the Land of Israel. To support the assertion, the PA argues that archaeological artifacts that unequivocally prove this connection are fake. The Palestinians on the other hand, so claims the PA, are actually a 4,500 year-old people who are descendants of the Canaanites. There is no honest way to deny the Jewish connection to the Land of Israel. Tens of thousands (if not more) of archaeological artifacts prove that connection. When the international community allocated the whole of Israel, in 1922, for the reconstitution of the Jewish homeland, they recognized that historical connection. When the Supreme Muslim Council wanted to describe the Temple Mount, it noted that "This site is one of the oldest in the world. Its sanctity dates from the earliest (perhaps from pre-historic) times. Its identity with the site of Solomon's Temple is beyond dispute. In order to explain away and negate the historical Jewish connection to Israel, the PA has invented an entire alternative reality. In the PA reality, Jews/Israelis have no history, and therefore they try to "steal" the Palestinian identity. The Jews, according to the PA, try to steal Palestinian foods and clothes, and even plant historical Jewish coins at excavation sites in order to invent a false history.

A series of quotes from contemporary Arab press were cited by Attorney Hirsch to back up his claims, among others:

[40] Maurice Hirsch, "When you lack any history, just invent one ", PMW, Sep 4, 2022.

> **Official PA TV host:** They are attempting to market the Palestinian people's heritage and the Palestinian garb as if it were part of the Israeli heritage and that they have a place here in this land. Even in the excavations under the Al-Aqsa Mosque and everywhere, they try to place some coins, as if [to say]: 'Here, we found coins, and this land is ours.' These are ongoing attempts at falsification.
>
> **Faiqa Al-Sous (a writer, retorted):** They lie. They know they're lying and the world knows they're lying... Look at the evil world, we whose narrative is reliable must not publish it, while they spread the false narrative, the false narrative of the occupation.[41]

The goal behind the false PA narrative is to convince the Palestinians that Jews are merely colonizers who came to inhabit a land to which they have no historical connection. This claim enables the PA to persuade the Palestinians that the Jews are simply thieves who stole "Palestinian land". However, for the PA narrative to be effective, it not only needs to negate the Jewish connection to Israel, but it also needs to invent the "Palestinian" historical connection that dates back thousands of years and provides the Palestinians with a history older than that of the Jews. To do so, the PA has even established the "Palestinian Clothing Day" to celebrate the Palestinian national dress, which it claims proves the Palestinian presence in the area going "back to the Canaanite period". In their words:

The Palestinians mark Palestinian Clothing Day every year on July 25, in accordance with [PA] President Mahmoud Abbas' decision on Aug. 1, 2018... Clothing Day was established to preserve the ancestors' history and protect it from theft and the Judaization that the Israeli occupation is carrying out... Palestinian clothing is one of the main supporting pillars that shape the Palestinian

---

[41] Official PA TV, *Returning*, July 16, 2022.

cultural identity, and it is witness to the Palestinian presence whose roots on this land go back to the Canaanite period. According to the historians, some of the shapes and images that were woven into the Canaanite royal garments (the queen's garb) [parentheses in source] are the same ones that exist today [in the Palestinian women's clothing]. Something that draws attention in most of the Palestinian women's clothing is the octagonal star. This is a Canaanite star whose roots go back to 4500 BCE. This star represented 'the goddess of fertility' among our Canaanite ancestors.[42]

When the PA refers to the "historians," claims Hirsch, it is clearly not referring to Palestinian Historian Abd Al-Ghani Salameh, who explained that even as late as 1917 there was no Palestinian people. He said those words in the same official Palestinian TV, verbatim:

> Before the Balfour Pledge (i.e., Declaration) when the Ottoman rule ended (1517-1917), Palestine's political borders as we know them today did not exist, and there was nothing called a Palestinian people with a political identity as we know today, since Palestine's lines of administrative division stretched from east to west and included Jordan and southern Lebanon, and like all peoples of the region [the Palestinians] were liberated from the Turkish rule and immediately moved to colonial rule, without forming a Palestinian people's political identity.[43]

The fact of the matter, concludes Attorney Hirsch, is that the Palestinians have no history prior to the modern period and no connection to the Canaanites. Had this ancient Palestinian-Canaanite people actually existed, it would certainly have been able to show centuries of history and culture. It would certainly have been men-

[42] Official PA daily *Al-Hayat Al-Jadida*, July 26, 2022.
[43] Ibid, November 1, 2017.

tioned in historical documents and would have certainly appeared in contemporary documents such as the 1922 League of Nations Mandate for Palestine, the 1947 UN Partition Plan and even UN Security Council Resolution 242 which the Palestinians often refer to as the basis for their false claim that Israel is occupying "Palestinian territory." The fact that none of the above mentioned documents make any reference to a "Palestinian people", let alone a 4,500 year-old Palestinian people, does not bother the PA. For the PA, in the absence of any real history, all you have to do is make it up. The bothersome aspect of all this fabricated history, is that no known decent Arab, Palestinian or Muslim scholars (and there are many of them, mainly living in the West and educated to scholarly accuracy and intellectual righteousness), has ever debunked those masses of lies and delusionary fabrications.

This reversal of facts is what characterizes the behavior of Muslim terrorists who seek refuge in the West, for the most part while on the run from their home regimes that they tried unsuccessfully to topple. Since they are persuaded that they fight for the path of Allah, they certainly do not regard themselves as terrorists, and, when they are arrested for terrorist activities within their host countries, which had generously, naively, and self-defeatingly given them shelter and provided for their needs, they accuse their benefactors and condemn their "barbaric behavior." This mechanism of denial, which posits Western democracy as a milking cow that owes them sustenance while they owe it nothing, allows them to deny the good and the protection they get and to even mount subversive cells that are liable to act in the heart of their countries of refuge. Their denial allows them to wreak havoc, death, destruction, and terror upon the nations that took them in, in spite of their repeated promises to the authorities that they will refrain from political or subversive activity as a condition of being accorded the status of refugees[44]. A

[44] *Executive Intelligence Review,* September 4, 1998.

sort of political denial is also adopted in the Western chanceries as well, under the belief that if they meant well for the Muslim refugees they would encounter exemplary behavior on their part in return. Even the al-Qaida entrenchment in the United States and Europe and their illicit activities were not enough to stir suspicions and to instigate the slumbering Western governments to take measures of self-defense until the Muslim radicals struck, first in the United States then in Europe. The new Muslim terrorists put the blame on the West for rescuing them from their own corrupt regimes, and therefore the host countries that have tried to fight terrorism are accused of racism, Islamophobia, an anti-Islamic drive, inhumanity, and the like. The democratic countries of shelter that have absorbed these streams of refugees, who have arrived uninvited, now become the oppressors of the poor and peaceful Muslims, like their original oppressive countries of Saudi Arabia, Egypt, Morocco, Yemen, Libya, and all the rest.[45]

Muslim diasporas in the West, which have vastly expanded since the 1990s and have acquired political power through sheer numbers of their coreligionists, have attempted to dislodge the older and more established, though far less numerous, Jewish communities from their advantageous positions. By doing so, they wish to eliminate the Jewish influence on the local governments and thereby shift the traditional political sympathies of the West from Jews and Israel to the Arabs and the Palestinians. This is why Islamic protests in Western societies almost invariably go hand in hand with anti-Semitic eruptions of violence. Again, this would seem an acceptable and legitimate way of political lobbying in any liberal political system, except that Muslim populations most often do not fulfill the two conditions that accompany political protest in the democratic West: they do not act in the interest of their host countries but rather against it, and they do not refrain from violence and the

[45] *Al-Ahram Weekly*, October 1, 2001.

breaking of the law. For Muslim immigrants do not seem to have internalized these restrictions at the same pace that they have mastered the benefits they can extract from their countries of shelter. Many naturalized Muslims—for example some of the perpetrators of 9/11 and then the London attacks of July 2005—did not hesitate to act against their hosts, who had showered them with benefits; and many other Muslims who have sought shelter in Europe, Canada, and Australia devote their time not to assimilating into new environments but to cultivating their separate identities and building enclaves of Islam in their host countries. For example, far from accepting their host countries' Middle Eastern policies or their anti-terrorist struggles, they protest against them, often violently. The second count of using violence, which is usually shunned in Western societies, raises even more concern, because it ultimately hurts public order and value systems in host cultures. Since the outbreak of the Palestinian al-Aqsa Intifada in late 2000, thousands of violent demonstrations by Muslim immigrant populations have unfolded from Montreal to Sydney, from Sao Paulo to Durban (South Africa), from Oslo to Rome—apart from the usual anti-Israel and anti-Jewish demonstrations that have exploded throughout the Arab and Muslim world. Anti-Israeli demonstrations are certainly legitimate, but when they involve bouts of rage, the burning down of foreign embassies and flags, the pelting of rocks against houses of prayer, and sometimes murdering of innocent civilians or when effigies of American and Israeli leaders, who are often personal friends and certainly political allies of the local leaders are burnt and abuses hurled at them, this is the limit that the rule of law can permit, of which Muslim immigrants often seem to be unaware. Indeed, few Westerners participate in these acts of violence, and conversely no Jews have responded by committing the same acts against Western or Muslim countries with which the host society maintains relations. What is more, although Jewish communities worldwide have rallied around Israel, they have done so with dignity and full respect for the law and have not allowed harm to be committed against their home countries or against the violent crowds of Muslims and their supporters.

The most distressing aspects of these outbursts of violence have been that Western countries have been turned by their Muslim communities into violent arenas where the Middle Eastern conflict has been exported. Not content with attacking American and Israeli symbols in Western capitals, these hooligans who terrorize the downtown areas of their countries of residence turned to brutal onslaughts of the local Jewish communities in France, Britain, Germany, Belgium, and others, thus signaling to the world that Jews and Israel were to be equated and that anti-Semitism meant also anti-Zionism, or even pure and simple anti-Israeli outbursts. The worst hit were the Jewish communities in those countries, where hundreds of Jewish synagogues, cemeteries, schools, and other institutions were torched or otherwise desecrated; Jewish adults were attacked on their way to and from prayer; and children on their way to and from school. All this has happened under the eyes of the local police, who have not dared to intervene forcefully for fear of the politically correct politicians. One can only imagine what would have happened if a mosque or a church were likewise burned, or non-Jewish worshippers or children attacked and harmed. Other places have also experienced the full extent of this pogrom, which in many Jewish circles was reminiscent of the infamous Kristallnacht of 1938. In most, though not all, cases, these horrific anti-Semitic attacks were orchestrated by the Muslim communities of Europe, at times in conjunction with local inveterate anti-Semites. The outcome of all this is that the Muslim communities in the Western democracies have shown since the 1990s that they can act in unison to undermine public order, to pose a serious threat to national security, and to harm their fellow citizens, Jewish and otherwise. This means that they can organize and demonstrate in the same fashion in their host countries when they judge an issue important enough or when local authorities are too lenient or reluctant to confront them. Polls organized in the United States after 9/11 found that Americans overwhelmingly tied Islam and Muslims to those horrific events: 68 percent of them approved of randomly stopping people who might fit the profile of suspected terrorists, 83 percent of Americans favored stricter controls on Muslims entering the country, 58 percent wanted tighter controls on Muslims traveling on planes and trains, 35 percent of New Yorkers favored establishing internment camps for individuals who the authorities identified as sympathetic to terrorist causes, and 31 percent of all Americans favored detention camps for Arab Americans as a way of preventing terrorist attacks in the United States.[46] This means that the threatened population found itself ahead of their authorities, which were more cautious in limiting civil rights, and the general public was prepared to a great extent to replay the unfortunate experience of the internment of Japanese Americans in World War II. It was to be expected then that if and when more major acts of terror unfolded in the West, the West would find itself compelled to curtail civil liberties and take radical measures against the Muslim minority in its midst. Only in this light did the very moderate measures taken by Israel against its demonstratively hostile Muslim minority, which had come under scathing criticism from the pre-9/11 world, look incredibly generous and even border at times on neglect. All these developments, which have swept through both Islamic countries and Muslim communities in the West, have created a mood that has evolved since 1989 creating awe, and often outright fear, in the West from militant Islam and from the chaos it can create if not addressed. The 2006 Cartoon Affair, in which Denmark and other European nations shamefully capitulated to the violent and murderous attacks against them, are a case in point.

[46] See Daniel Pipes, "Fighting Militant Islam, Without Bias," *City Journal*, Autumn 2001. http://www.city-journal.org/htm/41/fightingmilitant.html.

Instead of defending the liberal ideas of the West, including the hallowed freedom of expression, as they were being dramatically and violently challenged, the Danes, the European foreign minister, and the United Nations elected to placate the hooligans and their supportive Arab governments, particularly Saudi Arabia, who threatened economic boycott of Danish dairy products. That show of muscular force, which ended up intimidating Europe, could not help but boost self-confidence in the Islamic world that their economic power could easily bring Europe to its knees, not only on the cartoon issue but on any policy that displeased them. How much more concerning when it involved the Arab-Israeli conflict, where unless the European Union took a clear-cut anti-Israeli position, the Muslim world would act, by force if necessary, to impose its views. And what has happened to Western ideas of fairness and support for freedom and democracy? Who cares? No one of consequence talks about that any more, and no one acts to stop the Western drift toward submitting to tyranny. So much so that Europeans have come to accept the Muslim thesis that the honor of the Prophet of Islam was more important than the lives of innocent people who were killed during the Muslim rampage as a result of the Cartoon Affair, or the material losses that were sustained by the boycotted countries.

If we look at all this, as it is customary today, from the vantage point of Human Rights, just like humans themselves, are native of places and of ideas which evolved in certain locations and under certain circumstances. So, humanity prides itself not only of its great thinkers, but also of the great homelands which gave birth to the idea of human rights. Chief among those are America and France, where their national revolutions, unfolding within 13 years of each other (1776 and 1789 respectively) and were nourished from the same sources, have become the world revolutions that came closest to implement that lofty idea. But Americans, while focusing on the affinities of their thoughts with their European roots, and believing that if they meant well, then the entire span of humanity would behave likewise, did not relent on their delusions, like most recently under the Obama Administration (2008-16) about the "significant common ground linking America and the Muslim world, which offered a real promise that working together [ "engaging"] with other leading international players [ specifically Muslims] to improve the human condition across the world in general, including the Muslim world, was possible and vital". Improving the human condition is what America's ideals have been all about, for "life, liberty and the pursuit of happiness" are not just hollow words; they embody the ideals that lay at the foundation of America's aspirations, not only for itself but for citizens around the world. Thus, they embraced the notion that human development has broad and highly relevant significance for humanity in general and for the functioning of harmonious international relations. Human development is a concept that embraces enhancing the quality of life for the whole world; it encompasses the key dimensions of economics, health, education, human and civil rights, democracy and freedom, all protected by an independent judiciary, and sustained by a high quality of life. But in practice, if America ever had any "common ground" with the Islamic world, it was based on economic and strategic interests (mainly petroleum and military positions during the Cold War, and mainly strategic common grounds presently, as its dependence on foreign oil has dramatically plummeted), never on shared values of democracy, freedom and human rights that radical Islam, and even less radical Westernized Muslim individuals have declared as alien and "hated" in and by their societies. And when the US tried at an exorbitant human and material price to enforce those ideas in Afghanistan and Iraq, it finally realized that its dismal failure to enforce and promote them reflected precisely the lack of such a common ground. Numerous have been the manifestations of this alienation between the Western world of Human Rights as described above, and the

Muslim interpretation and application of its ideas, as amply sampled in the above text. On 9 and 10 November, 1998, the Office of the High Commissioner for Human Rights at the UN, under Mary Robinson, in cooperation with the Islamic Cooperation Conference (OIC), organized at the UN Office in Geneva a seminar, entitled: "Enriching the Universality of Human Rights, Islamic Perspectives on the Universal Declaration of Human Rights", to mark the 50th Anniversary of the Universal Declaration of Human Rights, ostensibly "to promote respect among peoples and a better understanding of the significance of cultural and religious backgrounds in the context of the Universal Declaration. It was said that twenty experts in Islamic Law and Human Rights were selected by the Hight Commissioner, in consultation with the OIC, though no final resolutions or conclusions were expected from that august gathering, due to its "academic character". Thus, all the High Commissioner could conclude was that "it had opened a channel of communication and indicated her intention of publishing the proceedings of the seminar", which was finally, done in a shortened version owing to "lack of resources".[47] Mary Robinson, like President Obama, highlighted the

> Greatness of Islam and its immense contribution to the dialogue between civilization and to the building based on respect of human rights of the global civilization based on respect for human rights...We all know the greatness of Islam and its civilizations and its immense contribution to the richness of human experience...through the profound belief and of the Muslim religion theology...It has shown itself to be universal in nature and has the dignity of the human person, tolerance and equity at the core of the message... It was in

[47] .HR/IP/SEM/1999/1 (Part I), 15 March, 1999.

> this context that I was happy to accept the invitation of the Foreign Minister of Islamic Republic of Iran to facilitate a process of preparing Islamic commentaries on the Universal Declaration, and today's seminar is a key element in that process.[48]

The three themes that were discussed (namely preached by the Muslim participants), were the principle of non-discrimination, civil and political rights, and economic, social and economic rights in Islam. But, due to Robinson's to preserve the "scholarly objective" nature of the speeches, the discussion was limited only to the invited experts (Muslims). In her ignorance of Islam and her extreme desire to please within the rules of political correctness, she defied the totally contradictory statements of those experts and rendered a disservice to the cause of human rights by legitimizing the revolting Islamic version of "human rights" as a worthy topic of discussion on the international state. Did not she not hear, or understand, the repeated statements of Iranian officials, including at the UN, of their wish to wipe Israel from map? Did not she see the murderous horrors that the radicals of al-Qaida committed all across the world? Did not she identify the cruelty and oppression that many Islamic regimes were practicing against their own civilians while she was praising the greatness, tolerance and contributions to humanity? Bat Ye'or's numerous books on the enslaved Christians and Jews under Islam[49]. If she had persisted in her job until 2022 she would have had to resign in disgrace when she took cognizance of the new specific studies of Human rights in Islam[50]. The other attempt of the Obama Administration at engagement

---

[48] Ibid.

[49] *The Dhimmi, the Decline of Eastern Christianism under Islam, Eurabia, Islam and Dhimmitude* are only a few samples.

[50] Raphael Israeli's, *The Rebellion of the Dhimmis, Human Rights and Human development in Islam,* both published by Strategic Books, TX, in 2022.

with a Muslim power was done when it thought that an agreed deal with Iran, to limit and supervise its nuclearization program, would contain, or at least slow down its pace, has proven futile, unwittingly aided by President Trump's (2016-20) determination to scuttle that deal and better rely on harsh, and growingly harsher, economic sanctions. Both of them ignored or simply were ignorant of, the ideological foundations of the regime of the Ayatullahs which hates, despises and is committed to resist any Westernization ("Westoxication" in their parlance) or reform which would obviate or weaken their "Death to America (and Israel)" slogan which seemed to endure as the most solid base of their rule. Both strategies were a priori doomed to failure due to the Shi'ite doctrine of the Hidden Imam which governs that regime, and came to its most brutal expression during the eight years of President Ahmadinejad, who came to see and present it not only as an apocalyptic vision or traditional belief in the end of times when the Hidden Imam will appear and bring justice and plenty to all humanity (under whom, who would need human rights?), but as an imminent divine program of action to be implemented under our very eyes. As a former Mayor of Tehran, that president, who had no clerical pretentions himself, seemed to be in constant expectation of fulfilling that prophecy in his own days, as the "pangs of the Messiah" indicated to his delusioned mind, namely that the more pressing and worsening earthly conditions in the world, the nearer the realization of that day of relief and redemption for the Shi'ite world. According to that logic, bad or disastrous events are the surest signs of messianic days, hence the vanity of the logic behind the great powers' balance of power, which was at the base of MAD (Mutually Assured Destruction) which alone prevented a new world war, each power being deterred from attacking or threatening the other by reason of their mutual capacity to annihilate the other in case of a nuclear conflict. Therefore, under the spell of that theory, owning nuclear power or being threatened by it, far from deterring the Ayatullahs in Tehran, on the contrary augmented their creed in the imminence of apocalyptic days, which under that scheme would invalidate MAD and make it obsolete and unnecessary. He and his coreligionists are firm in their belief that it was precisely that threat of annihilation which augured the return if the Imam, i.e. that the worse was the best, the darkest was the most promising.

# Chapter Four

## *Muslim Radicals Defying the West and its Values*

In the past several decades there has been talk among scholars, journalists and politicians alike about an Islam of the minority "bad guys", those extremist, fanatic, radical fundamentalists, who resort to violence, in order to enforce their brand of Islam on the rest of their coreligionists, who are the peaceful and moderate_members of the majority of Muslims. This distinction, which was quantified by some in percentage points-15% for the minority and 85%for the majority, has created the temptation to produce the wishful but erroneous difference between a "moderate" Islam of the "peace-loving" majority and a "radical" Islam of the belligerent minority, as if there were two separate doctrines of Islam, the one amicable, to be placated and befriended, the other bellicose to be shunned and fought. What has been termed "Islamic terrorism", when this construct was at all permissible in many Western countries' government systems, where one can still speak freely and reveal the truth, was attributed to the bellicose and violent type of Islam, while the rest of the Muslims, like the rest of humanity, were dubbed the "victims" of Islamic fundamentalism. This distinction has allowed the critiques and victims of violent Muslims to condemn them in the most blatant terms without exposing themselves as "Islamophobes" or "racists", as if multi-ethnic and multi cultural Islam were a race; or if they were themselves Muslims, as "traitors" to their faith.

Never mind that 15% out of 1.5 billion Muslims are in themselves a big enough threatening mass even if there were no positive majority to dilute them. The eruption of this distinction between two brands of Islam in the past few decades was not without antecedents, if we bear in mind that at the beginning of the 20th century Salafi Islam had made its attempts to assert itself against the background of colonial rule in Islamdom. In the second half of the 20th century two momentous events shook the Muslim world, both external, and as Hassan Turabi put it, necessitated a Muslim response:

> The historical test for Muslims has always been to recover after every setback, seeking through the revival of faith, the renewal of thought and the resurgence of action to salvage religion from temporal containment and ensure its progressive development, relevance and continuity in history[51]

As Turabi has viewed it, the present cycle of Islamic resurgence reassures that "the Unitarian principle of Islam shuns any variance or discrepancy between status quo and ideal, for the basic religious doctrine of Islam is one that unites the relativity of human existence to the absoluteness of the divine". Regarded in this light, and though Islam remains one, based on the same Unitarian doctrines, like the Five Pillars *(Arkan)* and the Roots of the faith *(usul-a Din),* it does recognize the distinction between the pragmatic Muslims who consecrate the status quo and fear violence which might reverse it, those we call the conservatives, and the revolutionaries that we dub "radicals" who seek the ideal, to attain it here and now, even if and when violence is necessary to reach that goal. And when they use violence it is precisely because they are as Unitarian as all the

[51] Hassan Turabi, "Islam and a Pan-National Movement", *RSA Journal*, August-September, 1992, pp. 608-19.

rest, and they wish to strictly impose the same doctrine of Islam that the others have neglected. Thus, we cannot speak of "moderate" Islam which does not exist, nor of "radical" Islam which its critiques accuse it to be, but of moderate and radical Muslims, both of whom distance themselves in fact from the standard doctrine in their daily struggle to practice it the best way they can, as long as the structure of the one-fit-all core of the doctrine is preserved. For example the obligation of Jihad, which is hallowed by all Muslims, may be in temporary abeyance for some Muslims who shun confrontation with the entire world in the present state of affairs, while the radicals advocate its imposition here and now, regardless of the present balance of power in the world, knowing that they are protected by Allah as long as they fight in His Path.

In view of this narrow and bigoted understanding of the world by Islam, these radicals have no compunction about literally terrorizing their rivals and enemies, be they Muslims who refuse to submit to them, or non-Muslims who oppose their abusive and horrifying *modus operandi,* which includes forced conversion of non-Muslims, mass massacres, live beheadings recorded on videos, mutilation of the dead, kidnappings, taking hostages for ransom or political blackmail, *Islamikaze* killings (what is called erroneously "suicide bombings"), and the like. This is all justified in their eyes either by the infamous Qur'anic injunction to sow terror *(irhab)* in the hearts of the enemy, hence the common appellation of those deeds as terrorism by the West, a proposition that has become current also among Muslim victims of organizations like al-Qa'ida, Hamas, ISIS or Boko Haram; or by the crimes they attribute to their rivals and enemies, who act in self-defense. It seems that especially non-governmental terror organizations, like Hamas, al-Qa'ida, Boko Haram, Hizbullah and Lashkar-e-Taibah, who are not accountable to anyone, nor can they be pursued by any international body, care little about human lives and do even less to protect them, and are more likely than others to take the most horrific measures against their victims. Consequently, little or nothing is done by the international community to counter these horrors, except by certain countries that feel directly hurt or whose interests are threatened, like the US and Israel, and feel constrained to act in response. Moderate Muslims often accuse the radicals, who are in fact common Muslims who behave in accordance with the accepted rules of the *Shari'a* which they apply strictly, of having "hijacked" Islam or "distorted" its "real" meanings, or misinterpreted it, and they in turn are condemned by their rivals for "having abandoned the Path of Allah", or for having themselves "been corrupted by Western ideologies", or simply as "heretics". But, for better or worse, it is the ideal standards of the radicals that prevail in the Islamic world, for even those who do not live by them hold them and their practitioners in high esteem. One can simply watch the mass demonstrations in the streets of Gaza, Quetta, Casablanca, Durban and Jakarta, or in the Muslim neighborhoods of Paris, London, Sydney, Amsterdam and Toronto to realize how much alive, universal, uniform and popular are the Muslim mantras that are uttered, and the rampages which are perpetrated daily by Muslim masses of men, women and children from all walks of life, including their leaders and clerics, of all ages. Are they all "Islamist radicals"? No, they are simply Muslims, and the common denominator which links them together in their hatred of the West and the Jews is Islam, standard Islam, under the justification of the *Shari'a*, which is promoted by their Imams. While some moderate and courageous Muslim individuals will fortunately always be there to save the honor of their creed when they raise their lone voices against the abuses perpetrated in the name of their faith, the mainstream in the world of Islam, including westernized and modern professionals, intellectuals and students, will also always be there to glorify in mirth the executions of westerners and Jews by Muslim terrorists, to write or broadcast in exhilaration in favor of the *Islamikaze,* and distribute in jubilation sweets in the streets to "celebrate" the death of Americans and Jews. Even when some Islamic governments turn against the Muslim radicals, like Egypt against the Brothers or Saudi Arabia against ISIS, the Muslim populace in those countries remains sentimentally loyal to them, especially when they hit the West or Israel. The best proof of that is their continued popularity and the steady stream of volunteers that swell their ranks. It is exactly this double standard of soothing the West on the one hand and expressing identification with their fanatic kin on the other, which has been engineered by Muslims to obfuscate substance and encourage the currency of Muslim terminology, while at the same time depriving the West from its arsenal when counter-attacking its aggressors in the battle against jihadism, which needs to be clarified and understood. Words were created to transmit conventionally agreed upon meanings. If each actor chose to lend to his words a different significance, or accuse others of "distorting" their meaning, then we would no longer be able to call a spade a spade or communicate with others on any issue. These are all indications of the spreading anti-Western antagonism in Islam. The zeal in the Islamic world has been directed not only against Israel and the West, but aims primarily to sweep out of power their own western-allied regimes which are regarded as American stooges. As the major Egyptian paper, *al-Ahram,* put it, "religious identity has replaced nationalist ideology",[52] and that applies not only to Muslim countries but also amidst Muslim minorities throughout their diasporas. This means that Muslim terrorism will continue to rise in both Europe and the Muslim world, hence the relevance of the present volume as a precursor and follow up to the saga of Sep 11 and its aftermath. One has to realize nevertheless the distortions of the basic data of Islam, by both scholars and politicians, who wish to depict a more benign and less menacing picture of the Islamic rise than it is in fact. This is done through the distinction that we have

[52] *Al-Ahram Weekly,* "Beyond the Vacuum", 13-16 April, 2006.

mentioned above, which has become conventional wisdom among both critics and proponents of Islam. It is the artificial bifurcation between the so-called "Islamists" or radicals, the minority "bad guys" who spoil the lot of the peaceful moderates by their violent deeds, lend a bad reputation to the majority of their coreligionists and wage war against the West and Israel; and the majority itself, which is arguably "peace-loving" and shunning violence and has no quarrel with the West. It is clear that this "scientific" distinction, though pursued by some scholars of reputation, and may have some empirical merit to it, has much more to do with political correctness and with a degree of sheepish *dhimmi*-like submissiveness, or fear of being accused of racism, than with historical reality. After September 11 a talk show was broadcast by *al-Jazeerah* network (representing what is known as "moderate" and "peace-loving" Islam) where the question was posed to the panelists and their viewers about whether Bin Laden was a terrorist or a hero. The only moderate panelist, a Tunisian, was mocked and humiliated by his co-panelists and by the moderator of the show for daring to dissent from the otherwise unanimous opinion which crowned Bin Laden as a national hero. Viewers who called or emailed from the entire Islamic world, were almost unanimous in the same consensus. That was not a "poll" among "Islamists", but among the rank and file Muslims, most of whom were supposedly the educated owners of PC computers. Yet, their reaction was "Islamist" in substance. So, where is the distinction between the supposed "moderates" and the alleged "Islamists?" Yes, there are *Islamikaze* activists who are ready to blow themselves up for the cause of Islam, in the process of killing westerners and Jews. But they are only a handful, who are recruited, trained, financed, indoctrinated and dispatched by a vast infra-structure of Muslim states, organizations and individuals, and are surrounded by the sympathy and admiration, often adulation, of the vast masses of the Muslim public and the mainstream press in countries that are clients of the US or have signed peace with

Israel. Who is then an "Islamist" among all those layers of activists and supporters, and who is the "moderate" and "peace-loving?". In the US and Europe, it was found that several Muslim intellectuals, leaders and clerics, who gained favor with the authorities and access to the highest echelons of power, for their supposed "moderation", and their openness to "dialogue", were later arrested for their illicit fund-raising for Muslim terrorist organizations, for incitement to terrorism or for suppressing women's rights. Did those suddenly turn from "moderate" to "radical"? No, they were the same Muslims who were perceived previously as "moderate" when they acted or refrained from acting in a certain way, and who became "Islamists" when they were caught red-handed when engaging in subversive acts. In both instances they acted as Muslims in the name of Islam. It was Western scholars and westernized Muslims who attached to them those epithets of "moderate" and "Islamists" which the Muslims themselves never recognized.

Matters are further complicated and made less comprehensible to western minds by the paranoia and conspiracy theories that are very widespread in the Muslim world, among "Islamists" and others alike, whether Muslims are modern and western-educated, or traditionalist and obscurantist. Those theories that are rampant even among Muslims living in the West, would insist that world leaders who support Israel are Jewish (like Presidents Reagan and Bush) and that the major violent acts that shook the world, like the world wars, the world revolutions and September 11, were all the fruit of Jewish premeditation and execution. Americans and other Westerners are accused of plotting against Islam, standing behind all the civil wars, divisions, wars and massacres that have plagued the Islamic world. Their minds are so permeated with these nonsense theories that they become impervious to logical, rational debate that is open to argument, discussion and to persuasion. Therefore, the difficulty of dealing with Muslim minds consists not only of removing the mountains of pure delusion that choke their free thinking, but also of persuading them that the very attempt to counter-argue against those futilities is not necessarily part of the world conspiracy that is being woven against them. It is possible to explain their imaginary picture of the world by their need to project on their enemies the analytical shortcomings that bewitch them, but it is impossible to move them out of the illusory scenarios that they have constructed around themselves, to which they cling with a tenacity that defies and contradicts western standards of logic and conduct. The result is that even when Muslims initiate and launch an act of violence, they accuse the West or Israel of it and dub it, or what led to it, as an act of "aggression" against them, of which they are the victims and which requires their retaliation/vengeance. The main thing is that they thereby escape the need to take responsibility for their deeds and for the policies they choose to embrace. This reversal of facts is what characterizes the behavior of Muslim radicals who sought refuge in the West that they detest and wish to undermine, for the most part while on the run from their home regimes that they had tried unsuccessfully to topple; or who carve for themselves all manner of "emirates" or "caliphates" in Islamic lands and strive to impose on them their *shari'a* laws, often amidst the use of violence. Since they are persuaded that they fight for the Path of Allah, they certainly do not regard themselves as terrorists, and when they are arrested for terrorist activities within their host countries in the West, which had generously, naively and self-defeatingly given them shelter and provided for their needs, they accuse their benefactors of sinning against them and they condemn their "barbaric behavior". This mechanism of denial, which posits Western democracy as just a milking cow which owes them sustenance while they owe it nothing, allows them to deny the good and the protection they get, as they mount subversive cells to act in the heart of their countries of refuge as of right. That causes them to wreak havoc, death, destruction and terror upon the nations that took them in, in spite of their repeated commitment to the authorities that they would refrain from political or subversive activity as a condition for being accorded the status of refugees, or else to perpetrate massacres and other abominable deeds among their own populations[53]. A sort of political denial is also adopted in the Western chanceries as well, under the belief that if they meant well for the Muslim refugees they have accepted, or refrained from interfering in the internal affairs of Muslim countries, they would encounter exemplary behavior on the part of Muslims in return. Even the al-Qai'da entrenchment in the US and Europe and their illicit activities done under various covers, was not enough to stir suspicions and to instigate the slumbering western governments to take measures of self-defense, until the Muslim radicals struck, first in America then in Europe, or acted atrociously against their own minorities in their own countries, and against foreign victims that they took hostage. The democratic countries of shelter which have absorbed these streams of "refugees" who arrived uninvited, now became in the eyes of the guest the "oppressors" of the poor and peaceful Muslims, like their original oppressive countries of Saudi Arabia, Egypt and all the rest.[54] And even the western countries that launch rescue operations against Muslim tyrants in their own territory, are perversely dubbed "aggressors" and "terrorists".

Three types of Muslim radicals are identifiable: firstly, those who operate established states, such as Iran and Sudan, where the state establishment uses its institutions and resources to sponsor its own or other Muslim radicals in the performance of their atrocities worldwide. These countries train, finance, indoctrinate, recruit and dispatch acts of terror worldwide, like Iran training Hamas operatives in its territory or sending its Hizbullah proxies to act against Jewish and Israeli targets in Argentina and Bulgaria, using the

[53] *Executive Intelligence Review*, 4 September, 1998.

[54] *Executive Intelligence Review*, 4 September, 1998.

immunity of their diplomatic pouch to smuggle in weapons and explosives; or Sudan recruiting and training its African operatives to blow up the American Embassies in East Africa in 1998, or supporting the *Shabab* in Somalia. Second come the Islamic movements which seek a territorial base whence they can launch their acts of terror, though they may not strive for or attain statehood. Such are al-Qai'da, which operated from Sudan first and then from Afghanistan under Bin Laden, until it was forced to decentralize worldwide when American counter-attacks disbanded and killed its leadership. Other such movements are the Hamas, Hizbullah, Muslim Brothers, Islamic Jihad, *ansar bayt al-Maqdas, ansar al-Shari'a* and *Jabhat al-Nusra* in the Middle East, or *Laskar-a-Taiba* in the Sub-Continent, or the Boko Haram in West Africa and the Taliban in Pakistan and Afghanistan. But there is also a third interim group of Muslim radicals, who have experienced a state, or are aspiring to it, or have declared one in the making but have not achieved yet a solid base for their statehood, nor a recognition by others nations. Such have been the Hamas and their rule in Gaza, the Hizbullah and their control of Lebanon, the Muslim Brothers which maintained an elected government for a year (2012-3) before they were removed in Egypt, or the Taliban who had ruled Afghanistan for 5 years (1996-2001 until removed by the American incursion into their country. So are the insurgents of Northern Mali who have declared a state there. The latest manifestation of this latter category has been the ISIS (Islamic State in Iraq and Syria, also known as ISIL), the latter appellation replacing Syria with Levant, which explains that Syria means Greater Syria, encompassing Jordan, Lebanon and Israel, so ambitious their program has been to widen the scope of their declared Caliphate, and so amazing their initial success, which matches that of the Taliban in Afghanistan. Lately, the epithet of "Islamic State" (IS) has been adopted by this group, hinting to their aspiration of an all-encompassing Caliphate, not necessarily confined to Iraq and Syria. Their success has been such that they already claim the fealty of local Islamic movements in the Sinai Peninsula (*Ansar Bayt al-Maqdis*= The Supporters of the Holy Place) and in Libya (*Ansar al-Shari'a* = The Supporters of the Holy Law), with others likely to follow. Characteristically uniting all of them, however, is their propensity to use violence, murder, terror and the most horrible ways of coercion to impose their ways.

In the Fall 2014, the success of ISIS was so sweeping, in spite of the persistent American air strikes, that some local and regional radical Islamic movements, especially those who did not achieve any stunning victories in their localities, such as *ansar bayt al Maqdis* in Sinai, *ansar al-Shari'a* in Eastern Libya or even *Jabhat al-Nusra* in Syria, which is the fountainhead of IS, that they have been swearing fealty to the Caliphate in Raqqa (Syria) and asking to be affiliated with it, hoping thereby to benefit from its worldwide popularity among Muslim youth and from its vast financial resources. Bayt al-Maqdis followers in Sinai already dub themselves IS Egypt, for example, admitted that the strikes of the Egyptian forces against them were successful and asked the people of Sinai to protect them and help them lift the security siege there. In a video, posted in early December 2014, appeared Osama al-Masry, the mufti and spokesman of the group, next to five bodies of members of the group that were killed by the Egyptian army, and urged the people of Sinai to fight the army, arguing that "the army does not want to apply the Shari'a". Conversely, he pledged that his group "would protect the people of Sinai as long as you did not cooperate with the army, but we will come after you if you do". He also vowed to cripple the whole of Egypt to avenge the group members who were killed and showed a video of the killing of three policemen in a car.[55]

The multiplicity of Muslim movements of all sorts, and sometimes even their tendency to fight each other, do not preclude, however their categorization under the heading of Muslim radicals, who

[55] *Al-Masri alYaum,* 5 December, 2014.

almost all share in common the basic traits that render them threatening in the eyes of outsiders, though for the world Muslim populace they may constitute a source of pride, hope, promise and even redemption. Those traits are: striving for Muslim unity, establishing a world Caliphate, a deep hatred for the West; a gut contempt for the Jews and Israel, a commitment to a *shari'a*-governed state and society, a world of illusions and delusions based on conspiracy theories, a disregard for human life and humanitarian sensitivities, a penchant toward the absolute even at the price of their self-annihilation, and the ready recourse to violence when they encounter resistance to their worldviews. Many of these traits, and others, are common to Muslims in general, and we shall examine them in the next chapter. Here, we shall elaborate some of them one by one, based on some examples, so as not to need to explain them again and again when we discuss each radical organization separately. Underlying all this is the basic perception in Islam that the times of the Prophet were ideal, hence the constant striving to emulate them and hold them as the yardstick to measure success and rightfulness in our days. The dominant penchant toward the absolute, even at the price of self-annihilation, has been the main plight of radical Muslims, which means for us that even when do not see any chance of success for movements like al-Qa'ida, ISIS, Hamas etc. to achieve their goals of overwhelming the US or the West globally and Israel locally, they still persist, and will try again and again, even if they suffer endless losses and fatalities, with new leaders quickly replacing the killed ones (Bin Laden, Mullah Omar, or al-Baghdadi and Sheikh Yassin) with new one rising from the ruins, as committed and determined to pursue the Jihad in which they are assured to achieve martyrdom. For the Muslim fanatics the Truth is one and absolute. For not only are they committed to make Islam prevail worldwide, but they see themselves obligated to enforce it and use any means, including force and compulsion, in order to rescue Unbelievers and heretics from themselves. In their world, nothing else but Islam is credible, therefore there is no meaning to anything but the absolute domination of Islam since no other faiths can compete and show the relativity of their validity. And that creed is so overwhelming, that Muslim radicals regard themselves bound to act upon it even at the cost of their lives. In the west it seems sometimes foolish that these radicals fight and devote their lives for causes that stand no chance to succeed: when Bin Laden declared a world war on Jews and the West, he knew and understood that he would not bring America or Israel to their knees, nor when the Hamas opened their missile barrages on Israel in July, 2014, knowing that they would not beat Israel, and only bring death, destruction and tears upon themselves. Nonetheless, they launched the war, broke every cease-fire they committed themselves to, cared little for the damage they underwent, and kept fighting to the end without respite. For them, their absolute commitment to wipe Israel out knows no compromise or concession, not even a negotiation directly with Israel, for negotiations are by nature a give and take process which should yield to a compromise and a settlement, and they have prohibited themselves from any of those concepts. Neither al-Qa'ida, nor the Hamas, or Hizbullah or ISIS have shown appetite for such processes, hence their self-obligation to fight to the finish even when their adversaries evince an overwhelming superiority over them. The capitulation of radical and fascist Germany and Japan at the end of WWII is not likely to repeat itself in the case of radical Islam which prefers death to surrender. At times it transpired that it was much more important for the radicals to take the risk of harming their enemies than safeguarding their own interest and security. A few examples will illustrate the point, but before we delve into them, it is necessary to explain the quantitative versus the qualitative ideological approaches to religious and semi-religious convictions. The quantitative approach usually deals in relative terms with the matter under consideration, meaning that all issues can be ironed out and resolved by a process of negotiations, namely a give and take procedure that produces a meeting of minds, born out of compromises which are translated into words that make up the agreement, pact or treaty. Successful negotiations or dialogues follow that model and no matter how hard and lengthy they are, they end up in agreement. Conversely, the qualitative approach followed by either religious fanatics or ideological diehards, is absolute in its demands, recalcitrant in its means and aggressive in its conduct. Its adepts are so one-sidedly persuaded of their truth that they have no need for negotiations, because they are guided by supreme or divine guidelines that are not given to bargaining or question. For example, if one believes that his creed or conviction is the final truth that cannot be compromised, then what is the use of negotiation? They are persuaded that nothing exists outside their beliefs, and they are so committed to stand for their creed that their universe is viewed only through that prism and they are ready to struggle for it and even put their lives on the fire line for it. They do not seek to convince others or debate their worldview in comparison to others, they simply wish to impose, even by force if necessary, their ideas since they are the only valid ones. They have a book, an idea, a platform, and all the rest are invalid fallacies that they denounce and dismiss or simply ignore. The outside world may consider their ideas unfeasible, "crazy", and incomprehensible, but they ignore the critiques and proceed on their way, with surprising stamina and often with unexpected and rapid success. On the other hand, unlikely and stunning as it may be, many young people adhere to those outlandish creeds and flock to reinforce their ranks. We see that in the conduct of ISIS these days, which the entire world is concerned about, but young Muslims everywhere converge on Iraq and Syria to swell their ranks.

1. <u>The Taliban Episode</u>- In the midst of the devastating civil war in Afghanistan after the Soviet Union was defeated by the *Mujahideen* and left in 1989, the Taliban, meaning literally

"students", grew literallyin the Islamic *madrasas* of neighboring Pakistan and in Afghanistan into a potent political movement, led by Mullah Omar in the city of Qandahar. In 1995, they took over that city, taking advantage of the chaos and factional conflicts reigned in the country and from there spread all over the country until they reached Kabul and formed their extremely puritanical and strict government which enforced *Shari'a* law. When they blew up the famous two giant Buddhist statues in Bamyan, in defiance of the entire world, people began to realize their threats to cultural values in the world, but they did not bend. But when Bin Laden sought shelter there, assured of the sponsorship of Mullah Omar, the spiritual leader of the country, who pledged protection of his guest no matter what, did al-Qa'ida dare to plan and execute the horrors of September 11, and oblige the Americans to move in December 2001 and remove the Taliban regime from its rule and put Bin Laden on the run, until he was killed in 2012. The Taliban knew that if they did not accept the American ultimatum of expelling Bin Laden and his gang, they would risk an American invasion, in which they could not emerge victorious. Nonetheless, they insisted on protecting their Muslim heroic guest at the price of self-perdition.

2. The Nazareth Confrontation - In the 1990s, as the Muslim majority in the mixed city of Nazareth became firm and irreversible, the Muslim population, propped up by the rising Islamic movement in Israel, decided to challenge the Christian minority rule of the city, and build in the plaza at the base of the Basilica of Annunciation, the tallest and most imposing physical feature in the city, a taller mosque that was to dwarf the existing Basilica. Those were the years the city was preparing to build the facilities necessary to welcome the Pope in the year 2000, having in mind the tremendous encouragement

that would constitute for tourism in the city. The Muslim radicals in the city refused to budge and installed in the interim period a tent-mosque, surrounded by provoking verses from the Qur'an which stated that "God was One, he was neither born nor gave birth", a clear allusion to the Christian doctrine of the Son of God. It took months of litigation until courts of law imposed the removal of the Muslim radicals from their tent-mosque where they squatted for months. Muslim leaders knew that they could not win that legal contest in Israel which was governed by law and order, even when they were prepared to lose the economic advantages accruing to them by the year 2000 festivities. Nevertheless, they went into that battle and lost it.

3. <u>The Hamas and Hizbullah Belligerence -</u> These two potent Islamic movements, both located on Israel's borders (in Gaza and Lebanon, respectively), one Sunnite the other Shi'ite, and both declared terrorists by the West, have caused havoc on the territories where they are based, by forcing themselves upon, and operating from among the civil population where they live. Their strategy, which has worked so far, is that they can engage Israel in a long war of attrition, with impunity because they can attack at Israel at will, forcing their enemy to retaliate massively against their bases and causing in the process huge losses to the civilian populations among which they hide. To exhibit those fatalities to the international media is always sure to bring blame and condemnation on Israel for its "disproportionate" reaction, while they, being movements which cannot be officially condemned by any world institution, emerge from the conflict unscathed on the propaganda domain. This was the case in the second Lebanese War of 2006, where the Hizbullah, and especially its host country- Lebanon, were so devastated that though Israel emerged as the condemned

party, prompted its leader Nasrallah to admit that had he known the consequences he would not have triggered that war. On the Hamas front, the 200-8, 2012 and especially the 2014 were also very detrimental to the Gaza population and caused untold suffering to the Gaza population, by the punishing Israeli air-strikes to silence the shower of missiles dispatched against Israel. The leaders of both movements knew in general that Israel could not contain their provocations and would have to retaliate in strength against the, inflicting in the process inevitable death and destruction on their bases. Nevertheless, they did not shy from repeating their provocations, while their own leadership hid in underground bunkers, while their populations were suffering devastation and death. It seems that deterrence only worked with the Hizbullah so far, which has to take into account the backlash against them by the suffering Lebanese civilian population; but the Hamas, which itself controls Gaza, has been less sensitive to the suffering civilian population because after each round of war, the international community rushes to donate money to rebuild the devastation.

4. The IS (ISIS) Megalomania - One of the offshoots of the Syrian civil war, which has been raging since 2011 and has cost some 300,000 casualties by the end of 2014, has been the growth there of such radical Muslim movements as *Jabhat al Nusra* (the Front of Victory), a branch of al-Qa'ida, and other similar factions, all committed to bring down the godless Assad regime in Damascus and install a Muslim state in his stead. That domestic war has not only devastated Syria and caused hundreds of thousands of fatalities and millions of uprooted refugees, but also attracted young enthusiastic Muslim volunteers from Muslim countries as well as from Western countries which host large Muslim minorities. One of the

consequences of that long and costly civil war, has been the emergence of ISIS (Lately dubbed as IS, or Islamic State), based in chaotic and unruly northern Syria, and in conflict ridden uncontrollable Iraq, under the leadership of a charismatic cleric Baghdadi, very similar to Mullah Omar of Qandahar, who aspires to create an expanding Caliphate under his aegis. This caliphate was fought by a coalition of western countries headed by the Americans, who try to bring in Muslim countries into the loop so as to make the ISIS threat seem universal. Unlike Hamas and Hizbullah, whose menace is "only" against Israel, and therefore it could be almost ignored and the Israelis who resist it can be blamed of "disproportionality" fighting it, the ISIS threat is seen by Americans and their allies as directed against them and their interests, therefore they are bracing for a protracted and costly war where no "proportions" are being considered. Despite all this, and the odds against which ISIS is operating, it continues to attract volunteer *mujahideen*, defy the Americans and their coalition and inspire other areas of the Islamic world, like the Sinai and Libya, to follow their model.

Common to all these movements is the idealization of the past, where lies the supreme model of righteous Muslim rule, for which it is worth to launch Jihad continuously, in order to achieve victory, and never be tempted by compromises or attractive temptations offered by West in its pragmatic conduct of policy, because they do not seek "progress" the way it is sought in the West, but a rehabilitation of the past. The Islamic instinct for restorative reforms every time a revolution looms in the horizon, also harks back to the ancient Islamic heritage, with its Prophet at its center, who had combined his prophecy with his temporal l rule of Medina, thus creating the perfect model of a ruler by the grace of Allah of the first organized Muslim community. That precedent had been achieved by the most perfect of rulers who had received via the Qur'an, the Word of Allah, divine guidance to the ideal way of governance. While during his early prophecy in Mecca, all the chapters of the Qur'an that were revealed to him were of an apocalyptic import, predicting on the model of the great Jewish Prophets, that the end of the world was at hand, the moment he migrated to Medina in AD 622 and began serving as the local rule, the burden of government obliged him to tailor-make new revelations which resembled more the legislative character of Leviticus and Numbers. But once those revelations were sanctified by inclusion in the Qur'an, after the passing of Muhammed, they could no longer be changed or improved upon, especially after the Prophet himself had followed their guidelines. Since then, those prescriptions of good government have been engraved in stone as the ideal Islamic rule for all generations to come. Ideal, since the Prophet himself practiced them. For, unlike the Prophets of Israel who were giant intellectuals, and usually inimical to the royal rule, and its greatest critiques, Muhammed was himself the ruler, some kind of philosopher- king, who understood the requirements of government and found solutions to them. Moreover, since he practiced that rule under divine inspiration and was himself infallible, his style of government could not have been afflicted by major errors or deviations which would require redress today. Quite the contrary, pretending to amend today what the most perfect of men did, would amount to insulting the wisdom and integrity of the Messenger of Allah. No wonder, then, that the era of the Prophet has become the perfect model of emulation, both spiritually and politically. Granted that after him no one can claim the gift of prophecy since he was the Seal of Prophets, his tradition (*sunna)* became the ultimate model of emulation, while the greatest scare of all in Islam has been innovation (*bid'a* -doctrinal, not technical). We customarily change things in order to improve upon them, but if it is determined that the best had occurred in the time of the Prophet, then what is the incentive to alter anything? The rationale is that the generations away from the Prophet keep deteriorating. In his time, the Companions (*Sahaba),* were second in perfection only to the Prophet himself, but their followers (*tabi'un*) and more so the followers' followers (*tabi'u al-tabi'un*), and so on *ad infinitum*, can only decrease in quality as they get farther from the Prophet's times. Thereupon, people can no longer attain the hereafter thanks to their proximity to the Prophet, but only due to their own piety and good deeds. This is the base for the doctrine that has been adopted especially by the two most puritanical schools of law (the Hanbalites and the Malikites), which reject the *bida*' and claim that after the worthy men who founded all four schools of law had passed away, the inspiration that moved them to legislate and innovate was terminated (namely "the gates of *Ijtihad* had been closed"), therefore any innovation after them would be hazardous and against any good counsel. Hence the Islamic precedents and verdicts of the past remain the exclusive reference for any judicious pronouncement, something which obviously precludes any free and open thinking, divine inspiration having been exhausted on earth. Paradoxically, then, the more the new generations become distanced from the Prophet, and in need for new interpretations to meet the emerging challenges and requirements of new modes of life, the more they are denied any such opportunities and they have to rely on the outdated judgment of the ancients. A classical example is Egypt, which in the 1920s and 30s was more liberal, open and democratic than today. Indeed, in these days of the Islamic Spring, as Islamic opinions and sentiments are reasserting themselves, the remnants of the liberal and democratic voices can hardly go on blocking the dam with their thumb to hold the threatening Islamic flood. To this trend there is one major exception, and that is Shi'ite Islam, where the Ayatullahs, due to their ongoing link to the Hidden Imam, can still get divine inspiration. This is what enabled Khomeini to lend innovative interpretations to the rule of the *mullah*s, as part of his *ijtihad* endeavors.Looking backwards at the past and finding in it all sources of wisdom and references to action, all that good and devoted Muslims can strive for today, is to attempt to recreate as close a replica as humanly possible, of the time of the Prophet, and this is exactly the meaning of the *salafi* movements, i.e. pious Muslims who strive to emulate the ancestors *(aslaf),* from the generation of the Prophet onwards. In Egypt, the Salafiya gained 30% of the votes to Parliament and came second only to the Brothers who secured 45% of the electorate in the 2012 elections which brought President Mursi to power. These Muslim tendencies profoundly believe that the truth is embedded in the sayings and deeds of their predecessors, and that pretending to improve upon them is blasphemous and a baseless and vain thought. Hence the tremendous magnetic appeal of these movements throughout the Islamic world, which do not advocate any new doctrine, but simply revive the ancient, venerated, but neglected and forlorn precepts which had made the glory of Islam in the past. And unlike the legendary Muslim Brothers, who are equipped with long-term patience and resilience, and invest in welfare to prepare a solid base for their future rule, the *Salafi* movements and their likes (the Algerian Armed Groups of the 1990s, the Egyptian *Gama'at* of the 1970s and 1980s, the Taliban, al-Qa'ida, and their ilk of the 1990s and 2,000s, and ISIS and *Jabhat -al-Nusra* of the 2014s), want everything and now, and are often violent in their demand for immediate application of their rule. The Brothers had in the past also embraced that road of impatience and violence in Egypt, Syria and Jordan, but when they were crushed by the authorities and risked annihilation, they elected to lower their profile and pretend that they had been moderated, giving the false impression to uninitiated foreign observers that they had indeed changed their ways. But now that Muslim Brothers have gained some legitimacy as a consequence of the Spring and their temporary rule in Tunisia and Egypt, they will also gradually revive the venomous discourse of their founding fathers- Hassan al-Banna and Sayyid Qutb, who continue to be deeply venerated throughout the Muslim world, and in practice merge with the *salafis*, there being no significant doctrinal and operational gap between them.

No less detrimental to the obstruction of the future by the past, when considering the era of the Prophet as the best of regimes and the most perfect of societies, has been the pessimistic state of mind this creates among Islamic peoples when they grow to believe that the best was and is gone, and is irretrievable, therefore things can only get worse. This does not encourage effort for betterment, initiative, entrepreneurship, but a spirit of fatalism and doom which leaves the individual apathetic, lacking in incentive to move and change, and not attaching hopes to learning, science and advancement. Even as the Islamic Spring proceeds, we watch the rebels against their tyrants not only cursing their oppressors and striving to remove them from power, but also doing that in the name of Allah, shouting war- cries of *Allah Akbar* (Allah is the greatest !) in response to their bombardment and shelling by their rulers' artillery and jet fighters. That means that they leave the revolution in the hands of God, while they, who expose themselves on the fire line, are only tools in His hands. It is doubtful whether Lenin or Mao could have achieved their grand revolutions if they had counted on any god instead of taking matters into their own hands, and risking their lives and the fate of their nations in the name of the alternative ideologies they pursued. The Islamic revolutionary passivity, as much as it sounds like a contradiction in terms, continues to lay at the base of the Islamic Spring today. The pessimistic view that all has been decided from above, also stands at the foundation of the annual UN reports on social and economic development, which have invariably cast the Muslim countries at the bottom of the world scale, in spite of the fact that these surveys are made by Arab and Muslim scholars who know and understand this hopeless situation, for otherwise this observation would have smacked of

"Islamophobia" on the part of scholars who would be accused of ill- intent to condemn Islam. In these annual surveys, the same sad themes are recurrent: this built- in chronic backwardness is due to Islam and its ramifications, namely the status of women, the lack of human rights, freedom and the Islamic form of government. The young people who have risen in rebellion in the 2011 Spring are aiming specifically at illiteracy, poverty, unemployment and sickness, which only if eliminated could salvage the situation. Paradoxically, however, the desperate people who ignited the rebellion, while shouting from the top of their lungs: "Democracy!", have often also supported the success of the Islamic parties, whose regressive views and worship of the past have precisely helped to generate this accumulated national lagging behind, which it has become urgent to remedy.

As against the Western idea of the nation-states, Islam posits the ideal of unity which is expressed in the yearning for a caliphate by Muslim revolutionary movements, while in practice the tribal fragmentation of Arab and Islamic societies make them nearly ungovernable, and the enormous 1,5 billion strong universal *umma* a pipe dream. The tribal structure of Arabia at the time of the Prophet, which connoted the absolute dependence of the individual on his family, clan and tribe for survival, was an almost impassable obstacle for the Prophet when he began spreading his message among the Arab tribes. Why would any individual who felt secure and comfortable within his tribe, risk his very existence by following a questionable preacher to an uncertain future?. The conditions in the desert did not encourage anyone to leave the protective wings of his tribe, hence the meager success of the Prophet at first, except for the first followers, who followed him in Mecca and then in Medina, and who lived in his proximity and learned to know him as a man they could trust. This is where the genius of the Prophet came to full expression: first, when he convinced the tribal heads to accept the Islamic call, usually most members of the tribe followed suit, a sort of collective undertaking, which in the beginning facilitated the process of conversion in Arabia, but later caused the most bloody war in the history of early Islam as upon the death of the Prophet, most of the tribal chieftains reneged on their personal fealty to the deceased Messenger of Allah and refused to transfer it to his successors. Then, the first Caliph of Islam, Abu Bakr, had to sink his two years of rule in a bloodbath against the renegades (*murtaddun),* which became the basis for the death penalty against any Muslim who relinquishes his faith.The *ridda* War has remained carved in the consciousness of all Muslims, to mean that rebellion against the ruler is harshly punished by death, something we observe every day even as the Spring unfolds. Since *Islam* means literally submission (to the will of Allah), anyone who seems to defy that principle cannot escape death. We have seen many heads cut-off by fanatic Muslim groups (like al-Qa'ida, Taliban, abu Saif in the Philippines, and the Janjaweed in the Sudan, or the Armed Groups in Algeria, who killed ruthlessly even other Muslim rivals who were accused of *ridda* or heresy). The ongoing massacres in Syria and Iraq, which are perpetrated by Jabhat-al-Nusra and ISIS opposition in the name of Allah, and by the rulers in the name of his prerogative to rule, just like the terrible slaughters in Libya until Qaddafi fell, and again after his fall; the tribal strife that was and is still brewing in Yemen; the almost daily explosions by Muslims against other Muslims in Pakistan, Afghanistan and Somalia, with hundreds and thousands of victims in all those places, have been pursued with nonchalance in the places of their perpetration, and accompanied by silence and indifference in the rest of Islamic world, seem to express the continuity of those mass killings in Islamic history. That is the reason why instead of looking inwards into their atrocities, of which they are unable to cure themselves, they direct their ire against America and NATO for their "slaughters in Iraq and Afghanistan", and against Israel, for its "massacres of the Palestinians", even when in comparison, the horrors they purposely commit of their own volition on their own people generate tenfold the victims that the West or Israel cause unintentionally, usually in collateral damage, to other Muslims. The second stroke of genius by the Prophet was his creation of the universal *umma,* an integrated supra-tribal community, which guaranteed to those who joined Islam that they would be protected and provided for, just as in their original tribes, thus encouraging them to relinquish their tribes and follow him. The growing Muslim community was no longer a matter of tribe or locale to satisfy, but an all-encompassing, and in the course of time universal community, where like in the ancient *ecclesia,* every new Christian convert became a member, literally one organ in its body of Christianity. In the outset, when the community was confined to Medina, all Muslims felt close and members of the same city, which they knew and trusted like the members of their original tribe to which they felt committed. And in order to boost their self assurance also economically, the *umma* created a fund, called the *zakat (*alms, which was in reality a tax) imposed on all members, which provided a public treasury to sustain the community. The *Zakat* became the fourth Pillar *(rukn, pl. arkan)* of Islam (the others are the declaration of Allah's unity, prayer, fast and pilgrimage), which when repeated on a daily basis by each believer became a sort of validation of their membership in the *umma.* This revolutionary device, which entrusted to the leadership of Islam a permanent source of income for the needs of the community, both encouraged and hastened its growth and also serves today as a powerful argument in the hands of fundamentalist Muslims who refer to the Umma as a first “”democratic” endeavor by the Prophet of Islam to establish a first social welfare system, and an incentive to return to the early days of Islam as a model of an ideal regime, as *salafi* Muslims would have it. These days, as modern taxation systems have replaced *zakat,* the latter is no longer levied in most Islamic countries, but it became voluntary alms contributed to the treasury of Muslim associations for their charitable activities, real or as a cover to terrorist organizations, or disbursed by donors for specific needs, like hospitals, orphanages, mosques and the like. Muslim associations have also learned to accommodate donors who are short of cash by accepting their payments in kind: building materials from constructors, food and clothes from merchants, expertise from professionals like doctors, lawyers and accountants, and labor by skilled workers. In this way, organizations like the Muslim Brothers and their affiliates could finance and run their operations in the days when they were banned from power and often persecuted by the authorities. In this fashion, they and other Muslim associations could accumulate the large pool of public goodwill towards themselves, which paid off later when the Spring was launched. The masses which appeared in the public square and celebrated Islam, and mobilized a million people to welcome Sheikh Qaradawi in Tahrir Square in Cairo at the outset of the Spring (2011), came from these social strata which had known poverty and despair, and owed much of their to the Muslim associations for their survival and livelihood. Naturally, these are also the masses which stream into the streets to voice support for the Brothers or shout: *Allah Akbar* !, or else to rejoice publicly for any western of Jewish setback. Since the concept of the *umma,* the universal congregation of all Muslims, was introduced by the Prophet of Islam, the idea of Muslim unity, ruled from one center, has been prevailing as an ideal if not as a reality. For while this notion was readily feasible in the polis of Medina in Muhammed's lifetime, it became increasingly difficult, and then outright impossible, to apply in the vast Muslim empire, as its conquests kept expanding. Indeed, far flung provinces, like Andalusia in the west and Central Asia in the east, that were ruled by independent – minded governors, soon found it more manageable and more lucrative to establish their own sultanates, with or without some vague submission to the suzerainty of the remote Caliph. Various attempts were made in the modern era to establish Pan Muslim organizations, like the Muslim League or the Muslim Congress, after the demise of the Caliphate in 1922, in order to rehabilitate Islamic unity, but none came to full fruition until the arson of the Aqsa Mosque in 1968 which gave rise to the Organization of the Islamic Conference (Later Cooperation), which has come to encompass since all the 57 Muslim-majority countries of the world.

What in the West the utopian idea of a world government has been finally laid to rest after the dismal failure of the post W W I League of Nations to prevent wars, and the same impotence to keep the world peace by the post W W II United Nations, has remained a lively ideal of the Islamic world government, which the radical Muslims are seeking to implement. Following the death of the Prophet in AD 632, the Muslim community in Medina was in disarray as to who should inherit him. It was clear to all that in his function as a Prophet and Messenger of Allah he was irreplaceable since he was the Seal of the Prophets and the last of the Messengers of God. But to fill his other functions as the Chief Executive of the community, its supreme Judge, its military commander and its spiritual leader, a replacing vicar could be agreed by the *Shura* of his companions. Thus, four of them were designated in succession: Abu Bakr (632-4), Umar (634-44), Uthman (644-56) and Ali (656-61), as Caliphs for the first 30 year consequent to his death, and later dubbed as *Rashidun* (the Rightful). But as soon as the first dynastic rule was established by the Umayyads (662-750), its ruling kings or emperors arrogated to themselves the title of Caliph without always deserving it. That supreme title was taken up by the successive rulers of every major Islamic dynasty thereafter until the demise of the Ottomans following World War I. But especially after its decline, the Caliphate has become the iconic system of government throughout the Islamic world, and every movement of revival of Islam, particularly the current one that radical Muslims have embraced, harks back to the caliphate as the ideal to be attained, so as to fill the yawning gap between the disunity and chaos of the present and the ideal government of past history and future utopia. However, even when there was no Caliphate, the tradition of authoritarian rule had already been well rooted in Arab and Muslim lore, and it facilitated its revival when it was resorted to. From its inception, Islamic government had to learn from the great imperial experiments of its time: the Sassanids in Persia and the Byzantines in Anatolia, which combined empire and religion. The Prophet Muhammed, consciously or not, adopted this model in his 10 years of rule in Medina (AD 622-32), for without his experience as a preacher in Mecca he would not have been invited to Medina, and without his ruling experience in Medina, it is doubtful whether his prophetic experience in Mecca would have served any practical purpose and accorded him his fame as the founder of Islam. The mould of government developed by Muhammed through his Medina experience while he was setting the first example of rule inthe first Muslim *polis*, consisted of five functions: prophecy and the legislative powers connected to it, spiritual leadership, executive power, judiciary and the military.

Muhammed's prophecy was his value-added quality over all humans, and when he moved from Mecca, where he was a "mere" apocalyptic soothsayer, who predicted the end of the world, and had not much to offer except to sermonize to the bourgeois merchant population of his clan in his city; to Medina where he was an invited ruler, his career changed completely. Now he had to care for the city's affairs, to deal with personal, clan, tribal and commercial issues which sought settlement before him. His prophecies continued, but this time tailor-made to respond to the arising problems he had to resolve in real life. Those revelations, as he and other Muslims came to see them, were being imprinted in the Holy Book as arising from his divine inspiration, and served later as the precedents and the base for the Prophet's legislation. But when he died, and having no successor as a prophet, it was clear that no Caliph could legislate like the Prophet, that the Prophet and his *Sunna* contained already all necessary legislation for all humanity for all time, and that only *'ulama'* (doctors of the Holy Law) could henceforth tell what was the law. Hence the important role the doctors of Islam have in the Muslim state as interpreters of the law *(Faqih*=jurist), as religious verdict renderers (*Mufti*) or as *quda'* (sing. *Qadi* = judge). Theoretically, the Caliphs could not legislate because they lacked the understanding of the scholars, but they could make other scholars who obeyed them pronounce the legal sanctions they wanted. In Muhammed's time, legislation was narrowly related to prophecy because as the Prophet's revelations were laws, and were later included in the verses of the Qur'an, they became laws by definition. But after his death, who else could legislate who did not possess the power of prophecy? In theory, the jurists retained that right for themselves, of legislation via interpretation, but not any more via inspiration, since the gates of *Ijtihad* had been closed, and most certainly not via innovation (Allah Forbid the *bid'a*). Except for periods of truly righteous and pious rulers, who would resort to the scholars of their time to determine right or wrong, most rulers could not resist the temptation of ruling daily on current matters and then asking their scholars to find rationalizations for their decisions. The Ottoman Empire already acted under the constraint of distinguishing between Shari'a Law which prevailed in the realm, and the *Qanun* covered the temporal issues that arose from daily necessities, be they financial, social, administrative or military. In our days, there is supposed to be a modern legal code that is partly based on the Islamic sources and partly on the civil code. But the body of laws in both systems is there to be violated by the rulers, who continue to play by the Islamic rules in public, but in private they do much what they like. Therefore, though no Arab dictator prior to the Islamic Spring of the 2010s would admit that he was the legislator, and would assert that he made sure that every item of legislation passed the Parliament, ever body knew that even the King of Jordan and the President of Egypt, who were among the mildest dictators, could suspend the Parliament at will; conversely, anything they wished the Parliament to pass, was done without much foot dragging. That meant, in fact, that the dictators were also the legislators. Concurrently, all those dictators made sure to lend lip service to religion, by declaring that the source of legislation was mainly or at least secondarily Islam. As far as executive power was concerned, the Prophet was truly limitless, even though his Medina Treaty which he signed (metaphorically, since he was illiterate) prior to his arrival, had stipulated certain conditions and obligations on him. In fact, after he Islamized the city and subjugated it to his will, and as his life style had become the model for all Muslims to emulate, no one could question his wisdom in his executive functions, especially as he was under the constant blessing of his divine revelations, thus he could not be contradicted or disobeyed. And so the Prophet, using his charisma and his leadership skills, could unite the Arab tribes, deal with the Jewish tribes quite harshly, expelling some of them, executing others and Islamizing still others; subjugate his rivals from within, launch military campaigns against other tribes, reform the inner structures of the city, launch the new religion and much more, all in the space of ten years. Executive powers are the area where the present day tyrants "excel" too: they make their own "constitution" upon ascending to power, thus taking over something from the legislative branch when there is one, they monopolize the appointments of all ministers and their Prime ministers, hold the reins of power at all levels, decide upon the budget, the rate of taxation to be levied, and the persons and institutions who enjoy public budgeting; they determine what the people will eat and at what price, and hold in hand all the entrances and exits to and from public power. Is this a continuation of the old privileges that the Prophet had enjoyed, or simply the place where all dictators are bound to slide? It does not matter, as long as there will always be people who find justification to their deeds in

Muhammed's exemplary life precedent.

The socio-political conditions of those days had indeed required that all those authorities be concentrated in the Prophet's hands, regardless of whether he knew or not that his style was not different from the authoritarian rule that he saw or heard about in his environment. The only model he was familiar with was the tribal one, where the *sheikh* concentrated all authority in his hands, thus he could not deviate much from what was known without producing controversy around him. Naturally, the *sheikh* was also committed to his tribe and its values, and to the consensus among the notables to preserve his dominant rule, therefore he could not turn his rule into a heartless and unrestrained tyranny without incurring the risk of losing it. There was an unwritten social pact, worded in terms of the classical *muruwa*, which included ruling justly (the judiciary aspect), managing wisely and effectively (the executive part) and leading heroically in battle (the military aspect). They, in return, undertook to obey him and his orders, and to follow his lead in all his endeavors. In other words, when the Messenger of Allah was asked to proceed to Medina and take over the rule there, it is reasonable to assume that he knew what was expected of him. The authoritarian rule in Islam naturally followed on the footsteps of the Prophet, who was, and still is, considered infallible and the most perfect of men, therefore he could commit no fault, in government or in anything else. It is also reasonable to assume that while establishing the fundaments of Muslim rule according to his needs, he also learned something from the imperial models he knew or learned about. Being possessors of an acute sense of obedience to his example, the Arabs as well as other Muslims have always felt that the great precedents set by him in his lifetime had necessarily grown to become valid for all times, especially after Muhammed died, and the Arabs sprang out of Arabia to conquer the world, and were in need to find a Muslim style of government that would respond to their growing and pressing needs. One has to assume that they were convinced of divine assistance to their vast and exciting enterprise of conquest, which was done under their authoritarian regime of the time, therefore after the death of the Prophet they pursued the same route, which was common to them and to the enemies they fought against. Moreover, at a time when their Sassanid and Byzantine rivals were tyrannical rulers dipped in luxury and opulence, in addition to authoritarianism, to the point that one spoke of the legendary "Byzantine Court" and "Sassanid ostentation", the Muslim court was managed much more simply and modestly, at least in the beginning of Islam, for the authority of the ruler was institutionalized in the *bay'a (*oath of fealty), without a need to resort to all the paraphernalia which inspired awe, splendor and authority in the rule and succession of those ancient imperial houses. That meant, that the Muslim ruler in place, who had been designated by the *shura,* as in the times of the Rightful Caliphs, or later inherited his mantle through dynastic inheritance, was recognized and accepted in the public square, as if the oath of allegiance to him were given personally by each Muslim. For, any time of rebellion or dissatisfaction with the ruler, dubbed *fitna*, meant that the oath (*bay'a*) lost its validity. Then, worshippers no longer mentioned the name of the ruler at Fridays' prayers, as if the weekly validation of the oath no longer held. Thus, the outside symbols of power were very much personal, direct and needed no elaboration or ostentation.

The charisma of the Prophet in his time was beyond doubt or question. Nobody challenged his sublime qualities and natural propensity to rule, as if he were a prince who inherited those qualities. But what about those who followed him as rulers? Did they inherit his charisma? How was the balance preserved between their nature as pious and righteous men and their ability to govern the people, for the people, and make their rule appear as just and beyond reproach as possible? Allah's Messenger, apart from serving in all the functions cited above, also created and enforced a systematic ritual, repeated daily and many times a day, which became one of the sources of his power, and made him also the spiritual and religious leader of the Muslim community, in addition to being the Messenger of Allah and His last Prophet. The first Pillar of the faith, the *Shahadah* (bearing witness), repeated at the head of each prayer the formula that "there was no God but Allah and Muhammed His Prophet". When it became the first of the articles of the faith, this formula made inextricable the connection between Him and the very belief in the religion. When repeated many times over, every day, in prayer, and preceding each important act one does, this accorded a central place to the Prophet in one's life. As long as the Prophet lived, and his contemporaries felt privileged to be around him, they could see in front of them the perpetual expression of Allah's grace, in sending to them the Seal of the Prophets and the most perfect of men to serve them and to guide them. There was never a possibility that anyone could question that charisma. Even in moments of friction with his closest companions, like with 'Umar in Hudaibiyya, Muhammed's unique and prevalent quality remained, because he always had the last word. When the Prophet suddenly died in A.D.632, there was an urgent need to appoint a successor, lest his entire heritage disintegrate. The *Shura* elected Abu-Bakr, probably by order or seniority since he was the oldest, but also the Prophet's father-in-law. What to make of his attribute of *Siddiq* (the Righteous) ?, probably not much, because it was accorded to him after his death. After him came the three others ('Umar, 'Uthman, 'Ali), every time following huge controversies and forceful lobbying for each candidate, which ended with compromises, horse-trading, bargaining, threats and pressures. The main issue was to designate a successor, lest the charisma of the Prophet be discontinued, and the authority of the Caliph be so diminished that there would not be much to inherit left. At the same time it was clear that prophecy was sealed for ever by Muhammed, and so were the divine legislative powers that emanated from it. Therefore, all that could be passed on to the Caliphs were the remaining functions of the Muslim ruler: civil legislation, executive, judiciary, spiritual and military command. This combination of so many top functions made sure that the Caliph would be no less omnipotent that the Prophet in the practical domain of rule, while the special and unique level of prophecy would remain sealed and out of bounds. Hence the attribute of *Khalifa* (Caliph) imputed to him, meaning a human figure, as even the Prophet had insisted upon characterizing himself, who served as a replacement, or Vicar in Christian parlance for the replacement of Jesus on earth. But there the vicars became infallible popes to a divine figure, while the Caliphs remained human all the way, with righteous qualities to be sure, but nothing divine, otherwise the doctrine of the unity of Allah (*tawhid)* would be seriously compromised. After the Four Righteous, many Islamic dynasties followed, often simultaneously, and struggling against each other, and sometimes the sons of the same ruler fighting for the succession of their father, like the bloody struggles between Aurangzeb and his brothers for the succession of Shah Jehan which while unfolding, the imprisoned ruler was helplessly watching his sons butchering each other. This war to the finish proceeded with every generation, for a new king could not feel safe on his throne, as an absolute ruler, unless all his rival contenders were eliminated. In the Arab monarchies today, there are families on the throne which try to ensure an orderly succession, and there is no telling when some outsider down the line might rebel and reverse the order, as had happened with the Nasser and Qaddafi anti-monarchical revolutions in North Africa. There are certainly various degrees of absolutism, like the one perceivable in Saudi Arabia, without any institutions to palliate the royal house, and where even the *Shura* is appointed by the monarch, and in Kuweit and Jordan which have some kind of Parliament. Some kingdoms, like Jordan and Morocco, boast their "constitutional monarchy", but either they do understand the difference between their kingdoms and those of Benelux, the Scandinavians and England, and they continue nonetheless their fraudulent pursuit, or they don't and they just play with words. But absolutism in these countries is not confined to monarchies, for in Saddam's Iraq, Assa'd Syria and Qaddafi's Libya there was also an extreme sort of absolutism, which even surpassed monarchies in cruelty and egotism of the rulers. Some of them were/are so full of themselves that they designated heirs among their sons to succeed them (Saddam for Iraq, Mubarak for Egypt, Ali for Yemen, Qaddafi for Libya, Assad for Syria, where Bashar had actually inherited his father in 2000).

The fact of the matter is that the Palestinians have no history prior to the modern period and no connection to the Canaanites. Had this ancient Palestinian-Canaanite people actually existed, it would certainly have been able to show centuries of history and culture. It would certainly have been mentioned in historical documents and would have certainly appeared in contemporary documents such as the 1922 League of Nations Mandate for Palestine, the 1947 UN Partition Plan and even UN Security Council Resolution 242 which the Palestinians often refer to as the basis for their false claim that Israel is occupying "Palestinian territory." The fact that none of the above mentioned documents make any reference to a "Palestinian people", let alone a 4,500 year-old Palestinian people, does not bother the PA. For the PA, in the absence of any real history, all you have to do is make it up. More worrisome, however, is the fact that no known Palestinian, Arab or Muslim authority (and there are many of them living in the West, free from the terror of "treason") has been heard to raise his or her voice against these distortions of history.During the illusory "Arab Spring " which began in Tunisia and Egypt in late 2010 and early 2011, with the relatively more humane, pro-Western and moderate regimes of Tunisia's Ben Aly and Mubarak of Egypt, it was paradoxically they who fell first at the beginning of the Spring, but their lives were preserved or they escaped to a protective exile. It seems that the more cruel among them, who were also ruthless in defense of their rule, like Assad, Qaddafi and Ali of Yemen, had to fight the longest and kill the most of their own citizens, to remain in place, or before they lost their lives. Islamic history had known both types of tyrants: those who ran away and others who were killed during the war of succession. But even the more benevolent types like Mubarak, when too long in power (30 years) tended towards corruption and "monarchic" rule. In effect, Mubarak was "elected" and "reelected" every time anew, by an obedient parliament, with no rival candidate allowed to run, lest he "caused division among the people". Lately, when old and tired Mubarak announced that his son would run for office after him, his people rebelled, because when they agreed to a republic in 1952, they did not mean a monarchical or dynastic republic. In Lebanon too, despite the full blown election campaign, Sa'd Hariri ran to replace his father who was murdered by Hizbullah on behalf of the Syrians, exactly as to replace the legendary Pierre Jumayel, the founder and commander of the Phalangs, his two sons followed: Bashir first, and when he was slain by the Syrians, his brother Amin followed to the presidency. Kamal Junblatt, the Druze leader, was replaced by his son Walid who is far from reaching his stature, and has even shown subservience to Bashar Assad, wrongly betting on the leader of Syria who began to stagger to his disappearance during the Syrian civil war. All these examples show that when it comes to authoritarian executive power, all the Arab countries of the Middle East have some affinity to it, one way or another. Only lust for power in this fashion can instigate a father to wish to bequeath his rule to his sons. It is not known what the Prophet himself would have done had he had a son. But since only Fatima his daughter survived, and she married his cousin Ali, who also became a contender for power, but it is difficult to conclude from that anything about the pre-Spring present day lust for the rule of succession in the Muslim world. One strong suspicion has to be mentioned nonetheless, and that is that the tyrants in place today are/were so much afraid of what might happen to them or to their memory after their death, that their only way to guarantee the posthumous survival of their reputation was to ensure the rule of their sons after them, because a) Only the son can assure the memory of his father, by making certain that he is properly commemorated and his heritage is respected and even worshipped; just imagine what would have happened to Hafez Assad's Memorial in Qardahah had his son not been around to defend and cultivate it; and b) without a pre-arranged succession, fathers, especially coming from a minority group, could not ascertain that their children would or could succeed, or even survive them. Imagine that Assad the father had been killed as a president-dictator, then his son Bashar would at best have remained an optometrist, or continued to seek shelter in London, and his father's memory may have been totally erased. Conversely, had the successions of Saddam, Qaddafi, Saleh and Mubarak worked out, then the dictators could still be in power, or put on the pedestal as elder statesmen, and in any case allowed to die naturally. As far as the Judiciary is concerned, judges, who were all religious (*qadi*) in old days, served under the various Caliphs and dynasties, but since they depended on the royal Court for their appointment to the job, they were also usually obedient, though they were supposed to enforce *Shari'a* law. But since the Ottoman rule, which had established the distinction between *Shari'a* and civil law (*Qanun*), all independent Muslim countries then gradually adopted such a system, and pressures began as to the degree and extent to which the law of each country ought to depend entirely, to a large degree, or partially on religious law. In any case the two systems exist side by side and both are apportioned their share by the administration in place. But under dictators the system does not matter and things are usually decided according to the whims of the rulers, when the the issue is important to him to the point that he cares to intervene.

We have mentioned above, that the first legal document that every ruler in the Muslim world has introduced, was a constitution, which instead of being left to the public or to assemblies of representatives to put together, is made by the tyrant or his underlings. Rather than constituting a legal framework which sets limits to the dictator's power, and promises protection to the citizens and their rights, this sort of "constitution" only draws the guidelines for the future action of the ruler, not necessarily to be respected, and to be altered by a new document of the same sort when the ruler changes his mind or the next dictator comes. And finally in the military field, the one that had been fulfilled with distinction by the Prophet, as he launched periodical wars of expansion in Arabia, or raids (*ghazwa)* against his rival tribes or across the Byzantine border, or to seize the holy shrine of Mecca to which he had not been allowed to enter by his fellow tribesemen of Qureish. Through his campaigns throughout Arabia where his Medinan followers never hesitated to tread, he ensured for himself the title of *Amir-al-Mu'minin* (Commander of the Faithful), a title he seemed to like in particular due to the frequency of its usage, when he was addressed by other Muslims. This was also the title favored by all the Caliphs and Sultans who followed throughout the generations. There were even cases of Muslim minority rebellions, where the local commanders who wished to rally larger Muslim troops around them, made their summons to their public using this title or similar to it[56]. In the modern Arab and Islamic worlds, most dictators also put themselves at the head of the high military command in their country, either because they mounted a *coup* as military men, or because they wish to appear as generals or marshals or admirals in their military uniform (Sadat was killed in a general's suit while watching a military parade; Idi Amin dressed like a marshal, Qaddafi liked to parade with either his officer's suit, or his clown outfit). In that

---

56 *Al-Masri alYaum,* 5 December, 2014.

fashion, they seem to send a clear message that whatever their generals' ranks, those they wear are superior. For all these dictatorships, the army has been their main sustenance in power, and it is worth recalling that in Egypt, when the army abandoned Mubarak, he collapsed; in Syria Bashar's army supported him, so he could fight for a long time while the outside world thought he was faltering and pressed him to abdicate his rule.

Even though dust is far from settling yet on all those countries which underwent the rebellious Arab/Islamic Spring, it is clear that what was will never be again and that new and uncertain paths are being carved into the rock, whose directions we cannot yet ascertain. It is also clear that the masses of Arabs and Muslims are loath to sustain the tyrannical rule that has ruled them hitherto. Yes, they all shout: Democracy ! as if they knew what it was, but what they mean is that they are tired of dynastic and absolute rulers. On the other hand, it is not easy to imagine in the Islamic world powerless "vegetarian" monarchical regimes like those in Europe, because for them a ruler is a ruler, a king is a king and an executive without authority is nobody. Thus, Saudi Arabia, Morocco or Jordan, or the Gulf States, which are proclaiming their wish to adopt reform, for example by instituting "constitutional monarchies" into their respective systems, will have ultimately to go, because neither can they relinquish their power totally, without which there is no constitutional monarchy, nor would their nations which they had enslaved for many decades, let them continue their rule unchecked, for then the monarch instead of becoming merely the symbol of the state would remain the main power broker in it, which is a recipe for more friction and future crises. The most amazing aspect of this is the fact that after years of intimate knowledge of the heads of states of the Spring, and of business dealings with them, and official representations in each other's country for years, during which they had the chance to examine the regime, gauge its feudalistic and dictatorial dimensions, evaluate the degree of oppression, suppression, corruption and exploitation which sustained it, Western powers, including their politicians, diplomats, military, intelligence and scholars, hardly ever voiced one word of alarm, of warning and of fear from things to come. They allowed things to deteriorate to their maximum, and only when open rebellion broke out and blood started to spill in the streets, have they had the decency to say: "Oh yah, we knew all along, but were ordered not to speak up"; or "we knew it was coming"; or else "we could have never believed this rule would be so easy to remove". We could even expect someone to cry out: "remember the Shah's island of stability, that Carter had turned into a swamp of Iranian hostility". Where were all those Presidents and Foreign Ministers in the West who invited those dictators to their capitals, sold them weapons, defended them in the United Nations, formed alliances with them, pardoned their violations of every law, forgave their crimes and allowed them to plant their tents (literally) in the hearts of Rome, Paris and London ? Didn't they know they were tyrants and corrupt? If they did not know, they should have dismissed their ambassadors and their chiefs of Intelligence there who submitted to them false and biased reports. Their late reaction would expose them now to two sorts of accusations that they would find difficult to refute: that they now admit their faltering policies in the previous years, for lending support to all sorts to corrupt and dangerous dictators and enabled them to survive for decades, knowing that they were robbing and exploiting their peoples; and secondly, if that is, or was, the case, why expect the countries of the Spring to have confidence in the Western powers which have disappointed and betrayed them with their conduct in the past.

Many secondary questions pop up in the public squares of all those countries which have chosen to change course, all leading to the main question of trusting once again the powers which have misled them more than once before. For example, America and the West now promise to support democracy. What democracy? How can we be sure we are talking about the same democracy? For years they had let Mubarak (and the others) rig elections, so how can they be trusted to ensure fair elections now? They had let Saudi Arabia and Libya to do without elections at all, and they were never heard urging those rulers to change course. What has happened now? Did westerners suddenly mend their ways? Why did they let Egypt suppress the Copts for decades, the Syrians to impose a regime of terror and to interfere in their neighbor's affairs, and Hizbullah to take over the rule in Lebanon, in submission to the Syrian and Iranian tyrannies? And when the West intervened in oil-rich Libya, dropping bombs without taking any risks for their troops, everyone expected to see the same unfolding in Syria. But NATO members knew the difference, because the Syrian army was and still is large, larger than the number of divisions NATO could field (except for the Americans), its air force and air defenses are formidable enough to challenge western air power save the American, while the Libyan military did not exist as a fighting force. No major European power could stand the domestic disaster of bringing home plastic bags with corpses, therefore no country volunteered to fight there. America, who could have done it, had her hands full in Afghanistan, and an election campaign approaching, and it was clear that they would not take any additional risk. Even though America has later taken the lead of the Arabo-Western coalition to battle ISIS, it has limited its intervention to air strikes and to training Iraqi troops, in an attempt to avoid a recurrence of the costly Iraqi and Afghani ventures.

# Chapter Five

## *The British Leading the Caving-in*

The multiplicity of Muslim movements of all sorts, and sometimes even their tendency to fight each other, do not preclude, however their categorization under the heading of Muslim radicals, who almost all share in common the basic traits that render them threatening in the eyes of outsiders, though for the world Muslim populace they may constitute a source of pride, hope, promise and even redemption. Those traits are: striving for Muslim unity, establishing a world Caliphate, a deep hatred for the West; a gut contempt for the Jews and Israel, a commitment to a *shari'a*-governed state and society, a world of illusions and delusions based on conspiracy theories, a disregard for human life and humanitarian sensitivities, a penchant toward the absolute even at the price of their self-annihilation, and the ready recourse to violence when they encounter resistance to their worldviews. Many of these traits, and others, are common to Muslims in general, and we shall examine them in the next chapter. Here, we shall elaborate some of them one by one, based on some examples, so as not to need to explain them again and again when we discuss each radical organization separately. Underlying all this is the basic perception in Islam that the times of the Prophet were ideal, hence the constant striving to emulate them and hold them as the yardstick to measure success and rightfulness in our days. But before we delve into them, it is necessary to explain the quantitative versus the qualitative ideological approaches to religious and semi-religious convictions. The quantitative approach usually deals in relative terms with the matter under consideration, meaning that all issues can be ironed out and resolved by a process of negotiations, namely a give and take procedure that produces a meeting of minds, born out of compromises which are translated into words that make up the agreement, pact or treaty. Successful negotiations or dialogues follow that model and no matter how hard and lengthy they are, they end up in agreement. Conversely, the qualitative approach followed by either religious fanatics or ideological diehards, is absolute in its demands, recalcitrant in its means and aggressive in its conduct. Its adepts are so one-sidedly persuaded of their truth that they have no need for negotiations, because they are guided by supreme or divine guidelines that are not given to bargaining or question. For example, if one believes that his creed or conviction is the final truth that cannot be compromised, then what is the use of negotiation? They are persuaded that nothing exists outside their beliefs, and they are so committed to stand for their creed that their universe is viewed only through that prism and they are ready to struggle for it and even put their lives on the fire line for it. They do not seek to convince others or debate their worldview in comparison to others, they simply wish to impose, even by force if necessary, their ideas since they are the only valid ones. They have a book, an idea, a platform, and all the rest are invalid fallacies that they denounce and dismiss or simply ignore. The outside world may consider their ideas unfeasible, "crazy", and incomprehensible, but they ignore the critiques and proceed on their way, with surprising stamina and often with unexpected and rapid success. On the other hand, unlikely and stunning as it may be, many young people adhere to those outlandish creeds and flock to reinforce their ranks. We see that in the conduct of al Qa'ida, ISIS and their likes in both the Islam world as well as the Western lands where millions of Muslims have migrated either by rejection and disgust of their native countries, or by an ambition to improve their living conditions. In both cases, they produced critical masses of Muslim populations which altered the landscape in their countries of asylum, and in some cases, like in Britain, France and Germany, where they migrated in the millions, they either founded bases of Islamic radicalism and terror, or joined existing ones. Terror. From there, young Muslims converged on Afghanistan, Iraq and Syria to swell the ranks of other Jihadi Muslims, or perpetrated acts of terror in their adoptive countries.

One of the countries mostly hurt by its own homegrown Muslim terrorist youth, was Britain, which on July 7, 2005, had the first taste of terror against its public transportation system when young British Muslims, who were reinforced by the generous and lax Muslim immigration into the British isles, adopted by the Tony Blair policy of multiculturalism. On Easter eve of the year 2009, we were faced by announcements of the British government, to the effect that it has ceased its dealings with the major Muslim Council of Britain (MCB), and by the Jewish organizations of France that they discontinued their "dialogue" with French Muslims. In both instances, the reasons cited were the same. Namely, the double game the Muslim groups were playing: on the one hand seeking "dialogue" with their partners, as a means of coexistence and of smoothing over difficulties in communications; but on the other hand supporting Hamas, which wants no dialogue with Israel. The non-Muslim parties in these "dialogues" were late in awakening to the reality, that Muslim culture understood "dialogue" not as way to facilitate rapprochement and understanding, by way of negotiation and clarification, but as a means to lend legitimacy to the monologue it wishes its partners to hear and to heed. When, after a few years of vain encounters, the non-Muslim participants finally understood, they withdrew from that exercise of goodwill once they realized that the other party did not respond in kind. The problem then lied in the juxtaposition of a resurgent Islam on the one hand, and a self-deprecating West on the other, unsure of itself, its values, or even what it stands for. Its people have made a virtue of instant self-gratification, and therefore they invest next to nothing in the future—hence they have stopped having children. Their preferred way of life amounts to a "credit card culture." They want everything, and they want it instantly. Never mind that their governments no longer raise sufficient funds from taxation to cover exorbitant welfare entitlements, or that a bleak financial future awaits tomorrow's pensioners. In short, the West has become a disgrace to its own heritage in sharp reversal of its fortunes when at the turn of the twentieth century the Muslim Ottoman Empire was considered the "sick man of Europe," and was therefore no match for a confident West. Former U.S. Defense Secretary, Donald Rumsfeld, was onto something apart from the obvious when he distinguished between "old" and "new" Europe—except that in their eagerness to grab some (necessarily short-term) economic benefits after emerging from Soviet control, the headlong rush of "new" liberated from Communism East European countries to join the EU, will inevitably contaminate them with the prevalent Western disease. There is another drawback to this constant resort to "dialogue." It lulls the Western populations into believing that their governments are doing something constructive to avert violence, or threats of violence, in the future. In reality, nothing could be further from the truth, for this non-policy simply serves to embolden and concomitantly empower those Muslims whom Western governments have chosen to act as intermediaries with the wider Muslim community. Invariably, Western governments have elected these Muslims largely because they are the activists, and therefore are prominent in the community, while the governments comfort themselves with the injudicious belief that these figures represent "moderate" Islam. However, these Muslims have been living in Europe long enough to have learned to tailor their vocabulary precisely according to whom they are facing across the table. They speak the language of peace, reconciliation, and goodwill to Westerners, and reserve their true thoughts and beliefs for fellow Muslims. In other words, they have learned to "work the system," admirably so. In effect, these "moderate" Muslim leaders gradually extract one concession after another from Western policymakers, rendering "dialogue" a one-way street. They enter each session with the full intention of testing the limits of the concessions they can extract, and it is a rare European government minister who would risk disappointing them—or else the headlines in the papers the following day would be sure to inflame the Muslim community with complaints and whining about Islamophobia, racism and xenophobia towards the very countries which had rescued them from misery and oppression and afforded them a relatively easier way to make a living and taste freedom.

Herein lies the value of the worldwide Muslim penchant for overreacting to every perceived slight, real or imagined, by demonstrating their "rage" loudly and violently. Temperament comes into play here too, for unlike other peoples who experience anger or humiliation, many Muslims are either unable or unwilling to contain those sentiments. One has only to recall the Arafat-orchestrated "days of rage" in the early days of the *Intifadah* against Israel, or the violent demonstrations against the Western embassies in Islamabad and Cairo when a Palestinian is killed in Gaza, a Rushdie had dared to publish his "Satanic Verses, or a Danish cartoonist took the liberty (and audacity) to depict the Prophet of Islam in some derogatory fashion, in order to understand that, in sharp contrast to Westerners, Muslims make a fetish of celebrating their anger. Such an uncontrolled behavior is unthinkable in the West, but not because of lack of Muslim provocation, particularly since September 11 (2001). Funerals too are manipulated to vent wrath and fury, emotion, general mayhem, and impromptu rifle-shooting. The total and shameless lack of dignity, even at what should be a somber occasion, is jarring to western eyes. Bodies are held aloft and bounced along the route, in a manner that would be regarded as disrespectful to the deceased in other cultures. Bodies have been known to fall off the stretcher amid the melee, and other processions turning chaotic as was recorded for posterity in the case of Iran's Ayatollah Khomeini's funeral. The explosion of the Cartoon Affair in Europe and the Middle East in 2006, which occasioned many deaths, boycotts, rage and world-wide demonstrations by Muslims, because some obscure artist dared to depict, in an obscure journal, the Prophet Muhammed in derogatory terms, in itself not only points to the pathological sensitivities of Muslims, but also to their obtuse attitude to others in their "dialogues". When the President of Iran vows to eliminate the Jewish people and to wipe Israel off the map, none of those dialoguing Muslim organizations raised its voice in protest; none also protested when Christian churches were torched, as a matter of course, throughout the Muslim world, or when the Joseph Tomb and the Jericho synagogues were burned and destroyed by Palestinians during the Intifadah. Only hurting the reputation of Muhammed matters, and justifies the use of violence, while the very notion of respect for other religions, simply does not exist in Islam, backed by their Holy book, the immutable Word of Allah, which condemns the Jews as "descendants of pigs and monkeys", and both Christians and Jews in the daily repetition of the opening chapter of the Qur'an (the *Fatihah*) for either " raising the wrath of Allah or going astray", or enjoining the Believers "not to befriend or associate with them". Worse, one of the authoritative Hadiths (*Sahih*) which is cited in the Hamas Charter, enjoins the Believers "to seek hiding Jews behind rocks and kill them".[57] Therefore, dialogue is only made to instill into Western minds the respect of Islam and its values, as the resolution of the Human Rights Commission, which was just adopted in Geneva, plainly

---

[57] R. Israeli, *The Charter of Allah: The Platform of the Hamas,* translated by this author and published both on Internet and in the author's book: *Islam and Israel: Essays in Interpretation,* University Press of America, Lanham, 1993.

attested[58]. As more and more western and Jewish organizations are finally grasping the meaning of "dialogue" for their Muslim partners, they may also try, at long last, to make it more egalitarian, reciprocal, and perhaps also efficacious.

The most disturbing aspect of this is that on the one hand, the British, like other Europeans and Americans seemed to understand the dangers inherent in the Muslim double-talk, but they were very formalistic and legalistic in their reluctance to take firm measures against the Muslim terrorist menace that was written on the wall, the FBI and the Scotland Yard both arguing that they were not allowed to act against ideologies, dangerous as they may be, and they clearly waited for the actual explosions to occur: in America on Sep 11, 2001 and in London in July 2005 (followed up by the rest of Europe, which culminated in the massive killings of 2015 in the streets of Paris). But while the Americans immediately launched war against Islamic terror and even he British also explained that even made deep incursions into Afghanistan and Iraq to root it out, the British authorities deluded themselves and tried to misinform their own people by stating their "surprise" about those acts, which descended suddenly and unexpectedly upon them, and that the "young British Muslims who committed the London Subway killings were criminals and would have to be punished". This author wrote a letter to PM Blair to debunk those delusions, determining two major facts that eluded the sophisticated British Intelligence and Scotland Yard:

1. There should have been no surprise, since years earlier, this author's research book on these matters[59] was published in London, which gave the names of some of the radical Muslim

[58] R. Israeli, *Duplicitous Constitutions,* Lambert Academic Publishing, Germany, 2022/3; *Human Rights and Human Development in the Arab and Muslim Lands,* Strategic Books, TX, 2022.

[59] .R. Israeli, *Islamikaze etc,* op. cit.

leaders and the mosques where young Muslim radicals were recruited for the mujahideen war in Afghanistan or for training in Pakistan. Relevant pages from the book were faxed to the Prime Minster

2. The perpetrators were not criminals, but Muslim ideologues, just like the Imams in the mosques of London and Manchester, who unlike regular criminals, did not act for their personal gain; quite the contrary, they put their lives on the line and even incurred expenses from their own funds to fulfill their religious commitment.

Many secondary questions pop up in the public squares of all those countries which have chosen to change course, all leading to the main question of trusting once again the powers which have misled them more than once before. For example, America and the West now promise to support democracy. What democracy? How can we be sure we are talking about the same democracy? For years they had let Mubarak (and the others) rig elections, so how can they be trusted to ensure fair elections now? They had let Saudi Arabia and Libya to do without elections at all, and they were never heard urging those rulers to change course. What has happened now? Did westerners suddenly mend their ways? Why did they let Egypt suppress the Copts for decades, the Syrians to impose a regime of terror and to interfere in their neighbor's affairs, and Hizbullah to take over the rule in Lebanon, in submission to the Syrian and Iranian tyrannies? And when the West intervened in oil-rich Libya, dropping bombs without taking any risks for their troops, everyone expected to see the same unfolding in Syria. But NATO members knew the difference, because the Syrian army was and still is large, larger than the number of divisions NATO could field (except for the Americans), its air force and air defenses are formidable enough to challenge western air power save the American, while the Libyan military did not exist as a fighting force. No major European power could stand the domestic disaster of bringing home plastic bags with corpses, therefore no country volunteered to fight there. America, who could have done it, had her hands full in Afghanistan, and an election campaign approaching, and it was clear that they would not take any additional risk. Even though America has later taken the lead of the Arabo-western coalition to battle ISIS, it has limited its intervention to air strikes and to training Iraqi troops, in an attempt to avoid a recurrence of the costly Iraqi and Afghani ventures.The faults that the awakening Arab participants in the Spring could detect and complain about against the West were not only on the military level, but on the diplomatic front as well. When America stated one year into the Syrian crisis that Assad had "lost his legitimacy", it simply revealed in public what it refused to recognize openly before, i.e. that Assad had never had any legitimacy for power, exactly as the other dictators. His father, who took over the rule by a *coup* and then bequeathed it to his son, had never been elected by anyone either. Bashar Assad's role in power has been sustained by Iran and by Hizbullah, externally, and the army domestically, themselves outlaws who have never got legitimacy from anyone to rule or to sustain dictators. Obama's administration had stated its policy of engagement which failed dismally. Before him, the Bush administration had successfully isolated Syria, cut off relations with it, put it under political siege, forced it to evacuate its forces from Lebanon, all this to punish it for the *al-Qa'ida* forces who had been allowed to infiltrate Iraq and cause damage to the American forces there. Came Obama with his new policy; he went to Riyad to prostrate before the King of that primitive and obscurantist country, a notoriously corrupt and human right denier, and then proceeded to Cairo where he made an incredibly hypocritical and sycophantic speech to the Muslim world, which produced no positive result, apart from the Spring of 2011 which Obama did not want in the first place. Then he enlisted Turkey to also sponsor

Syria back into the fold, by granting it back its place among nations and by re-establishing diplomatic relations with it. Assad and others came to believe that America needed them more than they needed her, and felt free to act at will on their domestic front. Within one year, Mubarak was urged by Obama to go, since he no longer represented the Muslim world, nor the much solicited stability. Assad was again boycotted, his legitimacy had gone and as he engaged in more killings of his own citizens, suddenly America discovered that he had formidable allies in Moscow and Beijing, even more so in Tehran and in Beirut, and that his allies would not let him fall, exactly as America and Turkey had tried to boost him one year earlier. Who could take seriously that zigzagging policy? Least of all the countries of the Spring themselves, who looked at pathetic Obama one week supporting Mubarak, the next negotiating with his sworn enemies of the Muslim Brothers; one week America boycotting and besieging Assad, then giving him long leashes with Turkish enthusiastic support, then banning him again and acting for his fall. Do they know whom they would support instead? Of course not, and they call that "foreign policy", as if it were all measured, calculated and considered. They regularly publish the State Department report about human rights violations, where the most liberal and human-rights guardian in the region, Israel, is censured, but Saudi Arabia, the most grievous violator of those rights, is kept hidden behind the scenes. One wonders what is going on. In Bahrain, an uprising of the Shi'ite majority was quelled militarily, with several casualties, but no word of delegitimation, censure, condemnation or blame came out of the State Department. The US has a strong naval base in Qatar and multi-billion deals with weapons, there, despite Qatar's shady relations with the Muslim Brothers, is providing a shelter and a home to the Chief anti-Western and Radical Islam propagandist, Sheikh Yussuf Qaradawi, and serves as the base of the international *Jazeerah* Network, in various languages which propagates radical Islamic messages.

Many Western countries (except the US and Britain's effort in Iraq) elected their narrow and immediate national interests over the fight of the eradication of Islamic terrorism worldwide, and instead of instilling into their citizenry the need to stand up to the new terrorist barbarians, preferring to behave like "soft" states who had lost the will to fight for their values and future. It is worth to recall that that in past millennia the rich, powerful, self-assured empires of Rome, Persia, Byzantium and China had much to lose yet were unwilling to fight anymore. These empires subsequently their battles to Vandals, Arabs, Turks, Mongols (and then Manchus), respectively, because the latter had nothing to lose, looked with contempt upon life, but coveted the wealth of their neighbors and concluded that it behoove them to seize it, rather than let it languish in the hands of those declining empires which they ultimately conquered, destroyed and replaced.People could learn, if not from others' experience, then at the very least from their own, from the antecedents that have tormented their own culture when not heeded by their peers, forebears and cultural equivalents. As we shall see, disturbing warning signs developing in Western countries were unnoticed or denied, while countries like Canada and Australia, and some countries of Asia, fell into a syndrome of denial until they were shaken up by events and forced to listen, often at a price. At the core of the Muslim presence in Europe are countries like Britain, France and Germany, which were lacking in law enforcement against Muslim radicals, since their executive and judiciary systems systematically preferred human rights, and apparent safety and security by appeasement, over defensive measures to protect their citizens and their way of life. Muslim immigrants, many of whom were accustomed to the often oppressive, and more so to their abusive imposition in their countries of origin, were flooded by millions who flocked, almost unchecked, to the heart of Europe and the rest of Western countries. Moreover, clear threats of Jihad were heard in London, Paris and Berlin, but the placid Europeans and Americans elected to ignore them, taking them as hollow rhetoric by frustrated immigrants who could not adapt to their countries of asylum. Few Westerners asked themselves why was it that Muslim immigration targeted the West and not the other way around. Even fewer lent an ear to the open urging by radical Sheikh Qaradawi to "conquer Europe by pacific ways", to compensate for the aborted previous attempts of the 7th Century from the southwest, when it conquered the Iberia Peninsula and was arrested in southern France; and then then the attack from the southeast into the Balkans by the Ottoman Empire. Both attempts were at first successful and lasted several centuries, but ultimately, Islam was refuted back into the Middle East. These days, the declining West was signaling to the world that it could no longer defend its turf and culture, which have been gradually diluted by the Muslim invasion, so the radical Muslims thought that their time has come to attempt for the third and decisive time.

The writing was on the wall, but British home secretary Jack Straw, for example, failed to read and hear it. His liberal policy, backed by PM Blair, for which he was to repent much later, was easier and more convenient to embrace, rather than to heed the menace of terror. In so doing, he acted irresponsibly, and that is the only yardstick to judge a government: not by its liberal intentions, good-hearted policies or idealistic values, but by its failure to defend its citizens, by allowing terrorists to abuse Britain's hospitality, allowing them to wreak havoc on its citizenry, and by its myopic understanding of the growing Muslim threat, permitted through his ideological blinders. It is a fact that too little and too late the same British government has had to reverse its policies and to seek even harsher measures than public opinion and Parliament would allow, which is an indication of its inability to foresee what was coming and prepare the citizens before terror struck.[60]. The US was no different in the outset, for in spite of the documentary evidence gathered on

[60] Tony Blair, for example, who had been the champion of multiculturalism and a supporter of Muslim immigration, reversed himself in his last speech in Parliament at the end of his decade's rule before he resigned and spoke of the need of a prevalent British culture into which the immigrants should be integrated.

film by eminent, diligent and visionary researcher Steven Emerson in the 1990s, under the threatening heading *Jihad in America,* the US approach to potential terrorists was very human and liberal: Muslim associations were allowed to raise money under the cover of "charitable institutions", and even to conduct military training with live ammunition in New Jersey, partly under the doctrinal supervision of the blind radical Sheikh Abdul Rahman, himself an fugitive expatriate from Egypt. But all this was ongoing, the FBI remained indolent, failing to take responsibility for domestic security, until that seemingly innocent Sheikh masterminded the first attempt on the Twin Towers in New York in 1993, and was caught and incarcerated, which, of course, did not prevent the second and fatal disaster of September 11 in 2001. Both models of Western democracy, the US and Britain, needed that traumatic jolt before they moved to act, and those were, respectively, the September 11 (2011) and the July 7 (2005) bombings. And in other Western countries: in March (2004) Madrid train bombings,, in France the violent riots of in 2005, in Amsterdam the van Gogh murder, in Asia, the Bali horror, and in Scandinavia the Cartoon Affair (2006). In all those instances the jolt was brutal for it would shatter the naivete of European populations who had believed in peaceful; co-existence with the Muslim immigrant population and in the feasibility of their integration into the European cultural and societal tissue. Previously, it was only exclusively Israel who had continuously suffered from Muslim terrorism, but it was condescendingly castigated by the Europeans that "if only she satisfied the Palestinian demands" all her suffering would cease, until they all of them got a taste of Muslim radicals, who the more they were welcome into their Western shelters, they more arrogant, aggressive and brutal they became. Take, for example, the case of Abu Hamza al-Masri, who took refuse in Britain in 1994. He never hid his destructive and subversive intentions, but was never heeded until he was convicted in early 2006 (several month after the London bombings) for the same crimes that he had committed with impunity throughout the previous decade. That means that what had changed was not the man or his deeds, but the permissive attitudes of Jack Straw and his peers, which was reversed by the London horror.. Abu Hamza' of Egyptian origin, arrived in London and became the Imam if the Finsbury Park Mosque. He headed the *Ansar al-Shari'a* (Supporters of the Shari'a), a movement that would have ssurely been outlawed in his native Cairo and wherein he promulgated the cause of the violent Algerian Armed Islamic Groups (GIA). Both his land of origin in Egypt and Yemen demanded his extradition, but liberal Britain would not response, in the name of the human rights that the man was trampling under his feet. He had emerged from a background of moral corruption, something that is sure to have made him more radical than others, as if he wished to catch up on his "lost years" of crime and depravity.[61]. Thereafter, he moved to Afghanistan as part of those Itinerant Jihadis [62] who wandered from one killing field to another in the pursuit to world Jihad. He stayed there with is family prior of the takeover of Taliban regime in the 1990s, when Islamikaze[63] camps were operating under local warlords to train Jihadi fighters[64]. He fought against withdrawing Soviet forces and was severely injured by a landmine which severed both his hands and destroyed one of his eyes. In 1994, Abu Hamza, a civil engineer by training, found refuge in London at a time when the entire West was off guard with respect to the international Islamic networks that were being erected in its midst, and there he founded his Ansar organization. Reminiscing about that period, he later complained that while he had never lived off his hosts' money,

[61] For Abu Hamza background, see *al-Ayyam*, (Yemen), August 8, 1999; and the *Christian Science Monitor (*Boston), September 27, 2001. Both cited by MEMRI, No 72, October 16, 2001.

[62] See R. Israeli, *Itinerant Jihadis,* op. cit.

[63] For this term, a combination of Islam and Kamikaze, see R. Israeli, Islamikaze: ``Manifestationos of Islamic Martyrology, op. cit.

[64] For the descriptions of these camps, see R. Israeli "Islamikaze and their Significance", *Terrorism and Political Violence, 9:3, 1997,* pp. 96-121.

those "British Infidels" had levied heavy taxes on his work when they employed him as an engineer, and therefore that justified in his eyes his latter attacks against the West, which had "plundered the lands of Islam. He never explained why he chose to live in the land of his "robbers", unless we take his words at face value: " I am a cripple and I use this country to spread good, to counter the British authorities who used to spread corruption". In spite of his continuous and repetitive complaints that he was constantly persecuted and harassed by the authorities, his Muslim activities, which clearly show his intention and will to take over Britain by Islam, he was released briefly after he was arrested in 1999, until finally he finally arrested and convicted after 2005. On his Internet site he claimed Yemen was the second best launching pad for Jihad after Afghanistan, to allow for the world Islamic revolution to prevail[65]. And it was from Yemen that he directed his attention in 1998 after having left his London mosque to take care of the " Aden Abyan Muslim Army". He apparently masterminded an abortive attempt against the life of Yemeni President and the kidnapping of foreign tourists. In a press conference that he conducted in London after his return in January 2000, he called for the overthrow of the Yemeni regime and urged foreign visitors to leave Yemini soil. In a letter to the London-based Arabic daily *al-Hayat*, he warned the Ambassadors of Britain of Britain and the US that they should depart from Yemen, lest a painful "strike against the enemies of Islam" might hit them. He also attacked Arab monarchs and depicted the deceased King Hussein of Jordan as "roasting in Hell", probably for his pro-Western attitudes.[66]

Abu Hamza also evinced an aggressive concern for Muslim communities under pressure or threat in foreign lands. In 1999, he convened a conference on Chechnian Muslims where he incited a group of Russian reporters who were on hand to cover the debates.

---

[65] www.al-bab.com/yemen/hamza/hamza.htm

[66] Ibid.

On the same occasion he voiced support for the Chechnian attacks on Moscow in the summer of that year.[67] All this took place under the open eyes of the British Government, who saw not and cared not, foolishly believing that words did not hurt and deeds would not follow that incitement, contrary to all known precedents of hate-literature, anti-Semitism and terrorism, where defining and dehumanizing the enemy is a precursor to de-legitimizing and ultimately using violence against him. Somehow, Jack Straw and his followers, under the concurring passivity of Tony Blair, assumed that Britain was immune to that rule. Abu Hamza's choice as the ideal launchpad to the world Islamic Revolution emanated from the fact that it was the only country in the Arabian Peninsula that "had not yet surrendered to the United Snakes [sic] of America", and he was certain that after the takeover of that country by the radical Muslims, the other countries would fall like a domino. (one must admit that the prolonged battle of the Arab Gulf states against the pro-Iranian Houtis, has been a partial fulfillment of that prediction). He denied in one of his interviews that he had called on his followers to kill foreigners in the Yemen, specifying that he means Infidels, unless they converted to Islam, paid the poll tax *(jizya)*that the *dhimmis* were obligated to pay under shari'a law; otherwise, he asserted "their blood and wealth are not protected". He admitted that he had also operated from Algeria and Egypt, but because reform there was impossible from within due to the corrupt regimes in place, he came to the conclusion that only a Muslim invasion from the outside would trigger the Islamic Revolution and the warranted change, and that the invasion he envisaged as stemming from the Yemen would fan out worldwide. [68]Abu Hamza's work consisted not only of promoting Muslim terrorism, recruiting volunteers for training in Pakistan or to fight in

---

[67] *Online Journalism Review,* November 15, 1999.

[68] *Al-Ayyam* (Yemen), August 11, 1999.

Afghanistan, indoctrinating others and raising funds for Muslim organizations, but he also launched a campaign to recruit, convert and train British Muslims, whom he was certain (and he proved right) that British suicidal liberalism would swallow and ignore. For that purpose he held "Islamic camps", usually in the grounds of his mosque, offering " military training for brothers, self-development skills, martial-arts, map reading etc", aimed as he said to "distracting the 30 men in attendance from television and the obscenities of Xmas" (he would have put the various "Smart phones" at the top of the list had he survived into the 21st Century). Incidentally, the website that carried this announcement was decorated with a picture of a hand grenade[69]. Some of those trainees found their way to Afghanistan and were killed there, but this did not come to the media attention until after the horrors of September 11 (2001)[70]. During the Second Conference of the Islamic Movements held in London in February, 1999 (thereafter it moved, very appropriately to Tehran),, Abu Hamza told the gathering of 500 Muslims of a plan to "blow up civil and military aircraft, so as to challenge Western monopoly on the skies". He even gave details, as if he were mad privy by al-Qa'ida on preparations to Sep 11, of "new flying mines connected to balloons, currently being tested in Afghanistan" and hinted that sometime in the future such an operation would be carried out against Britain or the US [71]. But the British apparently thought that he was hallucinating until they were awakened on Sep 11, to find out who was fast asleep and forgot about his national security alert. There are even indications that Abu Hamza knew of the September 11 plan, that he was involved in masterminding a scheme to kill President George Bush during the G-8 meeting in Genoa, two days before the attack in New York and Washington so that an America

[69] *Christian Science Monitor*, 13 January, 1999.
[70] *Daily Telegraph*, October 5, 2001.
[71] *French News Agency* (AFP) 23 February, 1999.

in disarray for the death of its President would be less able to respond and retaliate for September 11; and that he held a meeting in his mosque in London on June 10, 2001 where the idea of the attacks using aircraft was raised.[72]

The most relevant aspect of Abu Hamza from the Western viewpont was his encouragement of violence, which he cultivated and elevated into an ideology in its own right. His advocated use of violence had a two-pronged purpose: to topple existing regimes in the Arab and Islamic world on order to replace them with radical Islamic regimes, namely militant extremist Islamic government which apply shari'a law, unlike the "godless" Islamic regimes whom Abu Hamza accused of "having sold out to the West, and to boost the diffusion of Islam in the world. At a gathering in early 1999 commemorating the removal of the last Ottoman Caliph by Kemal Ataturk, the father of modern Turkey, he openly urged Muslims to resort to the sword in order to achieve his blueprint for domestic and international upheaval. One of his supporters, Muhammad Yussuf, seconded his mentor's ideas by urging his followers to fight back against the West in the Balkans and the Middle East, but also to establish a strong "fifth column" within the Western world[73], something that would have explained his own self-imposed exile in London and his cultivation of violent Islam there. But at that time, Jack Straw was still in deep slumber, and he again neither saw nor heard. IN 2001, Abu Hamza became involved in a press debate geared "to clear" his name from the "abominable accusation" that had relinquished the use of violence, something that would have been antithetical to the nature of his struggle. Indeed, according to the London-based *al Quds al-'Arabi,* Abu Hamza had been "accused by Abd al Hakim Dyab, another Egyptian fundamentalist expatriate who had also sought asylum in London, of having dismissed a

[72] http//dsc.discovey.com/news/briefs/20010910/abroad/html

[73] *Middle East Times, issue 13, 1999, MEMRI no 72,* October 16, 2001.

*fatwa* of the Palestinian cleric Abu Qatada, that Muslims should kill wives and children of Egyptian police and army officers as part of the struggle Arab regimes[74]. Expectedly, Abu Hamza denied this allegation and defied the accuser. But the accusation was too much of an affront for Abu Hamza to bear. In his rebuttal in the same paper, he said that he did not recognize the term "violence", because that very word had become a tool in the hands of the world media to designate anyone who defend his faith and honor against existing Arab regimes which "rule through legislative and oppressive measures". For him, therefore, the term violence seemed deceptive and incompatible with Islamic Shari'a and the struggle for the survival of Islam. He asserted that mujahideen had never recognized that term because it was the ruling regimes who utilized it to sustain their own monopoly of their own recourse to terrorism, while conversely using it to eliminate the Muslim religious precept of " doing good and avoiding evil".(this precept, as interpreted by the terrorists themselves, means that they do the good while their enemies and rivals and anyone who opposes them does inherently the evil). This thinking also helps explain why for the Muslim radicals, the Western definition of terrorism is inacceptable inasmuch as it addresses itself to the means of combat or struggle, namely acting against allegedly "innocent" civilians to attain a political goal, instead of addressing the essence of the issue, that is the "Islamic good" against the "Western or anti-Islamic evil. It is instructive to heed al-Hamza's words in their full context:

As a rule, Islam teaches that those holding opinions different from one's own, should be treated gently and flexibly, provided that they are ready to listen [to the Islamic counter-arguments] and comply, and provided that one's tolerant efforts do not lead to blurring rights and borders… Treating gently anyone who blocks his ears and forces perversion, heresy, abomination and humiliation

[74] *Al Quds al-Arabi* (London), 21 July, 2001.

upon Muslims in their countries through the use of force, is a kind of idiocy and loss of rights and religious precepts... What can be said about Arab regimes which have enacted abominable laws, implemented them, and then used tax money to finance military personnel for the protection of such abominations, instead of protecting Jerusalem and its people? That is the mark of Cain, which is unprecedented in the history of Egypt[75].

According to such analysis, the Islam that Abu-Hamza wished to impose was tolerant only as long as the challenger to its rules ultimately accepts it and complies with it. For Islam alone can distinguish between right and wrong,, holy and profane., acceptable and abominable; and anyone opposing it is no longer to be subject to the "gentle treatment and flexibility" suggested in his definition of tolerance. Getting to the point of resorting to violence of having abandoned, that he had been "outrageously accused". He wrote:

> My position is as clear as the sun, praised be Allah, and it will not change... I do not recognize the term "violence" and will not agree to abandon Jihad or to sign a truce with the regimes of the tyrants. As Allah said:" Fight them so there will be no internal strife *(fitna)*,and so that their religion be exclusively Allah's religion". The Muslim nation to which I belong cannot come to terms with anyone who does not have mercy on and respect on the people... Physical exile, far from my homeland is much easier for me and for many like me than the exile of our souls, the slaughter of our faith and of our values, and the amputation of our tongues as the price for returning to our homeland... [76]

---

[75] Ibid.

[76] Ibid.

Apart from providing another justification for his forced exile, in which he seemed to thrive, Abu Hamza liked to be in the limelight of the media in which he became accustomed, as his "charisma of cripple" which predominated and brought out his many personal accomplishments emboldened him to make audacious statements to the world press that "within ten years the Islamic flag would flutter over the Elysees Palace in Paris and Downing St 10 in London", as the proof of the Islamic takeover. Moreover, in defense of Islamic violence against the West, he now denied that Bin Laden was its author, though he had had boasted before that he had been privy to the preparations for it. He said to the *Christian Science Monitor*[77]:

> It was when the Americans took the knife out of the Russians [in Afghanistan] and stubbed us in the back.... In the meantime, they were bombing Iraq and occupying the Arab Peninsula [he was referring to American bases in Saudi Arabia and Qatar], and then with their witch-hunt, everything became clear: it was an all-out wat against mujahideen... The Americans wanted to fight the Russians with Muslim blood and they could justify that only by invoking the word Jihad. Unfortunately for everyone, except Muslims, when the button of Jihad is pushed, it is not eradicated so easily. It continues and continues until the Muslim Empire swallows every other existing empire... I do not condone what happened [on September 11] nor do I condemn it. If someone has done that just for mundane gain and political advancement, then obviously it is a cheap cause. But if it was done because people are desperate and their lives have been threatened, then it is a respectable cause...Then,

[77] *Christian Science Monitor, and The Radical, both* cited by MEMRI, No 72, 16 October, 2001.

> those people who have carried out the attacks would be martyrs. Martyrdom is the highest form of Jihad, and if you do things for the cause of Allah, losing life for it is the most sublime expression of faith. This is in the Qur'an. America thinks that life come first, but Muslims believe that the Believers come first. When you damage people and they have no home and no hope, and their babies and children are killed, then they retaliate. America took decisions to give weapons to certain people and deprive others from them.. What happened would be self-defense ... I have sympathy for the victims, but also for Bin Laden who is a victim of an American witch-hunt, but who is unable to commit an act like this though he probably has millions of sympathizers [who could have done it.]

Abu Hamza's was not the only writing on the British wall and on any number of other walls throughout the Western world. But the authorities were blind, or simple wished to avoid trouble by pretending, as most liberal democratic governments do, to pretend it is not there. They regarded these ominous warnings as mere rhetoric that in fact amounted to an early "prophecy", made by many other Muslim radicals about what was to come, as in the case of Sheikh Umar al-Bakri, of Syrian origin, who also operated as an asylum seeker on British soil, and propagated the same messages with equally vicious vitriol[78]. Extraordinarily enough, most of these rebellious and revolutionary radical Muslims, whose hold the world over seems to solidify are mostly Muslim clerics of one sort or another, who continue to inspire authority in the heart of their followers in line with the traditional authoritarianism that is inherent

[78] See R. Israeli, *Muslim Minorities in the Modern States,* Transaction, NJ, 2003, especially the Introduction.

in Muslim societies. We have seen several elements of authoritarian rule in Islamic tradition, which have all found expression during the turbulence in the Islamic world. For example, the tradition of the *Sheikh,* which generated the Caliphate and the dictatorships which are still extant in our days; and by contrast, the other tendencies which somewhat palliate that harsh aspect, like the *Ijma'* (consensus in religious practice), the *shura* (principle of the Council with notables participating), the lack of hierarchy in the clerical system, the mythical equality between all Muslims on the floor of the mosque, from the King to the last worshipper. We are suggesting here a contradiction, as it were, between principles that look proto-democratic, down to earth and popular, and harsh autocratic principles of government. There is a tradition in Islam that the Prophet and the first Caliphs were simple, accessible and were wary from elevating themselves over the masses, versus the later kings, emperors and sultans, who hid in their palaces and could hardly be seen by the public. Partly that stemmed from the size of the growing Empire and its bureaucracy, where it had to grow impersonal for the state to fill its pressing needs. But partly it was also due to the changing interpretations of things. For example, coffee was considered in the beginning of Islam as a drug or equivalent to alcohol or narcotics, and there were people who were arrested for using it. But popular custom was stronger, and at last coffee was not only permitted but became an essential tool of socialization. But one has also to pay attention to the fact that while *Ijma'* did gather momentum as a social and religious consensus, it was no longer possible to implement it in practice when the *umma* grew beyond the city *-polis* of Medina, to extend over large parts of the medieval world, and then over the entire universe. It was then necessary to confine the validity of the consensus to the scholars of each community only, since it was impossible that a consensus between all world Muslims be attained, especially under the transport and communications conditions of the time. But that too was too vast for a practical consensus, and in time it became imperative to consult only the main scholars of each generation, and even that became increasingly impractical. Of course, there was there neither democracy nor anything resembling it in that vast and varied Islamic world. But this was the closest one could come to some kind of representative body. Moreover, unlike the *Shura* and other councils of appointed notables, the consensus of scholars was, and still is meritocratic in essence, because it is self-selected, just like the Ayatullahs in the Shi'ite system, and elitist, due to the participation of a select few. There is another limitation here, which is that supposing a consensus requires at least a majority, if not the totality of the main scholars, namely that the minority does not even have the right to express its minority view, let alone implement it under the inundating sweep of the majority. In other words, to seek democracy in this society is equivalent to sending a blind person to a dark room to look for a black cat which is not there.

In the West, legitimacy is achieved by freely electing a parliament and a government at the end of each term specified by law, and when power is smoothly transferred from the incumbent to the elect. In the Islamic world there is no democracy of the western type, though in Saudi Arabia one could hear arguments in favor of the *Shura,* which is appointed by the monarch, as the "mother of all democracies". So, in what way would those who seize power justify or rationalize it? Except for the Prophet himself who ruled by the grace of Allah, who had dispatched him as His Messenger, all his successors had to prove their legitimacy one way or another. One way to gain legitimacy today, is to follow the spirit of our time and hold "elections", whose results are pre-programmed and whose unfolding is choreographed in such a style as not to expose the rigging. In the communist world, there were also elections but with candidates from a single party, namely the ruling party, and they were "elected" without opposition, a pattern that has been generously and uncritically copied by most Islamic countries if and when elections were held at all. In Iran, there is a Supreme Screening Commission which decides whom to permit to run for elections and whom to ban. In that system, there is a permanent Supreme Spiritual Leader, who does not run or stand for election, just like a privileged monarch. He supervises from above and nothing can be done without his agreement. The entire bureaucracy, from the President down, is supposed to be "guided" by him, due to his aura of "sanctity", deservedly inaugurated by Khumeini but allowed to continue even though no one was found so far to fill that position convincingly.

In monarchic systems, kings and princes are not elected, and when they don their crowns they act as authoritarian, and sometimes as absolute as the other sorts of dictators. They preserve their clan's laws of succession, going first through the collateral members of the family, brother by brother, and only when they are all exhausted, usually in their 80s, does that generation skip one or two generations forward to start a new count of kings, heirs and princes, the others becoming ministers, governors, military commanders, Court councilors, ambassadors and senior officials. In that system, proximity to the King and loyalty to him, rather than skill or proficiency for the job are the main criteria for senior appointments. In other systems, like Qaddafi's, Saddam's, Assad's, there was even no pretense of election or legitimacy, they simply took over and ruled, with the help of a military clique which supported them, in return for benefits that accrued to them after the success of the *coup*. After they take over power, they organize "elections", to signal to the world that the Arab Middle East is no different from the American Middle West, and very often misinformed and naïve western correspondents report about those "elections" with enthusiasm and statistics as if the data were credible, ironclad and authoritative. This grotesque farce continued for years and decades and the West kept its silence, pretending it did not know and did not hear.

The Islamic regimes also pretended that all was well, since very rarely did any western country protest against any disorder in the "elections" or in the transition from fake elections to rigged power. Quite the contrary, every President who was thus "elected" was inundated from western capitals by a cascade of greetings upon his "election". Even before the coming of the Arab Spring in the 2010s, the autocrats in place started feeling the push from the bottom, through Internet and social networks, to open up and democratize, something which compelled them to devise new rationalizations to their illegitimate rule, because they realized that their previous pseudo-democratic measures had encountered only contempt and anger in the street. So, they at first reverted to their old, irrelevant and rusty pretexts. The President of Egypt boasted the "strongest military force in the area" which would stand fast in defense of all Arabs; the Syrians were proud of their resolute Arab nationalism and their unconditional support for the Palestinians; the King of Morocco invoked his descent from the Prophet, and so did the King of Jordan who also added to his arrows the title of "the Curator of Al-Aqsa" which he obtained from his peace deal with Israel; and Saudi Arabia, as the curator of the Two Mosques, of Mecca and Medina, the holiest in Islam. They thought that if they all were so wonderful, idealistic and caring only for their countries and peoples, who would want to replace them? But in fact, they were all illegitimate, because no one chose them; they took power either by royal inheritance, or through succession of revolutionary leaders (Nasser, Sadat, Mubarak), and if not for the Spring which discontinued that apostolic chain, successions would have gone on to the sons or to the underlings of the leaders in place *ad infinitum.*

In World War II, G. Ferrero wrote his book *On Democracy*, which since became a classic, where he coined the idea of "fraudulent democracy" to describe the fascist regimes in Europe (Hitler, Mussolini, Franco, and some of their short-lived supporters in the Arab world like Rashid Ali in Iraq, the Brothers in Egypt and Haj

Amin in Palestine), part of whom had experienced something of the democratic system, but ended up borrowing its rules in order to distort its substance. For example, "elections" were held technically, but only to leave the arena open to the autocrat, and to him alone. In the Arab and Islamic world, which had almost never experienced democracy (even in Turkey, the classic border-case, the elected governments were removed by the army on several occasions), one can suspect that not a fraud was there, but an act of ignorance of the essence of democracy. Indeed, how could they know what it meant if they had never experienced it? If the UN wants to extend assistance to a new country to organize elections, it should not dispatch as its messengers the delegates of Syria, Sudan or Iran, but those of Sweden, Britain and Luxemburg, who know and have experienced something of it. In any case, "democracy" has become even prior to the Spring, a mantra repeated by every leader as if it were part of his platform, his belief or his understanding. In fact, it was meaningless, not only because those autocrats did not mean it, but also because they did not comprehend it. Mubarak's party was called "National Democratic", which like the popular democracies in Eastern Europe, namely Bulgaria, Romania, Poland, Czechoslovakia etc. purposely added to their names the appellation "democratic", knowing full well that they were not. Britain, France or Sweden, never needed to underline that they were democracies, because everyone knew it. China, similarly, boasts its "popular" attribute, intending to distance its image from the autocracy that it is in fact. The bottom line is that where there is a democracy, autocrats cannot rise, and vice-versa: where there is an autocrat there can be no democracy. When Ariel Sharon headed the Israeli government in the 2000s, President Mubarak was interviewed by the international press and he stressed, that unlike "Sharon the dictator", he himself was a "real democrat", voted in by a 90% of the Parliament. It was clear that Mubarak never understood how democracy worked, nor the very stringent rules and controls over Israeli elections, so that there should be no doubt or question over their results. What he said indicated more his ignorance than any flaw with the free and democratic elections in Israel, that are supervised by an impeccable Supreme Court Judge. Or take Bashar Assad. He inherited his father in 2000, following a speedy process of amending the Constitution (as if it mattered) to make the young age of the successor (34) eligible for the presidency. But the members of Parliament and the public at large who were interviewed after the amendment, all pointed to the "democratic process" which regulated the succession. No one dared to raise the issue of an inexperienced son inheriting the mantle of his murderous father, proving once again a case of a very simple-minded self-delusion rather than a sophisticated fraud or an effective system of succession of the rule.

We have already mentioned the fleeting constitutions, introduced by every new tyrant as a way to lay his future plans before his constituency, which he did not consult when he seized power. He and everyone else knew that he would not be restrained by those rules and that he would pursue his autocracy with or without constitution. But lacking any other legitimacy for power, he feels that his proclaimed goal serves as some kind of justifier, and he would throughout his tenure hold on to it and show it as his achievement even if there is no real substance to it. That "constitution" was aimed at replacing the previous one which had been written and promised by the previous ruler, full of rosy wordings and sublime pledges, which when the day comes and the autocrat is removed, would be replaced by another paper of that sort and of similar value. A plurality of constitutions, one succeeding the other, means that there is no one binding constitution. Only now, in view of the changing realities under the Spring, where public commissions were established to assemble, discuss and formulate new constitutions, is there any new public awareness of the vanity of previous ones, and is there a chance that the new versions would be more open and liberal and reflective of the public mood and not necessarily of the ruler's whims. Two more obstacles stand in the way of removing tyrants: to return the armies to their barracks as has been done by Erdogan in Turkey and Mursi in Egypt; and searching for some working compromises between the fundamentalist Muslim governments, who are getting the majority but are almost totally shorn or any governing experience, and those parts of the civil population which fear them, lest the entire infrastructure erected by the tyrants in the past decades come to total paralysis. In the West an asymmetry is created between the outrageously and audaciously vicious deprecation of non-Muslims in Qur'anic writings in the extremely irreverential attitude by Muslim radicals towards the West in general and its clerical representatives in particular; and the reverse, bordering with hypocrisy, of educated Westerners towards all religions, especially Islamic clerics (sheikhs, Imam and such), showing over-sensitivity not to hurt them and being accused of Islamophobia, hate of Muslims, racism and what have you. Muslims interpret that dissonance as "proof" of the superiority of Islam which no one dares touch and the other faiths which one can live without and can contain any insult blurted against them. The proof ae the cartoon, movies, documentaries and other forms of expression that are made against other faiths in the name of the freedom of expression, and the world upheaval the cartoon Affair of the Salman Rushdie *fatwa* have caused around the world

The Muslim Brothers, and for a while ISIS, like the Hamas and other such revolutionary movements, advocate the takeover of government in their countries and the enforcement of *Shari'a* there, as they did in Gaza. In Egypt, the Brothers tried to achieve the same goal by peaceful means, but they held to power merely one year (2012-3) before they were removed from the scene by a military coup. In neither case did those in power begin any practical process of forming a Caliphate. Salafis, like the Taliban, profess the creation of a Caliphate first, that would by definition be mighty and comprehensive enough to impose *Shari'ah* on all Muslims. The

Brothers in Egypt have embraced a cautious and gradual method of introducing the Holy Law to all citizenry, lest a sudden and all-encompassing Islamization in one stroke might deter and frighten hesitant and uncertain souls who had been, to their minds, corrupted by modernization, secularization and westernization. But there were also aggressive currents like the Taliban when they held the helm of power in Afghanistan in the 1990s, the Gama'at in Egypt before they were wiped out by Mubarak, or the Armed Groups in Algeria, who fought and killed their countrymen mercilessly in order to impose their way. Only now, in the post Spring era, after the failure of the Egyptian and Tunisian examples to impose and maintain power, and the trauma caused in much of the Islamic world by the horrors committed by ISIS, will any new attempt to Islamize societies have to rely on much more circumspect, gentle and slow piecemeal measures. Where there is no decision yet, like in Syria, Libya and the Yemen, it is early to know who will rise and who will fall, and for how long. One can imagine, however, that everywhere a settlement is agreed upon, the emerging ruler will have to explain where does his legitimacy come from. In Egypt and Tunisia we saw a genuine effort to conduct a fair election campaign, to keep restraint and to distance the military from the election process. These are signs of legitimization of government. But came the new wave of ISIS, and Jabhat al-Nusra in Iraq and Syria, and once again Islamization by force and terror is their agenda. Conversely, in places where the struggle is going on, there is no telling how it might be decided. But one thing is certain: the previous illegitimate rulers will not be back, i.e. there is a necessity and urgency to replace them by others who can inspire legitimacy. But who are they? What do they stand for? Who can guarantee their behavior as long as the democratic game is not digested well enough to become an organic part of the local politics?. And what is legitimacy after all? It can follow the Ferrero model of democracy, or the Caliphate precedent as the fundamentalists would have it. Democracy has never been tried to its full in the Islamic world, and we are hardly watching its first steps and holding our breath for them to succeed. It is true that most current Spring movements in the Islamic world have advocated slogans of democracy, but it is not clear at all that any of them knows what it is talking about, for none of them had ever experienced democracy western style. Democracy is not only elections, because beyond a given method of electing the leadership, it also means a state of mind that lets the media act freely, respects the majority but protects the minority, does not pursue investigative journalists who publicize the corruption of the system, like it is the case in Pakistan and Turkey today, respects human rights, gives top adjudicating power to an independent judiciary, does not arbitrarily arrest its citizens, accusing them of "plots against the government", refrains from incitement against its citizens and neighbors, advocates an open and liberal mode of government, and pursues a policy of good neighborliness with its neighbors. Where was there ever a paradise like this in the Islamic world? And where could such a regime materialize after so many years of oppression, corruption and travesty of justice? For a regime to be able to operate on such a standard, it has first to be legitimate. It is obvious that the Spring broke out precisely in countries where the young people have had enough of tyrannical rule for decades, with no chance of change, for the rule of the fathers was to be taken up by their sons. Namely, the hopelessness of change was what pushed the young people to rebel. The demonstrators shouted: " Freedom !! Democracy!! Expel the Tyrant !!". But we do not know what they meant, nor did they indicate what ought to be done in order to alter the situation. In most places we saw the same hypocrites and servile aides of the previous rulers, who had served them obediently for years, suddenly turn over to the rebels. So, people are suspicious and confused, not knowing whom to trust, convinced that whoever steals for you today, will steal from you tomorrow.

At the height of the crisis, the only alternative to the crumbling rulers has seemed to be the Islamic state that the Muslim Brothers had consistently preached since their inception. They are on record as opposing democracy, for being a human-made system that cannot compete with divinely inspired *Shari'ah*. Thus, the latter, despite its problems and anachronism, and the Caliphate after a millennium and a half of experiments which never lasted indefinitely, still looks to the Believers as the most trusted, known and promising avenue. In other words, that was the only system that could still lend legitimacy to the rulers, being based on Islamic tradition. For that reason, each time an existing system threatened to crumble, the Caliphate alternative loomed in the horizon as the only acceptable alternative. But when we begin comparing it with democracy, we immediately realize that not only are they incompatible, but they contradict each other in some very fundamental respects. Some believe that fundamentalist movements which negate democracy totally, would have stepped immediately into a *Shari'ah* Caliphate-like state, as did the Taliban during their short stint in power (1996-2001) in Afghanistan, and as the Islamic State is trying to do in Iraq and Syria. But the masses in the world of Islam have become so open to world media, to television, to the customs and standards of living in the West, to Internet and the social networks, and to the benefits of liberal democracy and human rights, that they cannot be easily deprived from all that after decades of exposure. They are no longer prepared to accept oppression as a divine calamity, therefore the idea of a Caliphate, which would be another kind of oppression from their point of view, would not be readily accepted without question.

Therefore, relatively pragmatic Islamic movements, like those in Tunisia, and those which ruled Egypt in 2012-3, were compelled to pretend to behave democratically, just the time to accustom the public to their style of rule, before they begin imposing restrictions and gradually trapping their public into the incontrovertibility of

*Shari'a* law, which no individual in an Islamic society can resist without incurring the wrath of his environment. This method has already been dubbed: "one man, one vote, one time", meaning that following the one voluntary vote which has lent legitimacy to their rule, such fundamentalists would need no more foreign legitimacy to rule, because they would be applying *Shari'ah*. For this reason, the early experiments we have witnessed in Egypt and Tunisia, as the test cases of the Islamic Spring, were decisive for the fate of the entire Spring. For if these tests had succeeded in operating a modern and efficient Muslim society, which enjoyed freedom, without the harassments that accompany puritanical Muslim societies, like restrictions on women, public morals police, but with fair elections to all levels of government and the like, then a newly reformed style of the moderate Muslim Brothers, which could have been more pragmatic and sensitive than what they have been preaching for almost a century since their foundation, could perhaps have produced a fresh, softer and feasible Islam, a sort of revolutionary reform, instead of the restorative reform that they have advocated since their beginnings.

Since all the ills, failures and drawbacks of Islamdom are imputed, if not to Israel and the Jews or to the West, then to the corruption of contemporary Islamic society, due both to internal shortcomings and external "Westoxication", it is imperative to revert to the times when Islam was at its height, Muslims were pious and Jihad-propelled, and the Caliphate was just, glorious and feared by Europe. On the domestic front, it is essential to revive aggressive Jihad, which has been neglected in recent generations, and re-install Shari'a Law, the Law of Allah, which alone guarantees the strength of Muslim society and is sure to produce devoted Jihad fighters who will return Islam to its past glory. It is also necessary to turn the present Muslim society, which has been infected with foreign ideas, back into Islam by enforcing Shari'a Law, as the Taliban had done in Afghanistan until crushed by America, and if it is impossible under the present tyrants to achieve that goal, then the radicals ought to follow the example of the Prophet, who had migrated (*Hijra)* from the pagan society (*Jahiliyya*) of his native Mecca to Medina in AD 622, in order to launch his Jihad for the conquest of Arabia and the world. So, if they cannot find a base for their struggle as Bin Laden had done in Sudan and then Afghanistan, then it is necessary to create a base (*Qa'ida*) by carving swaths of territory in Islamic land, as the ISIS and the Jihadi fighters are doing in Syria, where they can start to enforce the Law of Allah.

However, as these experiments did not succeed, and one is entitled to suspect whether the eternal values of Islam will prevail, with their conservative and fundamentalist leanings, as in the days of Ibn Taymiyya in Egypt and Syria or the Wahhabis in Arabia, or the days of Banna and Qut'b in Egypt, and the clerics once again regard themselves as the watchdogs of the integrity of their faith in the face of the Western cultural and civilizational onslaught, then major confrontations are to be expected between two styles of life, where not necessarily the stronger wins, but the more doggedly committed to his version of Islam in the world, as has already been evident in many arenas of the Spring today, especially in Syria and Iraq. The days of the Islamic Spring have shown that even in Islamic societies which had taken large strides towards civil government, like Turkey and Tunisia, it was still possible to arrest the process with the help of the backward societies of the conservative and illiterate countryside in both places, while the urban bourgeoisie was watching with horror, but helplessly, its great modernizing achievements rolled back toward their abrogation. What model of Islam will these countries choose when the dust settles, only time will tell.

# Chapter Six

## *Israel- Lone "Defensive Shield"*

Many historical and political circumstances have compelled Israel to become the first-line defense shield against the most militant and aggressive radical Muslims, precisely when moderate Muslims throughout the rest of the Arab and Islamic world are showing signs or reconciliation, repentance for past tensions and boycotts and a newfound will to reconstitute more open and beneficial with Israel. Somehow, due to Israel's privileged relations with America, and to the particular American efforts to promote a new architecture of peace between Israeli and the Arabs, many of the Muslim countries which are turning around and making up with Israel (Gulf states, Sudan, Chad, Morocco), are convinced that the new endeavor would also facilitate their way to Washington too. One may also put on the strategic scale Israel's assumed nuclear capacity, and its proven military capabilities, in the face of powerful Iran which many Arab countries regard as a historical threat to their security and an irremediable religious-Shi'ite rival in their vicinity, which strives for a world Revolution, to seek a possible defense and economically to compensate for America's retreat from her role of "protector" and partner which had guaranteed their security umbrella for decades before. So, while many Western countries have caved in to the Muslim radicals for all sorts of interests, little Israel has remained in many way the sole shield of the region from Iranian threats, because unlike

America which can withdraw its forces, Israel is in no situation to retreat anywhere, therefore will always be compelled to stand fast, reinforces its military capacities and destroy all threats directed against her survival. However, one must also take cognizance of the fact that until the Abrahamic process began, under President Trump initiative and encouragement, the Arab world, together with much of Muslim world, had formed a more of less united front of hatred and hostility towards Jews, Zionism and Israel. This means that the new structure is still fragile and still under test. In that regard, there was no great difference between radical and moderate Muslims, their being separated mainly by the urgency of dealing with the "enemies of the Arab and Islamic world". While those characteristics which were common to many Muslims, have been gradually narrowed down to the radicals among them, they certainly also share many other cultural traits with the rest of their coreligionists in the Muslim world, as far as modes of thinking, customs, world views, relations with others and more, which dominate their attitudes and conduct as well, side by side with their specifically radical modes of behavior. This explains their dazzling attraction to Muslim youth worldwide, who continue to flock into Islamic battle areas from the entire Islamic world, undeterred by the extremely negative and contemptuous reputation they have acquired in the West and among many Muslim governments, and often in defiance of their pro-western authorities, much like during the Afghani War of the 1980s. Moreover, since in the past four decades the presence of Muslim migrants in the West has grown by leaps and bounds, much of the convergence of Muslim youth to Iraq and Syria in the 2010s originates from Europe, the US, Canada and Australia, the very countries that have coalesced with the US in their battle against ISIS. This phenomenon, which keeps growing to alarming proportions, signals the persistence of these Islamic traits even among Muslims who had migrated to the West, and were thought to have mellowed by their adaptive cultural environment. To try to comprehend the attraction of Muslim youth in the West, who are usually closer to Western culture and grown in bourgeois societies of plenty and comfort, to the desert and pristine living of the Muslim revolutionary groups, and to the battlefields of the Islamic State, or to the Syrian civil war, or to the inner unrest of Somalia, Yemen, Libya or Kashmir, one has to bear in mind the underlining common grounds of all these Muslims which the roving volunteers find much more attractive than the alienation they felt either in their own Muslim societies of origin, or amidst the western host cultures where they found refuge. Hence their sense of familiarity and instant identification and adaptation even with the most abhorrent deeds of the radical warring society where they have chosen to implant themselves. Before we enumerate some of those basics which have become part of Muslim civilization almost everywhere, some introductory generalizations will be not be amiss:

1. That the home-grown Muslim youth in the West, was not only not overtaken by Western culture, and not domesticated to western thinking, but often kept fanatically loyal to its Islamic heritage. This phenomenon had already began in the 2000s, after the September 11 events, followed by the London and Madrid bombings by local homegrown Muslims.

2. That the bulk of Muslim volunteers who flock to the radical Muslim battlefields in the Middle East usually originate from the same "moderate" and "pro-western" Muslim countries like: Saudi Arabia, Jordan, Morocco, Libya, Egypt, Yemen, Chechniya, Bosnia, Pakistan and the like. This shows that not only do those countries pursue a pro-western policy contrary to their peoples' sentiment, but that the volunteers who fight in the ranks of al-Qa'ida, ISIS and Jabhat al-Nusra, head to the front knowing that they would have not only to aid their radical groups but also combat the West and its allies, including

their countries of origin or their adoptive host countries in the West.

3. That this is a long term battle for the souls and minds of the next generations of Muslims who have enough of their corrupt regimes which submit to the US, and are also so blinded by the glamour of the revolution brought by ISIS and other radicals, that they disregard the murderous reputation of these movements as long as they can attain their revolutionary dreams.

4. The struggle against ISIS and al-Nusra, like the long term challenge posed by the various branches of al-Qa'ida, exemplifies the waning away of state structures in the Islamic world and their takeover by transnational, trans-territorial and amorphous movements, which though they may declare universal statehood like the Caliphate as their goal, operate as states in the making which envisage no boundaries and no cultural frontiers.

5. The Muslim civilizational imprint is so deeply incrusted in the souls of young Muslims, that no Western style re-education in their host countries, nor the pro-western political orientation of their original governments can palliate their views of Islam nor their feelings and attitudes towards the outside world. In short, the mass mobilization of Muslim youth in the West to the ISIS project, means that you can take Muslims out of the Muslim universe, but you cannot take the Muslim universe out of them.

**Visceral Hatred of the Jews and the West built into the Culture**

Jews and the West are not popular in the Islamic world, even though some Islamic governments like the Saudis and the Arab Gulf

Emirates, may regard the US as their ultimate protector and guarantor. Jews and Israel are usually lumped together in anti-American and anti-Israeli demonstrations across the Muslim world and the western countries where large Muslim minorities have been established. Thus, Israel and the Jews are hated not only for their own sake, but also as the long arm of the West, which had arguably been implanted in their midst by the pro-Zionist West in order to undermine Islamdom from within. Often, as Muslim countries are unable to attack the US directly, they direct their hostility toward much weaker and fragile Israel, in what psychologists call "an aggression of impotence". At any rate, Muslims regard the US internationally and Israel locally in the Middle East as the only powers capable of scuttling their blueprint to overwhelm the West spiritually and culturally, and as they cannot counter for now western domination, they envy it and hate it in their guts. Perhaps since Nazi Germany no amount of vitriol was poured on the Jews as such, not only Israelis and Zionists, as has been the case in the past few years by Arabs and Muslims, beyond what emanates from Islamic sources. We have heard nauseating repetitions of anti-Semitic attacks in the high echelons of Arab politics, not only in intractable Iran and Syria and their underlings, but even in the Egyptian mainstream press, which shamelessly recounts its lies and fabrications as "history," and avidly "quotes" from the *Protocols of the Elders of Zion* that never were, and retells with a sadistic delight that can only match its joy at the carnage in the Twin Towers, the Blood Libels of which Jews have been accused. This, of course, reflects the vitriolic attitudes towards Israel and Zionism, because if the Jews are evil, then by nature their state and their movement of national liberation can only be equally evil. Not one voice is there to stand up to the calumniators and intercede for ceasing that orgy of hatred, even in Egypt and Jordan decades after their "peace" with Israel. All one has to do is to rummage through the hundreds of hate sites that are fed by Muslims and Arabs across the world, to realize the width and depth of anti-Semitic sentiment in the Muslim world, which has so poisoned Muslim minds in recent decades, that it is doubtful whether "peace" treaties are able to overcome it.

There has also never been any society since the Nazis which so cultivated and boasted of its hatred towards the Jews, as Muslim society does today. Its preachers denigrate and humiliate them, incite against them, justify massacres against them, and associate them with America and the evil West. Reasons for this contemporary outburst of hatred, which has been manifest also throughout the democratic West where Jewish and Muslim communities live side by side, emanate perhaps from the reality in which Jews represent the successful middle-class that has made the West prosperous. For the Muslims it is painful to admit that Jews succeeded where they have failed, and the jealousy in this regard cannot be contained or suppressed. The same envy of Israel's success, as a neighboring society and a state to the Arab and Muslim worlds, compared with their continued state of backwardness, feeds their intense hatred and generates stereotypes and pipedreams of destroying it. They compensate themselves by their prophecies about the "cowardly" Jews who in the end of days will run away and hide from the Muslims who will seek their destruction. There is no need, as some counsel, for Israel (and the West for that matter) to go into any soul-searching and to dig up the "reasons" (there must be reasons, right?) for this hatred, any more than there was one when the Jews were made the scapegoats of the Nazis, and were murdered for what they were, with the burden of the "guilt" accruing to them. If anything needs to be investigated, it is the sick minds of the anti-Semites, today and of old. Beyond the enumeration of some traits of character of the Muslims in general, which make them so prone to accuse others in general, it is essential to dwell on anti-Semitism and anti-Israeli attitudes, as the spokesmen of ISIS, al-Qa'ida and even mainstream Muslim media attest in their daily pronouncements.

Muslims and Arabs in general are indeed so fond of Hitler and of citing him, that they miss no opportunity to analyze "scientifically" the "reasons" for his victimization of the Jews, and they expectedly find the Jews themselves guilty of bringing upon themselves. In this context words like "reason" and "cause" have been depleted of their meanings, and one is dragged to the realm of the emotional, the incomprehensible and the irrational. But then, side by side with that, the Holocaust that the Jews were accused of having brought upon themselves, is vehemently, and again "scientifically," denied, and the Jews are relegated to the role of the Nazis themselves in their dealings with the Palestinians. Such a web of lies, presumptions, pretenses, denials and contradictions, was created by modern Arab and Muslim minds following their own Islamic anti-Jewish tradition and their generous borrowings from the classic bi-millennial European anti-Semitism. In any case, the delegitimation of the Jews, of Israel their state, and of Zionism—their movement of national liberation, is so thorough, total, and irreversible, as to turn them into the target of Islamikaze massacres, a fate which they deserve a-priori. By turning their hatred of Jews into a pathological phenomenon, as inseparable from their own being, they immunize themselves against any human compassion. Otherwise, it is hard to understand how crowds would jump from joy in Palestinian and Egyptian streets, at the sight of Jewish children blown to pieces, or entire families wiped out in one stroke of madness. They have turned so obtuse and cruel when Jewish victims are concerned, that it I necessary to remind them, from time to time, that they are evil to pursue civilians and murder them in streets, restaurants, and buses; and they must be excluded from the human race. Moreover, the beheadings of westerners and Jews which we have been seeing on the screens performed by ISIS or other Muslim radicals, should not surprise us because they emanate from the same sources of mainstream Islam. Muslim countries and governments pretend to be "horrified" by them only when their own regimes seem to be menaced by these rampages. Otherwise, they dub these massacres "Jihad", and murderers "martyrs", so much is their judgment blunted by hatred, to the point that they can no longer differentiate between good and evil, human or inhuman. True, radical Muslims profess the evil of indiscriminate killing, which is dictated by their blind hatred, even if they should themselves be consummated by its fire in the process. They have no use for facts (for example the Holocaust), nor respect to values (the mass-murders they commit without a hitch), nor concern for the victims. Because only they, the fighters of Jihad, who are awaited in Paradise, count, and anyone in their way should be eliminated. They turn their own plight onto the Jews and accuse them of their own backwardness, oppression, and poverty; and they impute to Zionism the "oppression of freedom" of which they themselves suffer, as do Muslims in general. Only a twisted mind beyond repair can accuse the Jews of the Twin Tower massacre, which they begin to believe themselves, and spread that lie as a fact, around the world. On Thursday night, the 6th of March, 2008, a lone Muslim gunman from East Jerusalem, (who knows whether he was radical or not ?) who was employed by Israel and enjoyed the services offered by its city government, surreptitiously made his way into a *yeshiva* (Jewish religious school) in the heart of the Jewish neighborhood, and opened gun fire on unsuspecting teenage students who were rehearsing the end of the month portion of the *Torah* and *Talmud* that they were routinely studying and debating. Eight of them lost their lives, many others were wounded more or less seriously, until a passing-by reserve soldier, who had incidentally graduated from the same institution a few years earlier, was alerted by the shooting, rushed to the reading hall of the library where the carnage was unfolding and put an end to the massacre. That rampage was not the initiative of a lunatic and lone hatred-filled man, or the idea of a hallucinating misguided fanatic, exactly as the perpetrators of September 11 (2001) in New York and July 7 (2005) in London, even if locally grown, were inspired by the satanic ideas of worldwide Muslim organizations bent on murder and destruction.

The next day, the well-to-do family of the killed murderer erected a huge tent at the entrance to their house in Eastern Jerusalem, to accommodate the Muslim well-wishers who began streaming by the hundreds to greet the bereaved family, not to present their condolences, for his feat of hitting their enemy at its heart, thereby attaining the hallowed status of *shahid* (martyr). To boot, the mourners hoisted the flags of Hizbullah and Hamas on the tent, all under the open eye of the Israeli forces of order and the liberal attitude of "non-interference with the lives" of the Arab Muslims in Israel's capital city. Soon the Hamas took "credit" for that senseless massacre, driving any sensible human being to wonder why a young man of twenty-one, about to wed a wife within three months, would take that harrowing step and destroy his own life and his future. It could not be economic want, personal despair, momentary madness or a family rift. It was simply hatred, inspired by the relentless Muslim "education" to despise the "unbelievers," demonize them, and dehumanize them to the point of making their lives cheap and unworthy of respect. It was more important to harm them than to bring relief to himself. But it must be more than that, for that horrific act, like the many other acts of terror and killings that we witness in the Muslim world, or emanate from it, day in day out, does not explain in full the intensity, the unbearable ease and the persistence of these unending and revolting manifestations of contempt and abuse of human life. Two weeks later, another Arab from East Jerusalem, who was employed by an Israeli contractor in the west part of the city, seized a bulldozer on his site and went into a rampage in the city shoving people and cars, including a bus full of horrified passengers, until he was gunned down by passers-by and police. Within two more weeks, that same horrible act was repeated in another street of Jerusalem, by another young

Arab of East Jerusalem, also using the same tool of shoving people and cars with the bulldozer he was supposed to operate on his construction site. He too was gunned down by armed citizens and police. This begs the question: why should such a succession of murders of innocent civilians be pursued by young men who were employed and living quite comfortably in the outskirts of the city and were holding Israeli identity cards, which they had sought for their own wellbeing in the first place? Why would they take the risk of depriving their fellow Arabs from such jobs that no Israeli would trust them to hold in the future? What other explanation is there of this successive orgy of murders than hatred of Jews? Maybe the answer lies in the theory voiced by French philosopher Jean-Claude Milner that today's anti-Semitism does not originate from old people, but from youth, and thus it is not likely to disappear but rather to become stronger, therefore it is the anti-Semitism of the future.[79] Judging from the widespread indoctrination in the media and textbooks for the young of the Arab world, such indoctrination is more likely to be perpetuated there in the future than among the youth of Europe that Milner was talking about. More often than not we are now talking about he same youth who are indoctrinated by the same people who draw from the same sources. In these outbursts of anti-Semitism by Muslim youth there is also an element of contempt and abuse of other faiths, as when in the first case cited above that same Muslim murderer indiscriminately shot and ripped to pieces *Torah* and *Talmud* books, which the students were consulting, and which they left stained with their blood when they fell to the bullets of the assassin. And save for a few human and courageous voices of reason in Kuwait and other Gulf States, the general

[79] Claude Meyer, "Interview with Jean-Claude Milner", the author of *The Criminal Inclinations of Democratic Europe, in Actualites Juives Hebdo, No 823, No 823,* 11 December, 2003. Cited by Manfred Gerstenfeld, "Antisemitism: Integral to European Culture", in *Post Holocaust and Antisemitism,* No 19, 1 April, 2004, p. 4, published by the Jerusalem Center of Public Affairs.

mood in the Arab/ Muslim world was not one of consternation, sorrow, shame or embarrassment, but when it was manifested at all, as in Gaza and among other Muslim circles, not necessarily "radical" ones, it was one of jubilation at the sight of the "feat" that their great "hero" had "achieved" in that religious school at the heart of the enemy.

It was as if a Jew, or a Christian, burst into a *madrasa* at the heart of the Muslim world and massacred students bent on their study. Can anyone in a civilized country imagine any sign of jubilation at that carnage? The rest of the Muslim world was busy with its own domestic massacres where people in countless thousands are eliminated on a daily basis in Afghanistan, Pakistan, Sudan, Iraq, and many other unreported places where human lives do not count. Expectedly, when the killings, intentional or incidental, are committed by non-Muslims, as in Iraq or Israel, they are invariably dubbed as "aggression" or "murder" against Muslims, which in every case is dubbed as a "massacre" or a "genocide." But the many more Muslims who are slaughtered by other Muslims and whose deaths cannot be directly blamed on the West, are simply disregarded and discounted and no grief seems to accompany them or any account taken of them. So, the real massacres by car-bombs and by Islamikaze assassins, of Afghani Muslims by other Muslims, Iraqi Sunnites against Shi'ites, Iranian Shi'ites against Sunnites, or Pakistani Taliban against their own kin, or Hamas adepts in Gaza against their Palestinian brethren from the PLO, and the ISIS rampages against non-Muslims in Iraq and Syria, go almost unnoticed and unreported in the Islamic world. What imports for Muslim propaganda is not how many Muslims are killed, but who kills them, regardless of the reason or the justification for it.

Anti-Semitism is an irrational phenomenon, which has defied definition, let alone explanation or justification in the past two millennia. Yet, the entire field of study of anti-Semitism has attempted for generations to analyze it by rational tools. For example, if we say that murdering Jews is the result of anti-Semitic contempt and hatred, then how to explain the massive physical elimination of other Muslims by their coreligionists: black Muslims by Sudanese-supported Muslim *Janjaweed* in Darfur, or the widespread cases of mass killings in the Arab and Muslim world, like Iraq, Syria, Lebanon, the Palestinian Authority, the Yemen, Algeria, Pakistan, Afghanistan, and all the rest? The inescapable conclusion is that the trigger-happy Muslims who are propped by Jihad, external or internal, and their innate disregard for human life, renders execution, capital punishment, beheading, hanging, mass murder, mutilation, and torture an acceptable norm of conduct. Implementing *Shari'a* rules in domestic penal law is in itself the best indication of the low value of human life in their eyes. When this worldview is practiced against Jews, it is rationalized as anti-Semitism; against other westerners, as "vengeance," "self-defense," reaction to western "arrogance," "humiliation," or "desecration" of Muslim values; and against others -by any amount of other trumped up justifications. Underlying all those instances is the burning desire by Muslims in general to impose by force their ideals and rules of conduct, both on their own nationals when they are viewed as apostates, thus deserving death, and certainly on their rivals and enemies, who are often considered as enemies of Islam and Allah, and therefore are equally deserving of annihilation. No debate, negotiation, compromise, or argument is possible with this "will of Allah," and therefore no perceived offense or deviation from these rules is tolerable or forgivable. It is often claimed that this strict interpretation of Islam with its abuses, including anti-Semitism, is only the lot of "fanatic," "radical," "fundamentalist" Muslims, usually quantified as some 15 percent of the 1.5 billion world Muslims, as if that were a different faith embracing different principles than those followed by the rank-and-file Muslims. In fact, we are talking about the same one creed, which upholds *Shari'a* law to various degrees, but those who do not follow it to the letter, as in any other religion, are not adepts of an alternative "moderate Islam," the one that is sometimes dubbed "religion of peace," to distinguish from the faith of aggressive "extremists." The truth of the matter is that no such separate Islam exists, though there are certainly many truly moderate Muslims, who have broken away from the bloody road of Islamic *Shari'a,* especially when they conveniently moved to the West, and could from a safe distance criticize the killings in their original countries of those dubbed there "apostates," or "traitors," or attack the phenomenon of the Islamikaze bombers against Westerners and Israelis, or the culture of death that is cultivated in many Islamic lands, or indeed the unbridled anti-Semitic calumnies that are rife in their own culture. But they have yet to produce an alternative doctrine and worldview that could rival official Islam and posit a creed and a set of rules which can attract Muslims to relinquish the *Shari'a* and embrace another way. If they did, they would no longer be Muslims in the eyes of established Islam. Moderate Muslims often accuse the radicals, who are in fact the common Muslims who behave in accordance with the accepted rules championed by the *Shari'a,* of having "hijacked" Islam or "distorted" its "real" meaning, or misinterpreted it, and they in turn are condemned for having abandoned the path of Allah and having been corrupted by western ideologies. But it is the standards of the former that prevail in the Islamic world. The particularly hostile attitude of the Islamic world towards the Jews and Israel has been founded on the times of the Prophet, when during his rule in Medina, he encountered four Jewish tribes which had lived there from time immemorial and he had hoped to convert to his cause. As they refused, some of them were slaughtered, other were Islamized and others were expelled from the city. These historical memories are preserved in the Qur'an and other Islamic writings, and even in Islamic countries which have made peace with Israel (Egypt and Jordan), or in countries which have never known Jews as a community, Imams in the mosques keep repeating every Friday the quotations from the Qur'an which evince a deep and foundational hatred against Jews, and contempt to them and to their culture, or cite abominable words of incitement against them, that in any civilized country would be counted as racial hatred and prosecuted accordingly. It is only natural that the rank and file of Muslims, including the more educated among them, keep repeating those insults as facts, and keep transferring those heinous anti-Semitic stereotypes into Zionism and Israel. Bin Laden, for example, like Yussuf Qaradawi, the most respected Muslim scholar and preacher in the Sunnite world, used to spell out anti-Semitic broadsides against Jews, Zionism and Israel, drawing endlessly from the delusory pool of anti-Jewish hatred that has accumulated in their tradition and became part of the Islamic heritage. In matters of hatred, Arab children, and many other Muslim infants for that matter, are imbued with large doses of it with their mothers' milk. The infamous passage from the Book, which is cited in sermons in the mosques throughout the Muslim world, and which depicts Jews as "descendants of pigs and monkeys", a-priori lends justification to any monstrosity attributed to Jews. We understand today that Muhammad had pronounced those derogatory words of the Jews when they rose against his authority in Medina at the outset of his political career there. But today, when they are repeated *ad nauseam* throughout the Muslim world in Friday sermons, by journalists and politicians, out of any context, they serve no other purpose than disparaging the Jews and insulting them. What is that if not anti-Semitism, irrational as it may be? That derogatory reference, which is seconded by many others[80], has had a profound and lasting impact on Muslim thinking, behavior, social norms and the education of their children, and not necessarily in areas of conflict with Israel or adjacent to it, sometimes even in parts of the world which have never seen a Jew.

Ayaan Hirsi Ali, the now famous Somalian refugee, who immi-

---

[80] See.eg. Suras 2:61, 4:44-46, 4:160-61, 9:30-31, 5:64, 5:82 and more.

grated to the Netherlands and was instantly catapulted to prominence there when she was elected to Parliament, recounted in one of her many press interviews about the religious indoctrination process she underwent in her country of origin in her youth. Her history teacher, Sister Aziza, used to take the class for an outing to the Iranian embassy and to promote a Muslim revolution. Gradually the girls in her class started to physically cover themselves. She herself took to wearing the *hijab* and to admire the Muslim Brotherhood. Aziza started to use the '*yahud*' (Jews) word. One day she said: 'You all sit up and listen.' She showed the girls a magazine from Iran (a Muslim, not an Arab country) with pictures of dead people, piles of bodies and blood, and said: 'look what the *yahud* have done to the Muslims.' The pictures were Iranian propaganda. They were taken from the Iran-Iraq war, showing Iraqi soldiers killing Iranian citizens. 'This is what the Jews have done, and Saddam Hussein was an agent of the Jews', Sister Aziza taught. She instructed the kids how to pray: "You hold your hands together, and you say: 'Allah please protect us from evil, Allah please keep us healthy, Allah please take care of my mother and my father, Allah please destroy the Jews.'" Hirsi Ali pursued her tale:

> For me, '*yahud*' [Jews] was not the same as human. It's the enemy. It's Satan. I remember a joke, well, it wasn't even a joke, from the time I was a very little girl. We were in Riyad and Jedda when the oil boom started. They were trying to build an oil pump; the construction project went on forever. At last, when the project was done, they opened the top of the pump, but instead of oil, water came out. And I remember my mom saying: 'See, the Jews are at it again.' And I think about the three most horrible insults you could think of in my world. The insults were '*yahud*', '*shuri*' and '*hanis*'. 'Shuri' means a communist. 'Hanis' means gay. You guys are used to laughing at it, but it's really not a laughing matter.

Because it's no longer just the Saudis who think like that. These ideas are spreading throughout Islam and all over the world to people who never met Jews, who know nothing about Israelis or what Israel represents. In 1993 I went to Antwerp with a friend. The friend said, 'We are now in the Jewish neighborhood' and pointed at an Orthodox Jew. And I lost my breath and said: 'Jewish?! Is he Jewish?! Wait, where? Where?' You see, I needed to visualize this huge fantasy of evil that I had in my head. And then he showed me a few people walking around and asked, 'What exactly were you expecting?' I looked around and said, 'Can you tell me, if a kid has two hands and two legs and he's walking, are there children who are Jewish as well?' And my friend responded: 'Yes, there are Jewish children as well. At that moment I felt something else inside me, that said it was shameful to voice what I had felt. I had to suppress that. So in 1993 I didn't talk about it again. It was in 1994, during history class, when I first saw pictures of what happened in the Second World War. I was coming from Somalia, and similar things started to happen in my country, along with Rwanda, Sudan, Liberia, Sierra Leone… There are many things I learned at that time in history class, but the story of the Holocaust made the biggest impression on me. I went to all the Holocaust museums. I've been to *Yad Vashem* twice. As I understood it, the Holocaust wasn't just the story of the Jews … I don't know if this goes for everyone, but knowledge enlightened me…As a Muslim, I belong to the universal tribe. Every human individual, regardless of his beliefs, faith, sex, deserves to live and is equal. My criticism is of religion, especially Islam, and not of Muslims. Therefore, my criticism of Islam is not a rejection of Muslims. It is the idea of race that makes us

> destroy each other. You have to change your mind and learn to accept the other. My case is to convince fellow Muslims. I call myself Muslim not because I believe in Allah any longer, but I come out of that culture, and I want to fight to modify that culture, and create a culture of love and human rights...[81]

If this was the case for remote Somalia, which has had other more serious problems to tackle and many more important values to impart to its miserable children, how much more so for the Arab children who are exposed, day in day out, to the bombardments of hatred in their schools, among their families, on their media and in their streets. Hirsi Ali' s enlightenment after her move to Holland, puts in perspective much of the education to hatred to which those innocent children are exposed in the Muslim world, and which bears no necessary relationship to deprivation or poverty (Hirsi was from a well-to do background). Add to that the universality of anti-Semitism in Islam (she heard the same derogation of the Jews in Saudi Arabia and then among European Muslims); the power of stereotypes land cultivated myths (Hirsi had never seen a Jew in either Somalia or, even much less likely, in Jedda); the fallacy of attributing these attitudes to the Arab-Israeli dispute (Somalia never was a party to it); and the lumping together of Jews and Israel as an inseparable entity, Muslim protestations to the contrary notwithstanding, and one begins to comprehend what we are talking about. Hirsi later also understood the systematic Holocaust denial current among Muslims, became a perennial visitor to Israel and to the *Yad Vashem* Holocaust Memorial in Jerusalem, and grew to castigate Muslims for the atmosphere of Jew-hatred that they cultivate in their midst. Much of the virulence against Jews in the Muslim world, is attributable to the constant flow of hatred propagated

[81] Gitit Ginat, "Freedom fighter", *www.haaretz.com* – 18 May, 2006.

among Islamic societies[82].

In much of the Arab and much of the Muslim worlds, there has been no let-up in this regard. Their publics are permanently inundated by biased information and one-sided propaganda emanating from their authoritarian governments, who have not educated them to think freely, to gather information from many sources, and make judgments for themselves. And the official version of news universally, exclusively and constantly transmits and diffuses the versions crafted by the governments in place, which invariably demonize the Jews-Israelis-Zionists, impute to them the most horrible monstrosities, heap on them the most horrible accusations and attribute to them the most evil intentions. History is also re-written and tailored to suit the evil nature of the Jews, in daily columns, in "scientific" books, encyclopedias, not to mention Friday mosque sermons and political speeches made by unscrupulous clerics, "scholars" and writers. Citations are invented which have no source to draw from, without concern for the false reporting to the readers or the distortion of the minds of children and youth who will grow in error, be bereft of intellectual curiosity and fortitude, and get accustomed to their "narrative" instead of to the truth. Arab media have no compunction about distorting reports, inflating negatives and attenuating positives when Israel or Jews are concerned, lest the stereotypes they are harnessed by their governments to propagate be corrected. Rumors and accusations that Israelis are killers of children, spread diseases around, undermine governments and diffuse corruption, are quick to travel in the Islamic world and adopted, lock stock and barrel, without critique or verification. Confirmed reports about a scientific invention by Israelis or Jews, an Israeli sports team which won a medal or a championship, or any international distinction awarded to Israel, like a Nobel Prize, or aid brought by Israel to Arab patients and

---

[82] See R. Israeli, *Muslim anti-Semitism in Christian Europe: Elemental and Residual anti-Semitism,* Transaction, New Jersey, 2009.

children, is sure to disappear from the Arab news reports lest, Allah Forbid, Jews might appear in a positive light and contribute towards the attenuation of the Arab hatred towards them.

No wonder then that children in kindergartens in Gaza are prone to vow for *Islamikaze* careers when they grow up, and for their mates to watch television programs of the official Palestinian Authority, or of Hamas Television, in which even popular international cartoon figures render Palestinian kids heroes who devote their lives to fight the "Zionist enemy", and the latter are dubbed the "scum of the earth" whose sacred duty of all Palestinians it is to blow up. The infamous Muhammed al-Dura case, which became *cause celebre* in France, after it was proved in court that it had been jointly staged by a French Television channel and the Palestinian Authority with a view of demonizing Israel, provides ample evidence of this manifestation of hatred. In Arab lore, Jews and in consequence Israelis and Zionists, are accused of racism, bigotry, corruption, undermining the world order, wielding international power on the media and finances, desecrating Muslim holy places, occupying Arab lands, discriminating against their own new immigrants; their leaders as devious monsters, their foreign policy as aggressive and expansionist, threatening the peaceful Arabs; accumulating a dangerous nuclear arsenal, and striving to the demise of the Arabs. As regards the Palestinians specifically, not only usurpation of their rights is invoked, together with the claim of their occupation, their exploitation and their persecution, but even genocidal accusations are occasionally raised against Israel. In the meantime, Israel and Zionism are routinely charged of eliminating Palestinian culture in order to replace it by the Jewish-Zionist one, and of diminishing the Islamic prevalence in Palestine and other occupied territories.[83]

---

[83] For details of such accusations, see R. Israeli, *Peace is in the Eye of the Beholder*, Mouton, Berlin and NY, 1985.

This image of the Jews, Zionism and Israel, which is cultivated in the Arab, and many Muslim, media worldwide, at the exclusion of anything positive which may be said about them, naturally channels public opinion towards a very deeply-seated hatred towards those entities, which is becoming gradually irreversible, even in the countries which have signed peace with Israel, like Egypt and Jordan, or used to be Muslim moderates, like Turkey, Qatar, Morocco and the Emirates, who sharply shifted their openness towards Israel the moment the first reports of Israel's "atrocities" in the Gaza War (2009) started to filter out. That hostile attitude persisted and even worsened during the subsequent incursions of Israel to Gaza in 2012 and 2014, which came on the heels of massive rocket attacks from Gaza against Israeli cities and towns. That there was a defensive reason for Israeli incursions did not matter, for it seemed that the infrastructure of hatred entrenched in the Islamic world towards Israel is there all the time, and all it needs is a trigger to re-launch it with ever greater vigor. Admittedly, even in many European countries where that same sort of anti-Israeli hostility was aired on the same occasion of the Gaza Wars, it was connected, at least in part, with the wrath of the Muslim minorities in the West which are fed by the same disinformation, hallucinations and hatred that they brought with them from the Islamic world, and continue to "update" their background "education" from the Arab media or from the anti-Semitic European media. In sum, the Jews, who were traditionally depicted in despicable terms in Islam, continue to be portrayed stereotypically in Arab writings, in cartoons and in the electronic media.

These perceptions of Israel also dictate the choice of items that the Arab press publishes about the Zionist state as well as the interpretations they lend them. Political controversies as well as political factions in Israel, for example, are seen not as arising from political conflicts within a democratic system, but rather as a sign of dissent, disintegration and failure to achieve unity. Former generals serving in the Israeli government do not signify a normal and legitimate way for people to move from one sphere of activity to another, like Generals Marshall, Eisenhower, Haig and Powell in the US, but are "proof" of the militarization of Israeli society or the "martial mentality" of its leaders. The careful screening of "facts" and outright fabrication of "data" that fit their negative image of Israel, sometimes generate contradictions which the Arab media choose to ignore. For example, while the Arabs keep repeating that neither Arab or Muslim tradition ever called for hatred of Jews as such, their verbal and graphic depictions are the most contemptible one could imagine; while they assert that the Jews in their midst have "always enjoyed equal rights", their leaders are exhorted to improve the treatment of their erstwhile Jewish minorities to allow for their return to their native lands, which they had abandoned in favor of immigration to Israel. When Israel develops industry in the Arab sector under her rule, she is accused of scheming to alienate Arabs from their lands, but Israel is also accused of preventing industrial development in that sector in order to keep it backward. When Israel takes a firm stand against Palestinian terrorism, she is accused of oppression, but when she shows leniency and flexibility, the Arabs claim that this was a maneuver to gain world sympathy for the occupation.

The second axis of continued and aggravated Arab hostility to Israel since 1948, in addition to the scrupulously preserved hatred towards Jews, Zionists and Israel, which has been elevated to the degree of an icon, has been the sense of humiliation which their rout at the hand of Israel had occasioned. The theme of humiliation was also mentioned to Secretary Kerry by all Arab leaders he met in his efforts to strengthen the coalition against ISIS in October, 2014.[84] Humiliation, which has been also invoked by Muslim

[84] In his press conference at the State Department on 17 October, 2014, broadcast live worldwide.

movements like al-Qa'ida, in the context of their struggle against the West, has two aspects to it: the first is the military defeats they have suffered, hence their permanent urge to take revenge, and the second is the exposure of their incompetence and backwardness when compared to the achievements of the West and Israel. Humiliation is born out of the sense of injustice done to them, which is another way of stating that defeat is undue to them, because justice would have justified their victory. Hence the Arab permanent clamor for justice ("peace with justice", a "just solution" to the conflict), as if justice were absolute and not in the eye of the beholder. Justice (*'adalah* in Arabic), which is also, incidentally, the name of an Arab civil rights group in Israel, is linked in Arab parlance to the notion of balance between the saddlebags on the camelback, short of which the camel cannot march at length to cross the desert. Justice is also connected to honor, and the maintenance of one's honor hinges on one's ability to protect one's property, including one's women, and on one's proven capacity to retrieve them if they are violated. Otherwise, one's reputation is irretrievably compromised. Thus, one's honor is constantly on the line, and it is always tested by one's daring in the service of one's honor. An Arab will not rest until the wrong done to him is redressed and his property is recuperated. Only then is justice done and the offended party can revert to functioning normally. There are no objective criteria to examine the feeling of right or wrong, or what constitutes an encroachment on one's honor; they hinge upon the subjective sense of the wronged individual. Only when the wronged party feels satisfied does he feel that justice has been redressed.

When the Arabs demand justice, they mean their justice, i.e. the retrieval of their rights and properties as they perceive them, regardless of whether, what arguments and how others might advance as disclaimers in historical, legal, logical or human terms, for all these are irrelevant from their point of view. First, the Arabs must get full satisfaction, in accordance with their sentiments and convictions, their rights must be recognized and stated, and only then they might show generosity and give back out of their own volition, not as a result of coercion or force. Thus, the whole notion of compromise does not come into play, because if something is yours, you must obtain it first, regardless of what others may claim. Sadat in his speech at the Knesset in November, 1977, and the Syrians in their various negotiations with Israel, the Hizbullah in Lebanon, and the Palestinians in their two factions (PLO and Hamas), have all demanded a total Israeli withdrawal of forces before negotiations can proceed, or at the very least an Israeli commitment to retreat at the end of the day. Not because, as some diplomats have thought, the Arabs wish to obtain the end results of the negotiations before they even begin, but in order to signal that what they regard as their property is not negotiable. It is theirs, period. The Palestinians, like the rest of the Arabs, sense in their deepest consciousness that the Holy Land in general, and Jerusalem in particular, with its innermost *sanctum,* the Temple Mount, have been the exclusive patrimony of the Arabs/Muslims, since they were included in the *futuh* (conquests of Islam), and were bequeathed to them by Allah, for all generations to come, as a *waqf* (holy endowment), never to be parted with or negotiated away. Hence, their "right of return" is not only a human and political need, but also a religious duty which imposes on them to struggle and pay any sacrifice so as to snatch the land from its usurpers who have subtracted it from Islamic dominion. This is valid in particular with regard to the *Haram- al-Sharif* (the Temple Mount) which was the very site of the Prophet's mystical nightly journey *(isra')* and ascension to Heaven *(mi'raj).* Thus, only after this right of theirs is recognized, as a matter of course, worldwide (what they call "international legitimacy"), may they evince *ex gracia* generosity and allow others to collect some crumbs from their table. Until then, all measures are allowable to retrieve the loss by peaceful means if possible, through violence if necessary, for in any case its holy character prescribes *jihad.*

As long as matters are not settled to their tune, the Arabs feel humiliated. This is the reason why every time they are close to the conclusion of a set of negotiations, after Israel has made far-reaching concessions to the Arabs for the sake of peace, but short of total surrender to their demands, they back down and retreat. Israeli negotiators, and many a Western observer, are stunned in disbelief, unable to comprehend how their interlocutors have once again missed another opportunity. Instead, they would rather wait to obtain the whole thing, without concession or compromise on their part, for the sake of satisfying their honor and sense of justice, rather than bend to the humiliation of accepting the part, which would signify that they have reconciled themselves to injustice. Justice is for them whole and indivisible, therefore they educate their children to claim it all and to deny their rivals any part of it. When they report to their own people about their clashes, debates or arguments with Israelis, there is never an understanding of the other's pain, sensitivity, loss or ambition. Conversely, there is in Israel a whole political camp which sympathizes with the Palestinians and even supports them, diffuses their grievances and expresses them in the media. No trace of that is found on the Palestinian side, and if there should be one "saint" who would dare, he would be condemned, arrested, or even gunned down or executed as a "traitor", so uniform is the wall of hatred and so unacceptable is the understanding of the rival. In "moderate" Egypt and Jordan, who have signed peace with Israel, anyone who maintains links with it or comes out in favor of peace and normalization with it, is excommunicated by his community and, more ominously, excluded from his trade union, which means in effect that he is denied the right to make a living, due to the "unforgivable sin" of reconciling with the enemy, who should have no longer been considered an enemy after the peace was signed. After every incident, Palestinian spokesmen are allowed to voice their grievances in the Israeli media, where the damages and casualties inflicted on the other party are reported and debated, while the Palestinian media never interview any Israeli or anyone critical of them, and they disregard the casualties and damages inflicted on the others, or rejoice in public when they learn about them. They always present Israel as the aggressor who pesters the life of innocent Palestinians for no reason, and cultivate the feelings among Palestinians that they are the eternal victims who can do no wrong. The very notion of being a refugee, which is perpetuated by Palestinians for generations as if it were a permanent status, became a state of mind which reflects their sense of victimhood. As they are the poor and eternal victims, the whole world owes them everything. They make children, but the UN has to feed them. The poverty and density of their camps, from which they make no effort to exit, are for the US and the rest of Western world (not the Arabs, not even the rich among them) to resolve. The Palestinian Authority has built 13 different security apparatuses, and the separate Hamas government is building many more, but it is the donor countries of the West which have to finance them. They are dipped in corruption and in inefficient government, but it is the rest of the world which has to foot the bills. It does not occur to them that if they had rolled up their sleeves and applied themselves to work, to pursue the road of construction and peace, they would have solved all those problems in the past decades, instead of perpetuating them and throwing the blame on others. Nor does it occur to the donors that if they had refrained from sustaining the victimhood with their donations, the refugee status would have been obliterated. Donations and humiliations go hand in hand: the recipient depends on the donor, but aches and hates him for that dependence and is humiliated by it.

The theme of humiliation widely reverberates throughout the Arab discourse with the world as well, especially with the US which is considered Israel's main sustainer. For some Arab writers and thinkers, Israel is considered a launching pad for taking over Muslim holy places, Judaizing Muslim land, killing, maiming and imprisoning innocent Muslims, and conquering more Muslim territories, so as to form a western base to "diffuse Jewish corruption, westernization, humiliation, enslavement and exploitation of Muslim society"[85]. Conversely, a Kuwaiti columnist, Ahmed al-Baghdadi, while lashing out at Arab regimes who persecute their own *intelligentsia*, and positing the Arabs and Muslims as "masters of terrorism", justified the aggressive reactions of the West, which "has turned to humiliating Arabs and Muslims and rejecting them from its midst ... Islam does not tolerate others' opinions and even undercuts its own intellectuals at a time when the "heretic" West and Israel do not practice that kind of terror"[86]. In a "letter to America", published in the Hamas' *al-Risalah* in Gaza after September 11 (2001), the message is clear:

> Oh America, the sword of oppression, arrogance and crime !!! Do you remember how you smashed man's humanity? Do you remember how you mistreated the Blacks under your aegis? Can you describe for us the humiliation, disgust and contempt you meted out to those unfortunate people, whose only sin was that they were born to black parents?... They were born free, but were enslaved in your virgin America, reexamine your decisions to cast hundreds of veto votes [at the Security Council of the UN), with a view of denying humanity its rights. Look at your humiliated face, and check whether it is not due to those votes. This will teach you to stand by justice and by the righteous, even if they are weak, and then perhaps the dust of humiliation will be

[85] .*Qira'a fi Fiqh al-Shahada,* (Readings in Islamic Martyrology) was published in 1988 as a special addendum to *al-Islam wa-Filastin* (Islam and Palestine) that appeared in Nocosia, Cyprus, and has been the ideological supporter of the Palestinian Islamikaze operations against Israel. See ibid. 5 June, 1988, p. 7.

[86] .*Akhbar al-Yaum (Kuwait),* 3 November, 2001.

removed from your sad face...[87]

Thus, in a fascinating reversal of projecting their own feelings which justify their *Jihad* against the West "even at the price of misery and humiliation"[88], their yearning is revealed of humiliating the West and Israel in return, because only counter-humiliation can remove the traces of humiliation. These manifestations of humiliation and the constant need to remove them by retaliation in kind, have been part of the Arab psyche since their defeat of 1948. But then, they were also cognizant of their inability to inflict defeat and to humiliate others in their turn. It is noteworthy that since the 1973 War, when they construed its results as a "victory", and more so in the two Lebanese wars (1982, 2006),and with the rise of the oil prices, the terrorist attacks that they inflicted on Israel and worldwide, their smashing victory against the Soviets in Afghanistan (1979-89), and the Israeli withdrawals from Lebanon and Gaza (2000 and 2005, under the pressure of Hizbullah and Hamas respectively), they perceive their ability to inflict humiliation as having gained the upper hand. But there is also another kind of humiliation, self-inflicted by those Arabs who have sought accommodation with Israel and the West. In a popular song sold on audio- and video-tapes throughout the Arab world, to celebrate Islamikaze acts of martyrdom, and savor the humiliation they have caused to America on September 11, such Arab leaders and their Israeli allies are castigated in harsh terms:

[Referring to peaceful Arab leaders and to Israel in humiliating terms]...
Your history is black and covered
Your ancestry is a tree whose branches are corrupt...

[87] *Al-Risalah,* (Gaza), 13 September, 2001, cited (in Hebrew) by MEMRI, *Terror in America, No 1.*
[88] *Al-Gumhuriyya,* 7 October, 2001. See MEMRI 289, 19 October, 2001.

And the Arab rulers in this homeland
Lie in a perpetual sleep
Eating from the fruit of your tree
And drinking of your humiliation
As if they were not Muslims [89].

Ultimately, for the Muslim world, humiliation should be the fate of the Jews, as prescribed in the Holy Qur'an, not of Muslims, and the present situation where these norms have been reversed, ought to be addressed and redressed. Saudi clerics, who usually deride Arab nationalism and pan-Arabism[90], insist that there is no way to defeat the "descendents of monkeys and pigs", namely the Jews, unless the road of *Jihad* is embraced. They say that as long as the Palestinians fight for their orchards, namely their material belongings and false nationalism, they will not achieve much, and therefore they ought to go back to their Islamic faith and fight in its name. They counsel their audiences to learn from the ways of the Jews:

> We have to realize that our defeats by the Jews are due to the fact that they did not let the Islamic *umma* confront them… These were defeats of Arab regimes which did not raise the banner of Islam… Should our lost [sons] revert to the Truth, then the Jews shall return to their wretchedness and humiliation that they were doomed to [by the Holy Book]. Then, when the ignorant wake up, nothing can rescue the Jews, they will never see victory, as long as they profess mistaken notions, heretic curricula and a humiliating peace…[91].

---

[89] By Ayman, a poet, in *Al-Istiqlal (*the Weekly of Islamic Jihad in Gaza), 13 December, 2001.
[90] Cited in R. Israeli, Islamikaze etc… p. 290.
[91] Ibid.

There is nothing which exemplifies and advertises the humiliation which the Arabs- Muslims painfully experience more than Israeli, Western and other non-Muslim presence in what they regard as "occupied" territory, be it Palestine, Iraq, Afghanistan, Kashmir, Andalusia and the like. Hence the urgency of expelling the occupiers from those lands in order to cleanse the spot of humiliation. *Jihadi* movements, like al-Qa'ida, Islamic Jihad, Laskar-e-Taiba and others, emphasize the recourse to *Jihad* to achieve this goal. The way Islamic ideology gave rise to the Islamikaze, and more so the way Islamic society rose to the defense of Islamikaze attacks, first against Israel and then against western countries and some Islamic countries deemed too supportive or docile towards the West, counsels us to try to understand the psychological make up behind them, beyond the themes of humiliation and hatred discussed above. Also in need of explanation is the fact that at the same time that there is great delight felt in the Muslim camp, in spite of the many expedient attempts to hide the phenomenon and explain it away, when Israelis or westerners are murdered *en masse,* there is a sense of a great shock and consternation in the face of the vigorous US or Israeli counter-attacks. Because when Muslims attack and sow death and destruction, that is mere defense against the aggressors, therefore, no counter-attack is deemed justified, and it would always be deemed aggressive by definition, thus deserving retaliation, and so on *ad infinitum.*

In its own lands, where it feels weaker materially, though it boasts its moral superiority, the Islamic world shows awe, if not respect, towards the West, and at the same time feels humiliated by it technologically, militarily, economically, and culturally. The frustration at the Muslims' inability to match up to the strong, especially since they were themselves the prevalent culture in the past, creates elements of confrontation between the two. This is a confrontation because, unlike Western culture which, at least in theory, accepts others for what they are, frustrated Muslims are eager to destroy the bearers of strength rather than try to lift themselves to their level. Frustration generates shame, and aggression is used to displace the shame. Several areas of comparison may be suggested, which point out the differences between the two cultures and can help explain why Muslims and the West do not perceive the world in the same fashion, and therefore it is so difficult to devise ways to compromise and co-exist. Israel used to be isolated in its understanding of the Islamic enmity towards it, but now that the confrontation has widened and grown global, more and more civilizations are drawn into the circle of those who try to crack the genetic code which characterizes Muslim societies. Thus, it is easy to understand the deep-seated hatred for the West, which is shared by most Muslims, although for utilitarian reasons of needing the technological and economic power of the West, most Muslim states do not quite evince the feelings of their populace. Suffice it to scan through the public relations surveys of such Islamic countries as Saudi Arabia, Iran, Egypt, Turkey and Pakistan, all at one time or another major allies of the US, whose successive governments have maintained close relations with the West, to realize the intensity of hatred and rage that their populations entertain towards the northern world of modernity, prosperity and domination. That sentiment may be engendered not only by the centuries of western colonization of Islamic lands, but mainly by the reversal at the gates of Vienna in 1683 of the glory and awe the Muslim Ottomans had inspired for centuries into a slippery descent into decline and demise of the last Muslim Caliphate at the hands of Russia and Europe. At any rate, in the modern world which is militarily and economically dominated by the West, it is America who gives, protects, guarantees and aids, and it is Islamdom, with the rest of The Third World which is needy, begging, supplicating for assistance and protection. And it is always the richest and strongest which is the most hated, despite its generosity' for those who cannot be like it wish to bring it down to their level, so as to erase the humiliation caused by the dissonance between the giver and the receiver. But since Muslim governments do not dare, nor have they acquired the power to act against America and the West, it is the Muslim radical movements who have taken up that mission with vengeance.

# Chapter Seven

## *Dealing with Pressing Issues*

Numerous are the problems and dilemmas plaguing the Arab and Islamic world, from basic issues of a dwindling food supply versus demographic growth and desertification of arable land and water supply, to chaotic governability, tribalism, civil wars, legitimacy of governments, rich and sparsely populated states versus poor and densely inhabited countries, political moderation versus religious extremism, state institutions versus rebellions revolutionary movements and what have you. Questions rise as to the connection between economic deprivation and religious radicalism, between Islamic piety and political legitimacy, between rational politics and emotional or religiously-provoked policies. Various ways have been experienced and tested, responding to national pride or religious conviction, or to the tension between the requirements of international politics and human and civil rights on the one hand, and the popular demands of tribalism and tradition. While democratization demands fundamental societal reforms, clerical and radical conservatism forbid them. Does every Arab and /or Islamic country acts on its own in defiance of all the rest, or is it obliged to conform to the corporative consensus within the Arab League, the Organization of Islamic Cooperation or the Islamic Bloc within the UN? And *ad infinitum* political, social, economic, cultural and religious problems which are at the top of the individual and collective agenda of this huge group of people amounting to 1,5 billion souls, spanning the two continents of Africa and Asia and gradually also spreading to Europe and the Americas.

Following the Arab/ Islamic Spring of the 2010s it is certain that the stature and torment of Islam have been higher in regional and international politics than they ever were in the modern era, and this signifies also more aggressive and belligerent attitudes and policies, particularly toward the Middle Eastern dispute, in which the Islamic world has noted a tectonic change in its midst during the 2020s, partly emanating from international developments, and in part evolving out of current local and regional politics. Even those who have accepted Israel and signed peace with it, like Egypt and Jordan and in part the Palestinians, and Israel's new allies in the Abrahamic Pact of 2020, will see their policies revised. The countries of the Gulf and Morocco, who have escaped the upheaval of the Spring, were and probably remain the most open and accessible to change in general and to Israel in particular, insofar as they maintain promising relations with it, and are clustering around new security and economic concepts under the specter of the menacing Iranian nuclearization. Evidently, the young people who triggered the Spring did not intend it to go the way it is going, given that the Muslim movements that stood on the sidelines in the beginning later joined the bandwagon of success, and being better organized and experienced, they soon took matters in their own hands when they were sure that the dictator had gone and no further harm could be expected from his machinery of evil. But did those young people who initiated the whole process find satisfaction? How will the new regimes address their frustrated hopes and unrealized dreams? Will their economic, social, and cultural situation, for the sake of which they rebelled, improve even a trifle, or after the dust settles will they sink again into a grey and grinding life of despair and poverty, with no horizon in the distance? Were the democratic dreams and slogans they voiced, which they probably did not fully understand, totally evaporate into thin air, or will they erupt again when they realize that their revolution, for which they made many sacrifices, was in vain? But unlike the republican models wherein the Spring has replaced tone sort of dictators with another, in the monarchies nothing has changed, for they seem impervious to democratic change, which will continue to knock on their doors until either they give way or the democratic forces give up. The "success" of the Spring amounted ultimately to turn what was initially supposed to be an Arab Spring into an Islamic one, like in Tunisia, Egypt, Libya, Sudan, Mali. In most of those cases, the Muslim radicals of the kind of the Muslim Brothers took over "legally" until they were overwhelmed by their rivals from the two edges: either military juntas who tottered them shamelessly in spite of the "legitimacy", or are continuously challenged by radical Muslim organizations which rebel against the new dictators who scuttle the Islamic revolution they wished to produce. So, the new tyrants, republican or monarchic, count among the "Moderates" due to their attempt to survive against Islamic attacks by repenting towards the West and Israel; while the Muslim radical, states or revolutionary movements, have elected to continue the rebellious way, against pro-Western and pro-Israeli realignment, but trying to put up a face of the "true representatives of Islam", to whom the West should yield. In places where the Islamic Spring began prematurely—like Iran, Pakistan, Afghanistan, Turkey; or within tribal or revolutionary societies like Mali, Palestine, and Bosnia, the Spring has simply confirmed the tendencies of unrest that existed previously (Hamas in Palestine, Taliban in Pakistan and Afghanistan, and Izetbegovic's Islamic republic in Bosnia) but it never, or only temporarily, came to fruition. This signals to them that they were heading in the "right" direction and had better pursue that road.

**The Food Problem**

But beyond the concerns about immediate political developments in the Islamic countries, there are some major issues looming on the horizon as likely tests of the success or failure of the new governments, and likely to dominate their agenda, be they republican or monarchic, moderate or radical, one of the them is the food problem, which is critical to the ability to feed a growing population, Others being the water supply, the inherent fragility of most of the Arab regimes, and the prospects of democratization in view of the Abrahamic Pact and the opening up to the world and to Israel. On the food front, an important article by Nadim Kawach analyzed the hazards of food shortages in the Arab and Islamic world and their impact on those regimes. The author claims that Arab countries have reeled under a cumulative food gap of more than $180 billion over the past ten years, to emerge as the largest single farm products importer despite their massive arable land potential, according to official figures. Except for fish, vegetables, and other minor crops, Arab nations are suffering from a persistent shortage in all types of farm products, and the gap has steadily worsened over the past two decades, as shown by the Khartoum-based Arab Organization for Agricultural Development (AOAD). Wheat accounted for more than half the shortage, and a decision by Saudi Arabia, the largest Arab economy, to stop costly cultivation of wheat in its desert climate and rely solely on imports, is expected to further upset that balance. Besides wheat, the Arab food gap is underscored in cereal, barley, sugar, cooking oil, corn, rice, and poultry, as the Arab World's self-sufficiency in some of these products does not exceed 50 percent[92].According to the findings of this survey, the farm gap, peaked at around $29.8bn in 2008 due to a surge in global food prices before it edged down to nearly $27.5bn. This widened the total Arab food gap to a staggering $182bn during 2000–2009, AOAD's staggering figures showed: This level is nearly quadruple the cumulative

[92] Nadim Kawach, "Arab food gap crosses $180bn over past decade,"*Emirates 24/7*, June 27, 2010. http://www.emirates247.com/eb247/economy/uae-economy/arab-food-gap-crosses-180bn-over-pastdecade-2010-06-27-1.259717.

gap of around $45bn during the preceding nine years, when the region's population did not exceed 240 million in early 1990s compared with around 334 million in mid-2008. At the end of 2009, the Arab population was projected at around 351 million. "Since 1990, it has grown by nearly 2.34 per cent annually compared with global growth of about 1.16 per cent," AOAD said and added that "The high population growth in the region is oneof the major factors for the persistent deficit in the Arab food balance. Another result of the high growth is that it boosts demand for food, which, in turn, pushes up prices. This means a large number of people will find it difficult to get their food needs." The report of AOAD showed total Arab food exports stood at only about $11.5bn in 2009, while imports were as high as $39.04bn, one of their highest levels. It also blamed poor water resources in the region, low land exploitation and investments, and what it described as "defective Arab farm policies." Nearly three years after they approved a fifteen-year common farm strategy in 2005, the Arab countries have become more reliant on farm imports, as such a strategy remains inefficient in the absence of right policies and sufficient funds, it said. What complicates the problem is that the most wealthy Arab nations are still reluctant to invest heavily in farming projects in fertile member states, for political and security reasons, while only around 12 per cent of the total available arable land in the region is exploited, said AOAD, a key Arab League organization[93]. The author found that there were several obstacles and challenges facing development of the Arab farming sector. They included "investments, defective government policies, poor water policies, inefficient use of available land and water and water reserves, and the low level utilization of available arable areas," the report said. "The biggest obstacle has been and will remain the relatively small water resources available in the region. This obstacle has blocked investment in the farming sector and will hinder any

[93] Ibid.

program aimed at exploiting those areas." The report said the Arab World "is one of the poorest areas in the world in terms of water wealth, with the quantities of available renewable water resources standing at only around 1.3 per cent of the world's total renewable water wealth, although the Arab region accounts for more than 10 per cent of the total world land area." It also says that the low water resources have sharply depressed the per capita share of water in the Arab World because of a steady population growth of more than two percent. "The Arab region is considered one of the most arid areas in the world and the per capita share of the water wealth is among the lowest as it has remained much below the global water poverty level of 1,000 cubic meters per year. In some countries, this level is even below 500 cubic meters," the report said. "As for arable land, it is estimated at nearly 550 million hectares but only around 12 per cent is exploited. Even in that 12 per cent part, the farming efficiency does not exceed 60 per cent of the world level. This means the Arab World is facing a real problem of not only low exploitation of arable areas but low efficiency in the cultivated land and its productivity."[94]

The absurdity in all this is that the Arabs' immediate neighbor, Israel, is among the world's top experts in water development and water conservation, land development and conservation, irrigation, and high productivity in agriculture. Of course, the AOAD's Arab League report makes no mention of this; and would rather see its compatriots sink in poverty and hunger than ask its hated and despised neighbor for help. This mental obstacle has been much more difficult for the Arabs to surmount than the physical ones, as Israel has learned from its experience. After the Israel-Egypt peace treaty in the 1980s, the former sent, almost secretly, its experts to develop two model farms in the delta of the Nile. These farms have achieved some stunning results. But even President Sadat, who

[94] Ibid.

initiated the peace, never dared to publicize this fact, lest he contradict himself when he was boasting of his oldest farming nation of the world since Pharaonic times, implying that Egyptians stood to learn from no one. To admit that despicable Jews could teach the noble Egyptians anything was a blasphemy that even Sadat could not utter. The end result was that the Egyptian press was only willing to publish this fact, in order to blame Israel and the Jews of vile conspiracies to poison Egyptian lands. This is precisely where the new Abrahamic Pact of 2020, with its moderating and pragmatic effects, which have already been in sight can raise new hopes in the Arab and Muslim lands: to use the extended hand and the unique expertise of their neighbor to help dramatically increase their farming development (and also other aspects of economic development like high tech) so as for Israel to dwarf into insignificance the insidious anti-cooperation trends among the radical Muslims. Israel has already done much of that in China, India, and many countries of Asia and Africa, and only narrow-mindedness and bigotry remain a major obstacle in the way of what can become a major channel to communicate peace between Israel and its neighbors."One of the solutions to this problem is the need to increase investments in the farming sector and adopt more active agricultural policies,"AOAD said. But it omitted the simple and straightforward recommendation of collaborating with Israel, apparently following the approach of the Arab League, which prefers to starve the people it purports to protect and defend, rather than to accommodate, even symbolically, a relationship with Israel that will benefit it first of all. The Arab League economists who wrote that report know of Israel's excellence in many economic and scientific fields, and of the fact that the GNP per capita is tenfold in Israel what it is on average in Arab countries, except for the oil-rich ones. The problem is clearly psychological, and the only hope of changing minds and shifting attitudes is through audacious leaders who might emerge as a result of the expanding Abrahamic Pact.

The surge in food prices in 2008 prompted plans by the UAE, Saudi Arabia, and other arid Gulf countries to fund agricultural projects inSudan and other fertile areas in the region. But such projects are expected to take time, and they are not large enough to slash the Arab farm import bill, according to experts. The surge in food prices in 2008 was one of the main reasons for a sharp rise in inflation in the UAE and other members of the Gulf Co-operation Council (GCC) given their heavy reliance on farm products. The GCC states, which control nearly 45 percent of the world's proven oil deposits, are among the largest food importers in he world, given their poor farm potential due to their desert nature. The bulk of their food imports comes from outside the Arab region and includes the United States and other Western countries. Official figures showed that the GCC's combined farm imports exceeded $75 billion during 2005–2009. They accounted for about 41 percent of the total Arab food import value of $180 billion, although the population of the six members, which hovers around 36 million, constituted only about 10 percent of the total Arab population. Arab officials have repeatedly voiced concern about the agricultural gap and growing reliance on food imports, mainly from the United States and other Western countries. Some officials considered such reliance as a risk to their security. According to AOAD and the Kuwaiti-based Arab Fund for Economic and Social Development, another key Arab League institution, most regional nations are suffering from slackening farm exports and rapid growth in the population, leading to a steady increase in their imports of food products. The shortage persisted despite an expansion in the cultivated areas in some Arab countries as a result of reforms aimed at increasing crops. From around sixty-seven million hectares in 1999, the combined Arab cultivated area widened by nearly 4.3 percent to seventy million hectares in 2002 and continued to expand to reach around seventy-five million hectares in 2009. But the report showed that the cultivated areas remained a fraction of the total arable land in the region, estimated at nearly fifty-five million hectares. "Arab nations have sought to improve farming policies and such moves have resulted in some positive developments," AOAD said. But they have also produced negative results, including the private sector's malpractices, which have hurt the interests of the farmers. New policies are needed to regulate these activities and encourage farmers. The report urged Arab governments, to take urgent measures to encounter the food price increases in the future, cut food imports from foreign countries, and achieve self-sufficiency in most farm products. The study said that the creation of a farm fund is crucial for the success of Arab agriculture projects aimed at achieving self-sufficiency, on the grounds that most fertile countries in the region lack sufficient investments in this sector. "This should prompt Arab nations to seriously consider the creation of a large joint fund to invest in farming projects in the region," the report said. "At the same time, Arab governments should take the proposal of setting up a strategic cereal stockpile into consideration, given its significance in ensuring the food needs of citizens and curbing sharp price increases. It could be a pan-Arab stockpile or regional silos. This stockpile should be sufficient for at least one year and should help Arab countries in collective purchasing agreements that will give them a better bargaining position."

Saudi Arabia's decision to halt local wheat production and rely on imports from foreign markets is final, as the world's oil superpower struggles to preserve its dwindling water resources, according to officials. The desert kingdom, which sits atop more than a fifth of the world's proven oil wealth, had produced nearly three million tons of wheat per year to meet domestic needs but output is expected to plunge to one million tons in 2012 following the government's decision to stop subsidizing local production. In the next two years, output could dip further, and the country will become almost totally reliant on imports, mainly from the West. "The decision we took two years ago to halt local wheat output is final and clear. There is no going back," said Fahd Balghaneem, Saudi minister of agriculture and head of the Grain Silo sand Flour Mills Organization. "The country is now giving priority to water security over food security...[T]his was a cabinet decision, which also directed us to stop producing wheat locally." Balghaneem said Saudi Arabia, one of the poorest nations in water resources, imported in excess of one million tons of wheat last year, and the imports are projected to surge each year as local output is steadily declining.

**The Weakness of the State**

The second issue the Islamic world will have to address in the post-Spring era is that of instability and weakness, especially within the failed states, as suggested by Yoel Guzansky and Benedetta Berti. The authors claim that the uprisings across the Muslim world that began in December 2010 signaled an era of change in a region that desperately needed to be shaken up. However, while the heterogeneous protest movements in the various Arab states were generally of one mind in demanding the end of authoritarian rule, in most cases they failed to produce a cohesive plan for the post-revolutionary transition. Apart from the partial (and temporary) exception of Tunisia (where the spark for the uprisings was first kindled in 2010), the divisions within the protest movements, along with the absence of a functioning and developed civil society, have inhibited the process of political change which usually ended up crystallizing around the dichotomy between illegitimate moderate Muslim tyrants and no less tyrannical but "legitimized" radical Muslims. Further complicating efforts to establish a new political order has been the legitimacy deficit of existing political institutions and the resilience of networks of power and patronage. As a result, the post-revolutionary period in countries where leaders have been toppled has been replete with challenges, including the exacerbation of preexisting divisions, rendering extremely difficult the creation of strong and functioning states based upon a universally accepted social contract. They claim that in general, state weakness is not a new phenomenon in the Middle East and North Africa (MENA) region, but has been significantly exacerbated during the years of the Spring since the end of 2010. State weakness can be measured by the degree of the regime's legitimacy, its capacity to deliver social and political goods, and its ability to guarantee a basic level of security. While states that fulfill these functions are considered strong and stable, a state that is utterly unable to meet any of these criteria is perceived as "failed."[95]

The authors emphasize that "lawlessness" may come to dominate the Middle East. They point to Yemen, Libya, Iraq, and the Sinai Peninsula as examples of this "cascade of state failure", to which Syria and Lebanon might be handily added due to their ongoing domestic turbulence, and their alliance with Iran and the one under the Russian "protective shield" while the other virtually dominated by Hizbullah. There seems to be truth that in the post-revolutionary stabilization period in most Spring countries we are witnessing the exacerbation of preexisting cleavages by virtue of the deepening confrontation between Moderate and Radical Muslims (leaders and states)that weaken central authority. Already prior to the Spring events, half of the twenty-two Arab League member states were defined as weak states, varying between highly dysfunctional states like Yemen or Sudan, and weak but far from collapsing countries like Lebanon until the latter's failure in the 2020s, due to the Hizbullah tightening control. However, if taken from the definition base of Islamic Spring, and including in the sample Muslim countries[96] other than the members of the Arab League, one identifies many more, and much more deeply failed states than in the Arab

[95] Moshe Dayan Center publishes *Tel Aviv Notes*, an analytical update on current affairs in the Middle East, on the tenth and twenty-sixth of every month, as well as occasional special edition, "Instability and State Weakness":http://www.dayan.tau.ac.il. "The 'Post-Revolutionary' Challenge in the Arab World," by Yoel Guzansky and Benedetta Berti.

[96] See R. Israeli, From Arab Spring etc..., op. cit.

sample (e.g., Afghanistan, Somalia). Indeed, since the beginning of the uprisings of the 2010s, there has been a general deterioration in the level of internal stability of MENA states. For example, the new Libyan authorities have been confronting monumental difficulties in their effort to reassert control, to over-bridge the regional gaps and accumulate sufficient legitimacy following their overthrow of the Qaddafi regime. The country is indeed highly fragmented—with competing tribal loyalties having always taken precedence over a common national identity— and lacking strong central political institutions. The proliferation of centrifugal forces is a particular problem given the fact that the Libyan security sector, already weak during the Qaddafi regime, has been in a nearly total state of disarray following Qaddafi's overthrow. Although security sectors reforms are being implemented and a large-scale DDR (disarm, demobilize, reintegrate) program is claimed to exist by the two competing regional regimes, the establishment of a cohesive and well-functioning unified Libyan state seems to be a remote possibility for now. The events in Benghazi on the eleventh anniversary of the September 11 attacks, where violent eruptions of Muslim radicals against the American Consulate there produced many casualties, including the American ambassador, and their aftermath, provide an ample example of the current disarray[97].

Syria, of course, provides the most stunning example of the volatility of these regimes, as an undone state structure that was held together by an authoritarian minority regime, cannot be welded again together, and has allen prey to sectarianism and tribalism. The initial clashes between the Syrian regime and the anti-Assad opposition forces have escalated exponentially throughout the months of fighting, leaving the country in a state of full civil war. The depth of the cleavage between the pro-regime forces and the opposition groups suggests that Syria's high degree of state

---

[97] Ibid.

weakness and instability will extend even to the post-conflict stage and will postpone indefinitely the permanent settlement. For, paradoxically, while only by force was any regime able thus far to maintain the state structure together, the "democratization" efforts pitifully deployed today by Assad the son's authoritarianism can only make the debate between the factions and the ethnic groups more bitter and more acute. There is simply no platform that can be acceptable to all factions as a base for a new agreed social contract. The case of Yemen, currently ranked as the eighth most unstable and weak state in the world, is even more extreme. This challenge is especially daunting, as Yemen is also among the poorest and least-developed states in the region, with the central government lacking internal legitimacy and the capacity to deliver social and political goods and being torn by a civil war where the Iran-supported and guided Houtis have been fighting to undo Saudi prevalence. The authors provide a few other examples:

> Firstly, failing states represent a challenge to regional stability. This is especially the case because of the large involvement of external actors in the domestic affairs of weak and failing states. The weakness of the central government and the proliferation of groups competing with the state, represent an excellent opportunity for external third parties seeking to expand their influence on the region. The Lebanese civil war between 1975–1990, and more so the disarray of the 2020s, serve as a reminder of the dangers of protagonists becoming surrogates for regional and international conflicts. Concurrently, both Iraq and Yemen are increasingly looking like potential arenas for similar struggles between the different regional and global powers invested in the region. Similarly, the conflict in Syria is becoming increasingly more perennialized and insoluble.
>
> Secondly, failing states are problematic from a human security

and humanitarian perspective. Such states are often unable to provide security as well as basic social and political goods, contributing to heightened precariousness of the living conditions of the population. The recent examples of famines in both Somalia and Yemen (and Ethiopia which is only semi-Muslim) tragically highlight the human cost of prolonged internal instability and endemic state failure. Similarly, apart from the hundreds of thousands of casualties, and many millions more maimed, bereaved and displaced persons, many of them exiled to refugee camps or to seek asylum in generous Europe, the ongoing disturbances and unrest are resulting in a humanitarian crisis, the pitiful evidence of which can be seen under the tents of the camps in neighboring Jordan, Lebanon, Turkey and Iraq and even in some Greek islands in the Mediterranean.

A third danger stemming from failing states is the terrorist challenge. Failing states present international and regional terrorist organizations with a convenient base of operations, and are more likely than other states to host such groups on their soil.

Fourth is the crime challenge. Similar to terrorist organizations, criminal organizations take advantage of governments' loose control in failing states to advance their interests

A final security challenge is the increased threat of proliferation of non-conventional arms. As Syria imploded, for example, the concern that its chemical and biological (and temporarily even an aborted nuclearization) weapons may not be secured, or may be aided by Iran and/or transferred by the regime to its Hizballah ally, has heightened.

The Spring, according to the authors, has also accelerated a preexisting trend within the MENA region (if this Spring is considered Arab and not Islamic), one characterized by state weakness and instability. This widespread weakness seems to stem from a number of factors, including the ruling political institutions, and the difficulties in preventing the proliferation of local militias and alternative pockets of authority within the country's territory. But given the problems faced by Spring states, it is unlikely that some of the regime changes induced by the Spring uprisings will lead to a rapid improvement of the situation, and it is fair to expect, more than a decade later, that continued instability and state weakness, with all the regional instability (a negative one as discussed above) implied, even given that a fundamentally evil stability is no better than a temporary instability that leads to a stable situation. What's more, the longer and deeper the crisis, the greater the likelihood that other regional or international, Muslim or otherwise actors, mainly radical Muslim movements which specialize in world Jihadism, will become more involved in the various flash points by supporting one or another of the warring protagonists. Based on this analysis of these two sober and insightful authors, the prospects for seeing the Spring as a positive watershed in the fortunes of these countries do not seem extremely bright. Quite the contrary, it seems that the Muslim Moderate/Radical divide has grown wider and deeper.

**Direct Effects of the Spring surge on the Relationship with Israel**

Few people realize how, in the long run, the current upheaval in the Muslim world will affect Israel in the most direct fashion. This is connected to the fact that Israel's 20 percent Muslim population (close to two million), which has seen its two icons, nationalism and then Communism, collapsing one after the other, has growingly become so attached to the Muslim alternative that the current Muslim upheaval is its best occasion to see the wind blow in its sails and push it forward to new, though unforeseeable directions. Already that current of Muslims in Israel has been on record as undermining state authority by acting in favor of Hamas, and their head, Sheikh Ra'id Salah, has been convicted for fundraising for terrorist Islam. For example, in their fixation on blocking the Judaization of

Jerusalem, Salah and his movement have been inspiring Islamic causes of the Palestinians as echoed by Hamas. In one instance, pamphleteers wrote a 2006 piece in *Sawt al-Haq wa-l-Hurriya* (Voice of Truth and Freedom), the journal of the Islamic Movement centered in Umm al-Fahm in northern Israel and led by Ra'id Salah, where the "plan to Judaize Silwan" is discussed in great detail. The Islamic Movement, a local branch of the Muslim Brotherhood, brought to bear its standing at the forefront of Israeli Arabs who identify themselves strictly as Palestinians, with Salah leading the campaign to defend "Muslim Jerusalem" from destruction by Israel and liberate it from Israeli occupation, while the country in general, and Jerusalem in particular, had never known such an enormous development *elan* and growth of its Muslim community and its prosperity and welfare, along all its history.[98] It is because Under Muslim occupation Jewish holy places had been mistreated and the Jews banned from them that Muslims cannot believe that Israel would act differently. In fact, they are amazed by the respect and care Israel has been taking of the Muslim (and Christian) holy places back to the Mamluk period when Jerusalem got to its glorious peak under Islam. They retaliate by spreading stories and myths so as to relieve their dismay and embarrassment. For example, they have been claiming in the past two decades that Israel has been digging under the Aqsa Mosque foundations in order to demolish the entire structure, but apparently their Islamic strength and resilience on the one hand and Israel's renowned inefficacy on the other, have dismally scuttled this far their sinister scheme.

Another unfounded claim of the Muslim Movement against Israel, which is and will be further enhanced as an offshoot of the

---

[98] See Raphael Israeli, "The Islamic Movement in Israel," *Jerusalem Letter*, Jerusalem Center for Public Affairs, Oct. 15, 1999; L. Barkan, "The Islamic Movement in Israel: Switching Focus from Jerusalem to the Palestinian Cause," Inquiry & Analysis Series, report no. 628, Middle East Media Research Institute, Washington, DC, July 30, 2010.

Muslim Spring, is the alleged Israeli plot to replace the al-Aqsa Mosque with a Third Jewish Temple—despite the fact that the Israeli authorities have consistently restricted the movement of non-Muslims on the Temple Mount to the point where they have been accused of discrimination against Jews and Christians to favor Muslims. A pamphlet from the Islamic group *Jihad-Beit al-Makdas* (the Jihad for Jerusalem), that is circulated in public, uses melodramatic language to further illustrate the "evil intents of the Jews," accusing Zionists of attacking Jerusalem and Silwan—"the gateway to al-Aqsa Mosque"—and al-Aqsa Mosque itself, which is "the rock of grace of Jerusalem and the crown of the whole Islamic nation." This is a total denial of the preceding Jewish history and the science of archaeology which have proved otherwise. According to this line of thought, Silwan becomes the doorway through which the contemporary "Jewish settlers are trying to pass to Judaize Jerusalem and at the same time, enter the Temple Mount in order to dismantle al-Aqsa and rebuild the Temple". The steps that are being carried out, according to Islamic spokespersons, will lead to a third intifada (the previous two had taken place in 1987 and 2,000). As Shaul Bartal, a prominent researcher on Palestinian affairs, has often noted[99] that the Palestinian Arab assault on the Jewish connection to Jerusalem continues apace aided and is abetted not only by radical Muslims or angry Silwanites, but by fellow travelers in the media and in academia, including Israeli Jews. Consider the tours carried out by *Emek Shaveh*, an Israeli nonprofit organization, and Palestinian residents of Silwan with a view to rebuffing the "political archaeology of the Jews" and to prove the area's "true" archaeological significance. *Emek Shaveh's* founder Yonathan Mizrachi, who has voluntarily left his job at Israel's Antiquity Authority, spares no effort to downplay the Jewish biblical history of the area. As he put

[99] Bartal is a lecturer on Palestinian affairs at Bar Ilan University and author of *The Fedayeen Emerge, The Palestine-Israel Conflict, 1949–1956* (Bloomington,Authorhouse, 2011.

it: "After three hours on [an Israeli organized] tour, you are convinced that you are at a totally Jewish site where evidence of Canaanite, Byzantine, and Muslim, and, of course, Palestinian [civilizations] are pushed aside. Jerusalem has 4,000 years of history. They only focus on the marvelous stories of King Solomon, David, and Hezekiyah, of which, by the way, they haven't found any archaeological evidence that ties them to the place." Mizrachi's website contains an essay of over 5,000 words—"Archaeology in Silwan"—which transforms archaeology into a handmaiden of social science pieties and criticizes even the use of the phrase City of David as a manifestation of "settler" objectives. In doing so, he also manages to rewrite history, claiming falsely that "during the main periods of prosperity under the kingdom of Judah [ which the Muslims deny lock stock and barrel]...the cultural identity of the town and its inhabitants was contested."

Bartal concludes that

> Sadly, the battle over Silwan (and for that matter the wider Palestinian-Israeli conflict) is likely to continue as long as Palestinian Arabs and their brethren refuse to recognize that another people, the Jews, have a claim to the Land of Israel.

Nothing has given more momentum to these anti-Israeli claims than the present Islamic wave of denials which is tightly linked to the discourse of Muslim radicals and of the Palestinian authorities, exactly along the lines of total denial of the Holocaust by radical Muslims and the Palestinians, like their leader's assertion that Israel "has caused the Palestinians 50 holocausts).Hence the supreme sensitivity of Israel to such claims and its vigorous reactions to them. Sensing the fatefulness of that trend, even the non-Hamas Palestinian leaders who negotiated and signed the Oslo Accords seized upon the nineteenth anniversary of that event which was signed in

September, 1993 (September 13, 2012), which coincided with the outbreak of the Islamic Spring in Tunisia, Egypt, and Libya, to signal their desire to withdraw from the Accords. For, under the upsurge of radical Islam, which vows that the Jews will be disinherited from the land, why should they hold on to their pledged compromises? They said that the Accords, which were signed September 13, 1993, and were in fact a DOP (Declaration of Principles), not a treaty, were meant to be an interim agreement leading to a final peace agreement and an independent Palestinian state within five years. Palestinian National Initiative leader Mustafa Barghouti said that the accords turned out to be "a transition to nothing," and had been used as a cover by Israel "to consolidate a system of apartheid." "We as Palestinians need to liberate ourselves from the terrible conditions of the "agreement", through popular resistance, national unity and boycott, divestment and sanctions," Barghouti told Ma'an News Agency.[100]He charged that the Palestinian side has committed to the agreement while Israel selectively implemented the accords to its benefit, adding that nineteen years on the concept of the two-state solution was at risk due to Israeli settlement building. He just forgot to mention that Oslo was signed to commit all the Palestinians, while half the Palestinian people (Hamas) elected to reject it, and that the first clause of Oslo was to put an end to violence and to fatalities, while Israel has suffered more casualties from Palestinian terror after Oslo than before it.

Together with some Fatah leaders like Mahmoud al-Aloul, who urged the PA to abolish the Oslo Accords, the Popular Front for the Liberation of Palestine also called on the PA to disengage from all agreements with Israel, and be free of political and economic restrictions imposed by the Oslo Accords. It also urged the Ramallah government of the PA to end security coordination with Israel and implement national unity. Chief Palestinian negotiator, Sa'eb

[100] Ibid.

Erekat, blamed the international community for failing to hold Israel accountable for its "violations". "Our hope for peace and justice has been destroyed by Israeli bulldozers and a culture of racism and hatred has been espoused within Israeli society. This horrific reality has been facilitated by the immunity which Israel has been granted by the international community," he said. He just forgot to mention that the final results of negotiations could not be predetermined before negotiations begin; for the issue of the West Bank as a disputed territory was something only negotiations and compromise could settle; and that the Palestinians have signed Oslo II, which divided the West Bank into three zones (A, B, C) between the parties until a new agreement supplanted that arrangement. No new agreement is known to have emerged all those years, and therefore those existing interim agreements were rule until they were replaced by others, and Israel cannot be accused of violating them. Since the beginning of the upheaval in the West Bank in September. 2012, as the Palestinians lost faith in Oslo and in their leadership, it became evident that the Islamic Spring no longer translated as a general Islamic malaise but as a peculiarly Palestinian problem which required its own particular Palestinian solution. The rise to power of Muslim Brother Muhammad Mursi in Cairo inspired hope in the West Bank too that it could rid itself of President Abbas and Prime Minister Fayyad, and expand the rule of the Hamas from Gaza to the West Bank. Thus, the Oslo Accords, which were opposed from the outset by the Hamas, became the topic of wide demonstrations, which only due to the danger they posited to Abu Mazen's rule, they were restricted. The protesters were also angry at rising prices, and complained that the economic sections of the Oslo process had been implemented by Israel selectively and mostly to its benefit, a position shared by UN agencies and economists. Israeli Muslims, led by Rai'd Salah, threatened to follow in open rebellion against Israel as part of the Islamic Spring, so inevitable their confrontation with Israel had become.

**Is the Democratic Alternative Applicable to Islam?**

Just because the demonstrators of the Spring had been screaming "Democracy!" without understanding what it involved, and without ever experiencing what it meant, many Western media came to the conclusion that democracy was upon us, and that with the fall of the tyrants—some of whom were convinced that their system was "democratic" to start with—tyranny would come to its end. However, it turns out that those who believed that words had a specific universal meaning often find themselves frustrated when other people from different cultural backgrounds use the same words in different ways, words that carry very different significances than the ordinary Western speaker comprehends. These differences can stem from words that are innocently used to express one thing but are understood differently or, vice versa, that can be said purposefully to make others believe something that was not meant in the first place. One can shout, for example, "Peace!"(meaning cease-fire), only to gain time to reorganize his troops for fighting. Another example: when fundamentalist Muslim ideologues would refute the concept of Western democracy and explain at the same why it cannot stand in opposition to Shari'a. For some of them, the words that are synonymous with, or that approximate Western democracy are the *shura* and *Ijma'*, not anything that is reminiscent of freedom of expression and conduct, clean elections, and equality of women, human rights, tolerance toward non-Muslim minorities, and the rights of expression and assembly for all. When President Muhammad Mursi of Egypt was elected, he made some moderate statements that raised hopes that he would force other Muslim fundamentalists of his kind to bend the doctrine by opening up to non-religious people and to a democratic fashion of speech as the Muslim Party in Turkey did after it won the elections in 2002, and then again in 2006 and 2010, and into its second and third decade in power. At least when it comes to elections and recruiting a majority to their side in Parliament, the Turkish Islamic party is playing the democratic game, though it still has a long way to go in matters of freedom of expression, persecution of journalists, incitement of fanatics, dissemination of false information by the state, encouragement of terror, and expression of hatred to political rivals (Erdogan himself had sat in prison for incitement as Mayor of Istanbul).)

In Turkey, as in Egypt under Mursi, there is a part of the public favoring the application of *Shari'*a there without delay, but in both countries a trend prevails that pledges to lead their respective countries the democratic way, at least on the surface. During Erdogan's visit to Cairo after the Spring broke out, he tried to convince his hosts to follow the "Turkish model". On the other hand, the unlimited support that both countries evinced then for Hamas, which forcibly took over the rule of Gaza from the Palestinian Authority in 2007, did not indicate the prevalence of a democratic spirit among them. In the meantime, Mursi was toppled by General Sisi, and Erdogan himself, in search of retaining the West's favor has been trying to rehabilitate his links with Israel and with Sisi's Egypt. What is the Turkish model? Are there models in democracy? When we speak about democracy, we have in mind the models developed over the years in liberal countries of the West, where democracy does not need any qualification, much as its ideal form had been developed by Giuselmo Ferrero back in the 1940s and became a classic model since. That concept of democracy leaves a vast gulf between itself and what Islam conceptualizes as democracy. That difference is expressed also in different words, but even when the same words are used they mean different things. Thus, every time we hear the words that are familiar to us, we must inquire what exactly they mean in their cultural context. Both sides of the aisle resort to that same formula: "democracy", although they do not mean exactly the same thing, out of a belief that since that Western word is positive, respectable, and has become an object of universal emulation, better stick to it than invoke some other terminology that would arouse suspicion and require definition. Democracy, everyone knows, will always be associated with positive thinking, with liberal politics, with human rights in mind. Therefore, in the eyes of many uninitiated Western people, anyone who proclaims democracy must be credited with good intentions and cannot be accused of any wrongdoing, much as Muslim radicals in Europe and America declare in their demonstrations that they hate democracy.

We have all learned from lived experience, that any novice in Islamic politics and any demonstrator in the Spring has learned very quickly that screaming that word in the street immediately draws sympathy from the West. Few are the Westerners who would care to inquire any deeper into what is meant by that—whether the people who proclaim the word understand what it means, whether they had ever seen it, experienced it, or have just heard about it. What we hear about "Islamic democracy" indeed varies widely from the democracy we know, both on the conceptual as well as the functional levels. Simply defined, democracy means the rule of the people by the people. But who is "the people"? What is rule? How do we connect between people and its rule? In the West, our need to define these terms stems from the necessity to determine the sovereign, who is also the source of legitimacy, the wellspring and fountainhead from which legislation flows. The idea is that since the entire people cannot themselves legislate, as had been the case in the ancient Greek polis, they must elect their representatives, whom they entrust with the mandate, over a set period of time, to make the laws of the country. At the end of that mandate, the power of decision returns to the sovereign—the people—in order for it to determine the sort of laws and the kind of administration that would administer it for the next term. This mechanism is founded either on an unwritten social pact, or on a written constitution, or a basic law, where the people, the authority, the source of legitimacy, and the way to express it are spelled out. When the elected representatives and officials do not fulfill their mandate, they are removed and others replace them according to the will of the sovereign. This is a matter of course that we have become accustomed to in liberal democracies, while Islamic countries have never heard of such arrangements. There were rosy and bombastic constitutions, like those of the Soviet Bloc and of Saddam and of modern Egypt in their time, but what happened in reality had nothing to do with them. The constitutions are customarily ignored there, until the next ruler comes about and imposes his new rules, takes over power, and determines the law, and no one can move him out of office because his term is limitless, and he draws legitimacy from his illegitimacy. Nonetheless, Assad the father and Mubarak, like the dictators of Sudan and Libya, Algeria, and Yemen, were convinced that their system was democratic.

The masses of demonstrators in all countries of the Spring were incensed that the issue of legitimacy did not much concern their leaders of twenty, thirty, or forty years, leaders who were not elected by anyone in the first place, and then automatically succeeded themselves without asking anyone's opinion or permission. It seemed a natural process to the leaders that they should be rulers in perpetuity, that they were not held accountable to anyone for anything, and that they ruled by the legitimacy of their force rather than by the force of legitimacy, which they did not have. Until the outburst of the Spring, their publics too were made to believe that proper "elections" had been held in their countries, that the presidents were "reelected" once and again, by the public or by the parliament, and that their rubber-stamp parliaments were not representatives of the people but agents of the tyrants. And suddenly their minds opened up, by force of the open media that transmitted proper elections in other places, where governments alternated, where prime ministers and presidents were sanctioned, dismissed, and even incarcerated for wrongdoing—something never heard of in those countries. The crowds wanted the corrupt leaders just to go so (the urge *Irhal*!! – Quit !! was on every lip) that something new should start, but they knew not whom and what to install instead. And when the dictators refused to go, they were fought with weapons, and as the fighting escalated, the stakes of the revolution went higher; and the heavier the sacrifices of the rebels, the more pressing and insistent their demands; and the larger the gamut of foreign powers who were brought into the conflict, the more clearly they took sides with the tyrants or with the rebellious elements who were pitted against them. The leaders, who did not understand at first what the rebellions were all about took those outbursts of violence personally, and either tried to quell them, or ran for their lives, or offered reforms too little and too late, or continued to fight to the bitter end. One can then conclude that the main reason for the bitterness that accumulated in the Arab street and caused the explosion of the Spring was due not only to the chronic problems of poverty, illiteracy, disease, unemployment, hopelessness, corruption, and disparity between the haves and have-nots, but also mainly to their despair as, instead of seeing their leaders legitimately elected to sort out their problems and to be accountable for their solution, they were faced with immutable dictators who ruled for life and did not have to account for any misdeed or mismanagement.

That was the reason why in all those uprisings, the most strident call of the demonstrators was against their rulers to go. For in almost the entire Islamic world, no one had elected the rulers who were either monarchs who needed not to be elected, and who regarded their countries as their own property, or military juntas who took over power and hold it by force, or ideologues of tyrannical rule like Arab Socialism or the Ba'ath, or maniacs like Qaddafi and Saddam, whose only ambition in life was to rule and to count their subjects as dust. Never were there any social contracts developed between rulers and ruled, and rulers persisted in their rule as long as their military might sustained them or outside powers supported them. The young people of the Islamic Spring countries, and certainly their elders, had watched twenty years earlier the Eastern European regimes collapse, live on television, and power transferred to elected systems, and they began to ask themselves, "why not us / ours?" And when the Internet allowed the young people to cover the gaps in time and space, as the spark that was kindled in Tunisia started to spread, the snowball effect began, rolling from one country to another until the fire caught everywhere in the Islamic world. As the hurdle of fear was removed, simultaneously with the rapid passage of the rebellion from one country to the next, one tyrant followed another into oblivion. It is always easier and faster to destroy the existing structure than to erect a new one. No wonder then that only in two of those countries, Tunisia and Egypt, is was any semblance of a permanent settlement, which held for only one year in Cairo before the military took over, and a return to chaos in Tunis, where regime instability is still plaguing that most Westernized country. But institutional and personal issues need to still be sorted out there and new modalities of rule explored and refreshed, so as to depart from the old tyrannical patterns and rework the relationships between the military and the civil, and the fate of the old regime is to be decided. For example, the military brass, which had a say in politics, as used to be the case in Turkey and Egypt and still in Pakistan, will have to be sent to the barracks, since they cannot possibly aspire to any sort of working democracy. The problem is that some of the competing new regimes of the Muslim fundamentalist sort posit a challenge to the Western concept of democracy by claiming, for example, that sovereignty belongs only to Allah, and that to pretend that someone else can possess sovereignty or share in it with divinity amounts to heresy, for all creation is the feat of the Creator, and to attribute to someone else sovereignty or part of it is also blasphemy. Any Islamic ideologue or thinker can try to circumvent this delicate issue by arguing that people, as part of creation, can participate in divine acts such as sovereignty, and go into hair-split arguments on how people can become the source of legitimacy for power. This was done by the new short-lived president Mursi of Egypt, a Muslim Brotherhood adept, who assured his Egyptian audience that he was founding a civil government, not a religious one. But it is doubtful whether any serious Muslim scholar could risk his reputation by letting any human being cross the red line of divine sovereignty over Muslim lands that is imposed by Shari'a Law.

The crucial significance of these definitions is their reverberation over the vital issue of legislation. If sovereignty belongs to Allah, and He had already dispensed to humanity the most perfect of codes of law, as incorporated in the Qur'an and the Sunna, then who would dare to try to improve on it without provoking a blasphemy? If not, would parliaments be needed to legislate laws? Defining divine law as final and unalterable means recognizing that legislation has disappeared from the human world and that all matters of this universe must be arbitrated not by legislators but by jurists who understand and can interpret the laws of Allah. Moreover, while humans legislate over years piecemeal, and then alter, amend, abrogate, and change laws according to their needs, and therefore constantly resort to their legislative bodies, Islam had accomplished that process since the times of the Prophet, and the entire body of Shari'a was dispensed to humanity in one stroke, or at most, by the tenth century A.D., when the gates of *Ijtihad* were closed. All that needs to be done, Islam says, is to study and comprehend the will and intentions of the Creator and his Messenger, and the interpretive power of the founders of the Four Schools of Law. And who better to do that than the jurists of the Holy Law? In Sunnite Islam, the ulema are only required to counsel the ruler, but in Shi'ite Islam as interpreted by Khomeini, they should be the rulers or the supreme guides to the rulers. The presumption to improve upon divine legislation by ameliorating it through parliamentary committees appears in this light (or, rather, obscurity) as an affront to Allah, and therefore it is ruled out of the question. On the functional level also, Western democracy challenges the Arab/Islamic practice in at least three aspects: the smooth transfer of government from one leader who lost legitimacy to a newly legitimized one; the ultimate focus of power; and the place of the opposition in the system. It is characteristic in Western democracy for those who lost legitimacy in free elections to admit their defeat, congratulate the inevitable winners, and transfer power in a gracious and peaceful way, bowing to the rules of democracy. After that, they can ponder the reasons for their defeat and pledge to try again next time around. All these gestures are admission and recognition that such are the rules of the game that are accepted without question. And if the results of the elections remain nebulous, such as razor-thin margins that can be interpreted one way or the other, then a court of law or the central elections committee, which is usually headed by a judge, are invited to decide, and if all that remains divisive and in doubt, then new elections are called for.

Nothing of all these smooth and civilized habits was recognized in the Arab/Islamic world prior to the Spring nor are they practiced almost anywhere subsequent to it. As the leader was replaced only after he died or was murdered, then of course no one was there to help usher in the new ruler or to transfer the affairs of the state smoothly to him. It seemed significant for a while that in Egypt, Libya, and Tunisia new parliaments were freely elected, the first time in many decades or ever, and they appeared on their way to attaining constitutional legitimacy and to usher in new democratic rules and habits. But the interference of the military and the ideological discrepancies, between moderate Muslims and their radical opponents, have shuffled the cards, some of their practices evoking the old practices of the new ruler who after performing his coup took over the broadcasting stations, the first tool of control of the crowds, in order to announce the change of rule and the execution of the previous ruler, both of whom were branded as "illegitimate", but that was considered the normal course of things.

And immediately upon the arrival of the new ruler, he would announce a new "constitution"—as if old or new had any effect—full of promising plans and rosy visions, but without any built-in guarantees except for pledges from the dictator that some of them might be fulfilled. The only assurance was that the next dictator would bring another "constitution" when his e time came. Against this background one could look with respect and awe upon the process of transition in Egypt, Tunisia, and possibly also Libya, at the outset of the Spring, until the military coups and chaotic politics reverted to the old games which won over the legitimate election campaigns that were launched with many candidates participating, and the winners were declared by seemingly independent elections commissions, to the applause of large crowds who campaigned for one candidate or the other and went to the polls to determine the results. True, this process was watched over by the military, the only remaining organized force in the country in the midst of this chaos, but this was probably inevitable as part of the transition. But after the orderly transition of power with the former office holder amicably shaking hands with the newly elected, even when not much love was lost between them, and we did see the newcomers welcomed, which was an immense innovation. We had been accustomed to seeing parliaments, presidents, and governments "elected" in most of these countries, but the ultimate power was always in the hands of the dictator, be he a monarch or a military tyrant or a religious or political figure or a prince who holds power. Those "elections", whose results were preprogrammed, were always held for a show of participatory democracy, but their rules are at variance from what is known in the West, and more like the one-party regimes of the Soviet Bloc, where the list of candidates was decided by the single party and no one else could run against them. In personal elections, like for the president and the mayors, the party announced the lone candidate, who was sure to be elected and reelected, so as to preclude divisions and rifts within the ruling elite, and to advance a sole and agreed-upon candidate for the position, as befits the dictatorship of the proletariat, except that those elites had forgotten long before what being a member of the working class meant. But the supreme position remained vested in one persona: the secretary of the party, the president, the head of the military commission, the chairman of the revolutionary council, and he like, all intended to point constantly to the supreme location where decisions are made. While in the West the elected representatives vote confidence in the government, and the head of state often commands the army and can dissolve the parliament under certain stipulations, it was the pre-Spring omnipotent dictator in the Islamic world who possessed the undivided authority to do it all: to act as the supreme commander of the forces, to suspend the parliament at will, to decide upon war and peace, to manage domestic and foreign affairs, while the parliament could only formally rubber-stamp what was decided by the leader, not debate him or try to impose control on the executive by which were conducted parliament.

In Iran, above the elected president and parliament there is a spiritual leader who can override them all. In those regimes, Egypt for example, the military always stood int he background as part of the power game in the country, since not only did it guarantee continuity of the regime but also took part in the economic and social life of the country. The first slice of the national budget was always assigned to the army, and the commanders of the army always held the controls of power, industry, and many economic sectors, including bread manufacturing and marketing, arms and ammunition factories, restaurants, clubs and entertainment centers for officers, and everything needed for the army to serve loyally the regime that provided all those amenities. The key to stability of the regime was always the tyrant who, as long as he was credible and long lasting, the army supported him, because in his longevity lay the continued prerogatives of the army. But when question marks began to be appended to his policy, conduct, determination to stay in power, or the support he elicited domestically and externally, the army would always be the first to sense in what direction the winds blew. In Tunisia, from the beginning the army aligned with the rebels; therefore it preserved its position as the guardian of the people in time of crisis. In Syria, on the contrary, since it was/is a communal army, whose command was founded basically on the Alawite sect in partnership with other minorities like the Druze and Christians, the army got its fate linked to the regime, and was bound to fall with it. In other intermediate situations like in Yemen and Libya, the army supported the tyrant as long as it could, and deserted when the ruler stood no more chance to succeed. In all instances, the national army was called upon by the rebels to defend the boundaries of the country, that is, to refrain from interfering in domestic affairs, where they remained the only power able to decide the fate of the revolution. In Turkey, where the army took over on four occasions—from its position of strength as the curator of Ataturk's heritage, and most recently it dismissed the elected government of Necmettin Erbakan in 1998 and outlawed his Islamic party by reason of its far-reaching rapprochement with Iran—a turnaround came about when Tayyip Erdogan's party took over power in 2002. That was the inauguration of the Islamic Spring in Ankara, which has become a general model to be followed by other Muslim countries and an example to be marketed by Turkey, with Western encouragement. Slowly, cautiously, lest he fall victim to the army like his mentor Erbakan who preceded him, but with farsighted vision and firm determination to see his quiet revolution succeed, he started appointing his people to the top echelons of the military—army, navy, and air force. Then he sent to retirement many others, arrested others for conspiring against the elected government, and effected a total change that sent the military back to their barracks and neutralized their capacity to seize power. Erdogan could do that only after he won a landslide in successive elections, which made him and his party so popular that the army could not move against him without provoking popular resentment. Europe and the United States certainly could not censure Erdogan for that measure, since they too considered putting an end to military meddling in government affairs as a sure sign of the democratization that Turkey was required to adopt on its way to candidacy for the EU. For Erdogan it was a totally different strategy that he was pursuing, in order to achieve Islamization, not democratization of his country, exploiting the usual European and American *naivete*(see below) to execute his plans.

The third yardstick for comparing Western democracy to the Islamic style of rule is the status and position of the opposition. In democracies, opposition is the next government, inasmuch as it forms a shadow government that hunts down the incumbent government, pursues it, and criticizes every step of its doings; its views are heard, and its head has an official standing. Opposition in this view is not made of enemies but of apprentices of statecraft who stand ready to replace the government when it fails. In other words, there is an expectation that a failing government would not last and others would inherit that power legitimately after they had learned from the mistakes of their predecessors. In the pre-Spring Islamic countries, this thinking was considered heresy, for the government's success was measured by its ability to overwhelm its rivals and subjugate them. Conversely, the opposition, which was viewed as the negative element that seeks to divide the people and incite them against their government, would by definition be the enemy who tries to scuttle all measures adopted by the government in order to replace it. Thus, opposition is nothing better than an opponent that one would be better off eliminating. The result was that while the Western opposition sits in parliament and its presence is respectably acknowledged, in the Islamic world it was either liquidated or sent to prison. There, it not only could not constitute an alternative government, but since it posed a danger to the ruler and his gang, measures had to be taken against it to protect the public from the enemy within the walls. Only time will tell whether Egypt, Tunisia,

Libya, and the rest are able to build vital and aggressive oppositions to act in the face of mounting Islamic regimes. If they do, there is hope that the foundations of democracy can be erected and strengthened, and strong oppositions would act without running the risk of retaliation. But if they fail, the entire democratic experiment will have to be questioned. All experiments of democratization will not necessarily follow the Western model but rather are likely to maintain authoritarianism of some sort, as in Turkey, even when other ornamental trappings of democracy are adopted. Because during the chaotic situation of the Spring only a strong-handed government can restore law and order and calm the moods after upheaval, the question being what sort of democracy will be installed, if any at all will be pursued. There is also the Iraqi model, where reasonably fair elections were held, but due to the direct Iranian involvement in the country, it is uncertain whether it will succeed to impose its own type of regime, or will be so violently opposed by the Sunni minority which had rules under Saddam, that it would settle for the present condition, where public and personal security are far from restored, and the Sunni portion of the population is not satisfied with the new dominance of the Shi'ites, who were previously downtrodden under Saddam. Similarly, the oil riches of the country have not yet been brought to bear in view of the electricity cuts, and the political arena is not yet serene in the struggle between the autonomy that the Kurds yearn for and the strong federal tendencies that have led the country so far. And then there is the Turkish model, which though more prosperous and modernized has also been plagued with the question ofthe Kurds, the Islamization that is resented by the bourgeois urbanites, and other problems of domestic and external affairs. And finally there is the Islamic model, where the Muslim Brothers champion a clear ideology of a Shari'a state, but their ability to enforce it in its totality remains slow and very uncertain.

# Summary

## *The Tectonic Shift*

Paradoxically, the more Jew- and Israel-related hatred has deepened among radical Muslims in recent years, both within Muslim states and world Islamic movements, the closer to Israel and the West were moderate Muslim states and liberal individuals drawn to the accommodation which produced the repentance and accommodation between the parties that we have witnessed with the Abrahamic Pacts of the 2020s. The universal negative consensus between Arab and Muslim countries, that are members of either the Arab League (22 countries) or the OIC (57 states) which intolerably denigrated Western culture and hated Israel and its heritage, emanated from the persistent Islamic belief that their creed is and will be the creed of the future, since Western civilization is exhausted and Islam is called upon to take its place in the world. Bernard Lewis has made the point that, unlike other civilizations which are essentially regional, Islam and Christianity have, by their very pattern of expansion, become universal, and exclusive in the sense that not only do they consider themselves the "fortunate recipients of God's final revelation to mankind, and therefore it is their duty to bring it to the rest of humanity," but that the clash between them becomes inevitable.[101]

[101] Bernard Lewis, "How did the Infidels Win?," *National Post*, June 1, 2002.

However, while Western culture has generally forsaken the use of violence to spread its message (unless it feels directly threatened), and pursues it by ways that the Muslims regard as devious (mission, the pop culture of jeans, fast food, pop music and coca-cola, television, cinema, alcohol, etc.), militant Islam and its supporters do not shun violence, as the Islamikaze phenomenon has been dramatically evincing. In other words, the humanistic idea of tolerance of the other in western culture, which has come to mean that the other is accepted as is, without value-judging him, has become predominant, and has paved the way to the free market of ideas that prevails in the West today. That thinking has not only permitted the renouncing of force, at least in principle, to spread Christianity, democracy, free trade, and other Western ideas, but has also allowed for Islam and other creeds to compete on its turf, without ever suspecting that the competition would ultimately become over the turf itself. Moreover, since the West accepted the idea of separating the Church from the modern secular state, the faith has become the domain of the individual while the public square was made impervious to it. In the Islamic world, practically all the "secular" governments, which for the most part lack legitimacy, must pay lip service to Muslim militants, at times by even including them in their governments. Even so, the militants appear as the most popular claimants of power, and if allowed to operate as political parties, like in Lebanon and Palestine, can often show their mettle and gain access to government. Therefore, no Muslim turf can be made neutral towards other faiths, and the frequent use of violence against them goes a long way to prove that, day in day out. To this day, while Islam can build its houses of prayer anywhere in the world, other faiths are prevented from doing so in some Muslim territory. And while tens of thousands of Europeans have freely converted into Islam, any Muslim who would entertain a thought to convert is considered a heretic or apostate and dealt with accordingly by capital punishment. Furthermore, Muslim radicals regard the defeat of their own illegitimate governments at home as a prelude to their restoration of the universal Caliphate of all Muslims, and therefore treat the Western governments who protect, aid, and sponsor the dictators in place as the direct enemy of the Muslims. From their point of view, then, not only is Western culture despicable in its own "right" and faulty due to its own deficiencies, but it invaded their turf in order to subvert it and undermine it from within, until it falls off like a ripe fig. It is the West that came to them, not they to it. This creates a paradox nevertheless, for while Muslim militants decry the Western cultural invasion, which is "worse" in their eyes than the physical invasions of the medieval Crusades, they and their less militant coreligionists at the same time crowd the queues in front of American, Australian, and European Embassies and Consulates across the world, to gain visas of entry into those bastions of Western values that they love to hate. Some explain their quest as a simple will to study in the West, especially value-free technical professions, which are not "soiled" by Western thinking, ignoring the fact that Western learning and protracted sojourns in the West by necessity will have an impact on them, to the point that they would at the end elect to stay and become Western; others, wish from the start to improve their economic lot by immigrating to the West, but once they get there they congregate around their kin and constitute fertile grounds for Muslim *da'wa* (Call, Mission); still others, the likes of Sheikhs Bakri and al-Masri in Britain in previous decades, who have declared their intention to alter the West rather than adapt to it, have migrated to the West as "refugees," because there was no other place left as a safe haven for them in their countries of origin, and the West was generous enough to accommodate them, ultimately to its own detriment.

Paradoxically, it is the adherents of the latter category who place themselves at the forefront of Muslim radicalism in the West and who, benefiting from the hospitality and social welfare arrangements in their host-countries, recruit local converts or already naturalized Muslims for training abroad, for indoctrination at home and for activities in the Path of Allah. It is they who were tolerated by societies against whom they are operating ideologically, who are the least tolerant towards their hosts. Their objective is loud and clear: to Islamize their host societies and let Islam take them over. If until now, under the decisive impact of the integrationists, namely Muslims who wished to assimilate into society, fit into its political, economic and social institutions and become part of it culturally if not religiously, the penetration of Muslim radicalism into the West has begun to change these trends around. More and more Muslims "rebel" against their host cultures and demand, as full-fledged citizens, that their original culture be recognized as a component of the national make up; that state symbols (for example the cross in Scandinavian national flags) be altered to become inclusive of them, and that mosques, foreign Muslim languages, and Muslim education should be subsidized by the state, thus changing the social and political make-up of their host countries. All this emanates not only from the absolute conviction of the Muslims that Allah's message to them, being the most recent is also the most "updated" as it were, but also that their way to Allah is the only valid one.

In contrast to Christianity, the other universal monotheistic religion that claims the same, however, the Muslims did not preclude force to enforce their beliefs and to "save the Infidels from themselves," by their own volition if possible, and by violence if necessary. Therefore, when they speak of "tolerance" they mean some sort of temporary measure of accommodation towards the Infidel, who has clearly been born into an inferior creed, until Islam is strong enough to prevail. The miscalculation of al-Qa'ida on September 11, and before and after that of the Hizbullah, the Hamas, and the Islamic Jihad, was that they thought Western societies, including Israel, were so ripe for their demise that a shocking trauma, or a series of smaller but frequent and consistently growing blows, would in the end overwhelm the enemy. Thus, every time the enemy responds forcefully, or in more unconventional ways than expected by Muslims, like the Americans in Afghanistan or the Israelis in the West Bank or Lebanon, or Gaza, they cry "Foul game!!" This is not how the enemies of Islam are supposed to behave, their very resistance to their subjugation by Islam is regarded as "blasphemous" for its failure to recognize the will of Allah, and their retaliatory strikes against Islam are seen as "signs of distress and despair" which augur their approaching end; hence the stepped-up activities by Muslims to speed that process up, and bring it to its conclusion, and so on and so forth. That point of view does not recognize the right of the attacked "for the sake of Allah" to self-defense. The Muslims can, and indeed are called upon, to expand, conquer, kill, enslave, dominate and rule, for the entire universe is theirs to be included in *Dar-al-Islam*, but woe to those who resist that "noble" process that is entrenched in the Will of Allah, and if they do, they are decried as "aggressors," "killers of civilians and children," "arrogant," and a perpetrators of "massacres. Thus, any hideous attack upon Western enemies, even when it involves innocent lives, as in the Twin Tower case, is "inevitable", "blessed", "well deserved," a "great success," and causes masses to jubilate and writers to sing its praise throughout the Muslim world, while every retaliation is lamented, condemned, and blasted as "unjustified," "out of proportion," "cruel," "wanton massacre," and "proof," if proof was needed, of the enemy's inherent evil. The idea of fair play, of attack and counter-attack, and in consequence of casualties inflicted on both parties to a conflict, is misunderstood in Muslim circles. Even the issue of aggressive and defensive warfare is foreign to them, because the Muslim definitions of warfare do not follow the accepted objective norms prevailing in the West, but strictly abide by the subjective rules drawn by Muslim jurists who have formulated Muslim political theory and international relations[102]. According to these rules, any attack by non-

[102] For the most comprehensive and authoritative study to date, see Majid Khadduri, *War and Peace in Islam.* Johns Hopkins, 1969.

Muslims on Muslims is inherently illegal and immoral, and therefore it is incumbent upon all Muslims to assist their co-religionists, regardless of what they did to provoke the attack. Conversely, any Muslim attack on the West, for example, since it can be justified as a "defensive war" against the heretical West, or as an act of self-defense against the spiritual invasion of the West, or as a battle to repulse the enemy from *Dar-al-Islam* (for example Palestine, Andalusia, Kashmir, and Southern France), is *eo ipso* a just war that all Muslims are called upon to sustain. In other words, once a war against the enemy had been entitled "Jihad," and any of the latter examples justifies a Jihad, the arena is wide open for war. Guerilla warfare, or Islamikaze terrorism and the like, which are the tools of the asymmetrical wars, are means of warfare that are hallowed in Islam, with all the attending ideological and doctrinal elaborations attached thereto.

The West has no standing in these definitions and what it says or thinks does not matter, because the Islamic position is Allah-inspired and *Shari'a*-dictated, which means that it is beyond discussion, compromise, debate or concession. Therefore, while external wars in the West are considered quantitative issues (over territories, interests, assets), and when they are terminated, then compromise, concessions and negotiations are led until an agreement emerges; and when it does, it is binding on the parties who signed the treaty, cease-fire, or convention; in Islam the wars are qualitative (over ideas, doctrines, "justice," "redress of wrongs", "retrieval of rights", "Allah's *Jihad*" etc), are never terminated until the victory of Islam and the imposition of its rule is brought about. And when an "agreement" is signed under duress (like after a military defeat), it always derives from the precedent of Hudaybiya that was established by the Prophet, namely that the agreement is temporary (*hudna*=armistice), and it is to be violated at the first opportunity, when Muslims feel they have regained superiority, or have found new ways of warfare that the enemy is unable to counter (like the Islamikaze). *Sulh* (peace-cum-reconciliation) can be concluded only under the terms of a *Pax Islamica*, when the non-Muslim has accepted the hegemony of Islam and submitted to its rule[103]. This is the reason why Muslim authorities in Egypt and Saudi Arabia justified the Camp David Accords of 1977, as well as the Oslo Accords of 1993, in terms of a temporary Hudaybiyya-like truce, which is open-ended and reversible, if and when the circumstances so allow. Like the Prophet's precedent, these "agreements" were only necessary in order to extort concessions from the enemy, but once they are made and cashed, they no longer necessarily bind. "Islamic interest" is then the key concept in that culture which does not include respect for the Roman law of contract, and the international treaties and conventions which derive from there. This was exemplified once again during and after the asymmetrical rules of Lebanon and Gaza which were initiated and led by Muslim militants. This worldview, where rules of war and peace do not apply equally on the belligerents, and clearly benefit the Muslims while they are expected to obligate only the non-Muslims, is the very reason why the Muslims see themselves free to violate their "agreements," while they constantly accuse their adversaries of "violating all agreements and commitments," at a time when they themselves faced no reproach because they had never expected to live up to their "commitments" in the first place, while their adversaries, who were truly obliged by them, were expected to keep them to the letter.

Thus, when the Palestinians, for example, committed themselves in Oslo (another Hudaybiyya, in the words of Arafat), without reserve or qualification, to end terrorism and violence in general, not to introduce to their territory any category of un-allowed weapons, to maintain their armed force at agreed levels and under one command, to put an end to incitement against Israel and the Jews,

---

[103] See Moshe Sharon, "*Hudna* and *Sulh* in Islam" (Hebrew), *Nativ,* Summer 2002.

to arrest terrorists and pursue them in justice or extradite them, as a prerequisite to receiving more territory from Israel and advancing into the peace-process, they remembered only the Israeli part of the agreement, and when not fulfilled they heaped all the blame on Israel, while their consistent violations of their main commitments did not matter. They became accustomed by the Rabin Government to the fact that they could break their commitments, but that Israel, for fear of arresting the "peace process," would swallow all violations and proceed with its one-sided concessions, and so it was. But when a new Israeli government came in, which made further Israeli concessions in accordance with the peace accords contingent upon Palestinian parallel implementation, they cried "Foul game!" once again, and that brought the process to a dead end. Intolerance based on a concept of superiority, whereby the superior does not have to conform like the inferior, is apparent also in the daily conduct in the Muslim world towards other religions. Rampant are the instances where Christian churches are burned down in Egypt, Nigeria and Indonesia, and synagogues are attacked and destroyed by Palestinians (notably the Joseph Tomb in Nablus and the Jewish Synagogue in Jericho during the Intifadah), and by Muslims throughout the Western world since the outbreak of the second Palestinian insurgency in late 2000, but rare are the occasions where Muslim mosques are attacked by anyone anywhere. The Muslims do not take this, and the fact that they can build their mosques anywhere in the West, as an indication of Western tolerance and acceptance of the other, but as a sure sign that no one dares to resist Islamic expansion while they, in their countries of origin, can curtail or totally prevent the construction of any Christian, let alone Jewish, houses of prayer. Muslims can be the inhabitants of any country in the world, including the Christian world and Israel on whose doors they knock for immigration or "right of return," but they would not, by law, allow any Jew into Saudi Arabia or Jordan. What is more, they still dub the countries to which they wish to immigrate as "racist" for not completely surrendering to their will, while Jews and Christians are severely restricted in various areas of the Muslim world. That suggests to them, once again, that while the whole universe is their domain as of right, other faiths are not, by their very nature, entitled to the same rights in the lands of Islam.No country in the West witnesses its citizens following the shameful scenes, current in the Muslim world, where American and Israeli flags, and the effigies of their leaders, are burned ritually as a matter of routine, save when Muslim communities in the West practice that same ritual. But no sustained burning of Arab or Muslim flags or effigies is known as a phenomenon in the West or in Israel. Once again, the inability of the Muslim world to accept as their equals the national symbols of others is striking, at a time when the West respects theirs as a matter of course, and when it does not Muslim violence ensues as it happened with the Cartoon affair of early 2006. This, far from awakening the consciousness of the Muslims to their own intolerance, in contrast with the publicly advertised and exhibited Western tolerance towards them, on the contrary has confirmed them in their belief in the hegemony of their faith and symbols that no one dares to challenge, at a time when they openly defy, with impunity, other creeds and symbols. This has encouraged the Muslim communities in the West and in Israel to demand the right to construct their mosques, or to perform their Friday rituals, in places known as holy sites to other faiths. On Temple Mount in Jerusalem they built their mosques on a site that they knew was the holiest for the Jewish creed, they transformed many churches and synagogues into mosques during their conquests and expansion, and turned every occupied land into a *waqf* (Holy Endowment) that cannot revert to non-Muslims[104].But woe to anyone who dares to turn a mosque into another house of

[104] See repeated references to this in the Charter of the Hamas, See R. Israeli, *Islam and Israel*, University Press of America, ch. 7, pp. 123-170.

prayer, or to occupy land that is or was Muslim, for that is intolerable. More recently, new challenges rose when Muslims began to illegally construct a mosque on the grounds and in defiance of, the Basilica of the Annunciation in Nazareth, to squat for the Friday prayers near the main cathedral of Florence, and to deny any historical rights to the Jews over Temple Mount, thereby declaring to Christianity and to Judaism, in Lewis' memorable words: "Your time has passed. Now we are here. Move over."[105]This is not exactly tolerance.

Incidentally, and significantly, the verse from the Qur'an that Bernard Lewis mentioned in connection with the inscription in the Dome of the Rock, to wit: "He is God, He is One. He does not beget, He is not begotten," which was meant to reject the basic dogma of Christianity about God and His Son, when the Muslims took over Jerusalem in the seventh Century, was also inscribed on the temporary tent-mosque in front of the Annunciation that awaited the building of the permanent mosque, obviously with the same intention and meaning. Coupled with the denial of Jewish rights on Temple Mount, this signifies, in the eyes of the Muslims, that they intend to indeed supersede both Judaism and Christianity, as Islam had taught them of old; hence, the hatred of the Muslims to the construct "Judeo-Christian tradition," which they regard as a passing episode in history, once the Seal of the Prophets, Muhammad, had dispensed to humanity the latest divine message that is Islam. "Your time has passed. Now we are here" is not only the statement of a factual chronological sequence, but also a declaration of mastery, dominance, hegemony, and exclusivity, backed by the will and the power to make it happen in the real world. For, a creed that was designed by Allah to replace all others and to bring all humanity under its aegis, cannot be expected to tolerate other faiths, let alone competitors for the same world constituency on the

[105] See Bernard Lewis, op. cit.

same site.

In stark contradiction to the dreams of world dominion that they entertain, radical Muslims tend at the same time to regard themselves as eternal victims of the West that they hate and want to displace, but whose help they need and implore; and they rationalize this contradiction by the plots and conspiracies constantly woven around and against them, as if the West had no other concerns than them, or could not do very well without their lachrymose complaints. First and foremost for them is the need to explain to themselves and to the world why and how they, who had pioneered civilization and sciences in medieval times, and had caused Europe to tremble and fear their successive mighty empires, found themselves, without preparation, warning, or transition at the bottom of the civilisatory heap and of the hierarchy of world powers when the modern era dawned. For a shame society like theirs, it is difficult, nay impossible, to take responsibility for their deeds and to devise a policy of adaptation that could help them pull out of the quagmire, for that would amount to admitting the deficiencies of their culture, the stifling restrictions of their faith, the pipe-dreams of their leaders, and the insufficiencies of their social systems. Thus, rather than admit their inabilities and seek succor elsewhere, it is easier to project their own ill-will on others, masquerade their jealousies and bigotry as "revivalism" and accuse the all-powerful West, the colonizer and imperialist of yesteryear, of all their ills, including their demise, suffering, backwardness, population explosion, dictatorial rule, corruption, and what not. They do not want to recall that when they were the powerful, the conquerors, the colonizers and the imperialists, they did not stop one moment to ask themselves what they were doing to their conquered peoples and civilizations that they gradually decimated.

Arabs and Muslims have resources, human and mineral, a great tradition of learning and a vast ambition to restore themselves to where they were before they began slipping in the modern era. But their self-inflicted deficiencies in government, economics, and antiquated social structures do not permit them to take off. Perhaps most stifling of all is the array of dictatorships of all sorts, monarchical and republican, one-party and military juntas, rulers who were never elected and self-imposed Presidents for-life. Illegitimate rule spawns corruption, helplessness, and hopelessness, and the near non-existence of civil society and non-governmental organizations and voluntary associations with the necessary clout to fill in when the government is deficient, make change difficult and nearly impossible. Uncontrollable poverty and population explosion are hardly the requisite processes to arrest these trends. When allowed to operate, Islamists often step in to fill the gap, but they are closely monitored or harnessed to the regime's goals, and therefore their operations are often circumscribed and cause them to become part of the problem instead of the solution. In this state of affairs, where the Western world, and Israel at their doorstep, advance and increase the gulf between themselves and the poor Muslim world, an eye-poking gap is observed on television screens and in neighboring Israel daily, which prompts people to find refuge in self-victimization: it is not their fault, it is the fault of others. This state of mind is aided in those societies by the dependence of the commoner on his corrupt government for food subsidies, for employment, for education and social services, for development, and for the individual's well-being. But the governments are incompetent, illegitimate, bent on staying in power and lacking in a blueprint for resolving the ever-aggravating problems of their countries and societies. The stronger the regimes, by virtue of the modern weaponry, which affords them a superior power of enforcement, the more disaffected are the populations who sense that their government's interests are not theirs; all the more so, since the maintenance of the rulers in place is often made possible by their Western "allies" who provide the money, the economic aid, the weapons, and the food that keep this explosive situation from getting worse and from blowing up in the West's and the regimes' faces. Another paradox develops: because when they are dispossessed, unemployed, and hopelessly classified as have-nots, the masses in those countries not only are victims of their rulers and their Western "allies," and, therefore, feel "entitled" to demand that both provide for their needs, but the more they receive to sustain themselves and ascertain their survival, the more humiliated they become for that dependence, the more enraged they are by it, and the more violent-prone they grow as the only way to air their frustration that only keeps increasing. In other words, the West and the local governments, who are held jointly responsible for the poverty and frustration of which the masses are the victims, not only are expected to alleviate the burden of the impoverished and the disadvantaged, but when they do so are all the more resented and likely to become the targets of the frustration. This is a no-win situation which *inter alia* causes massive departures of immigrants to seek their livelihood or the implementation of their revolutionary dreams elsewhere, notably in the West. Bin Laden, for example, is no less enraged against his own Saudi government, which is sustained by its alliance with the U.S., than against America and Israel. If it is so with a Saudi system, which is not needy, and a Bin Laden who is not impoverished, how much more so with other Arabs and Muslims where both government and people are in dire poverty!!

The eternal victims also believe not only that everyone owes them everything, and they themselves are exempted from any self-strengthening effort, but also that they can use violence to redress the wrong done to them. So, for example, Palestinians who have been living on UNRWA's handouts and sacks of flour for the past sixty years, and where their population in the squalid refugee camps has quadrupled since then, believe it is the duty of the world to continue to feed them indefinitely. They make children and the West has to take care of them. They have resisted all attempts at resettlement in their host countries, which are also Arab and

Muslim, but prefer to leave the refugee problem seething, and to continue to depend on the world's goodwill for survival, rather than force the refugees to take up a constructive life and end their refugee status. They maintain the illusion of the "right of return" in their refugee standing, which is the ultimate victimhood, and they are not about to relinquish it. What is more, the U.S., and other Western countries that shoulder the brunt of the UNRWA budget, are also the most hated and threatened by the Muslim radicals who feed from their hands. If they had learned, if they had been willing to learn, from Western nations and Israel, how to absorb refugees in their own territory and put them on a productive track, rather than to implant in them hatred the mentality of the eternal victims, much of the bitterness and frustration that engender violence and terrorism could have been spared. And this is not only a matter of money or of development (Bin Laden and Saudi Arabia being the ultimate example), but a matter of culture. If one is educated to not accept any handouts, to rise on his feet and help himself, to shed the feeling of victim and be proud of a self- made and self-sustaining livelihood, then one's dignity is restored, the humiliation effaced or diminished, and the paralyzing jealousy and stifling apathy replaced by aspiration, ambition, and striving.

No wonder then that among Palestinians a high ratio was found to support terrorism, which is for them, to be sure, the "right" of the eternal victim to both avenge his situation and to have it redressed. How exactly this will happen, they do not say, unless they think, as part of their world of delusions that we shall address below, that they can bring the West to submission or destroy Israel and replace it. There is also no wonder that al-Qa'ida, the Hamas, Hizbullah, and the rest rationalize their wild terrorism as "retaliation" for their humiliation and victimhood by the strong, the arrogant, and the powerful who had rendered them victims. Therefore, while their terrorism is to be "understood" in their eyes, and justified as the cry of the desperate victim, any Western counterattack or defensive act, must be construed as "aggression" against and "massacre" of the eternal victim. They insist that for every one of their orgies of killing, one must seek the "roots" and comprehend the "reasons," and address the "causes," exactly as for every burning of a church or a synagogue; however, if a mosque is hit, or Muslim children are injured, even incidentally, that is intentional "murder," "desecration," and "blasphemy." For that reason, they do not recognize the difference between intentional damage and collateral casualties. It is the result that counts, no matter what the intention of the enemy planners may have been. America and Israel are always "children killers," "heretics," aggressors, arrogant, and perpetrators of massacres. Americans "killed" Iraqi children by "preventing food and medicaments from reaching them," even if it was Saddam who preferred to purchase weapons or compensate the families of the Palestinian Islamikaze, rather than import food and drugs for the sick. The dead corpses of the Iraqi children were there for display, for if they are clearly the victims, then the Americans must be their killers.

Thus, a reversal of roles is effected, whereby the West and Israel become the "terrorists" and the Muslims the victims thereof; it is the West who terrorizes the Muslim world and is arrogant and condescending towards it, and the Muslims merely act in self-defense. Hence the failure of Muslim countries, including in their Kuala Lumpur Islamic Conference of June 2002, let alone in international gatherings, to accede to the Western definition of terrorism, which is, in essence "the use of violence against innocent civilians to attain political goals." They refuse to relinquish the mantle of victimhood to others, therefore terrorism is what is done to them, not what they do to others. They struggle at all international forums to show that the Palestinians and Hizbullah cannot be considered terrorists, no matter what they do, because they fight for "liberation" from "occupation"; many of them also rationalize the Twin Tower horror as "liberation" from the choking American tutelage, or a "message" to the "real terrorist," which is America (or Israel for that matter), or a "lesson" to the arrogant, or a new "mode of warfare" against the threatening and aggressive West; or the "desire for death" of the audacious Islamikaze martyrs, matching up to the "desire for life and comfort" of the cowardly and decadent West. That is also the reason why they remind America of its own "terrorist attacks" against Hiroshima and Nagasaki, proof that what matters is not what is done, to whom and under what circumstances, but who does it. "Victims of the world, Unite!!!,." if, of course, America or Israel is the reason of your misery.

Other victims, such as the Americans murdered on September 11, or Indians obliterated in Kashmir, or now Ukrainians killed by invading Russia, or Israelis who are blown apart in pizza parlors, or in the bus on their way there, are not victims in the eyes of Muslim radicals, and more and more in the eyes of plain Muslims in general, even when Muslims are the recognized and avowed perpetrators of the terror in all those cases. The victims of terror do not deserve compassion, because they "had brought that upon themselves," or better, "have concocted it themselves" in conjunction with the CIA or the Jews, or the Mossad. The wide acceptance of those theories of conspiracy, including among intellectuals and opinion makers, adds to the universal sense of victimhood that is rampant in the Islamic world. Another important corollary of this attitude is that, while in the Judeo-Christian tradition martyrs are usually the victims of external aggression inflicted on them in the pursuit of their faith, in Islam it is the perpetrator of the aggression, who also immolates himself in the process, who becomes the Islamikaze martyr. In other words, it is not he who suffers death or torture or misery on his way to martyrdom, since he had chosen that course avidly and advisedly, but he who must kill in order to gain his place in the hierarchy of martyrdom. This dramatic shift, from those who were killed in battle or by accident and thereby became martyrs in classical Islam, to the Islamikaze intentional mass-killing of others in order to go to Paradise and enjoy the seventy-two virgins promised by the Qur'an, is the mind-boggling thought that baffles the West today. The hard-core Muslims are therefore shocked that the West battles them and resists them, instead of submitting to them and recognizing that Islam is their only salvation. We have seen appeals to President Bush to convert to Islam and astonishment at his procrastination to do so. They cannot comprehend how and why Westerners are failing to see the light and do not hurry into the fold of Islam. In their world of delusion, they already see "thousands of Americans" repenting for their previous obdurate misunderstanding of Islam, and their "coming to tears when they listen to the Words of the Qur'an recited to them." Their worldview, which cannot accept a plurality of creeds, cannot also understand why they themselves, the disseminators of the good of Allah and His message, should be held in low esteem, feared and persecuted by the West. All they did on September 11 was the fulfillment of the Word of Allah:

> For them [the Unbelievers], garments of fire shall be cut and there shall be poured over their heads boiling water, whereby whatever is in their bowels and skin shall be dissolved and they will be punished with hooked iron rods[106].

Infidels will not only have to live in "disgrace in this life, but in the Day of Judgment, He Shall make them taste the penalty of burning."[107] To have precipitated the Day of Judgment upon the victims of terrorist massacres, was therefore nothing anomalous, just the early fulfillment of the Word of Allah. Then, the stage of denial sets in, as Muslims realize the outrage they caused and the

---

[106] 22: 19-22.

[107] 22:9.

havoc that their delusions have impelled them to commit. Be they acts of terror against Israel, the Karine A weapon smuggling, or the September 11 horror, Muslims first of all denied they ever did, intended, knew, or participated in those acts, paradoxically while at the same time evincing unrestrained jubilation about them. In their stage of denial, they wish both to dissociate themselves from the atrocities they had committed and to "enjoy" their results at the same time. The first major terrorist act against Israel, committed at the height of the Oslo euphoria in mid-1994, for example, when twenty-one young Israeli soldiers were murdered, was immediately denied by Arafat, who "had no knowledge" of it, and as "proof" of his innocence, denounced the "act." In an interview to Israeli media, he speculated that it must have been the "deed of the Israeli security services" who "were interested to wreck the Oslo Agreements." Why wreck them, when the Rabin government who signed them was in power, full of goodwill and leniency towards Palestinian violations, and eager to show to his suspecting constituency in Israel that they "worked," Arafat did not explain. His conspiracy theory and instinctive sense of denial was stronger than any rational consideration he might have invoked. When the *Achille Lauro* was hijacked by Palestinians in the Mediterranean in 1986, and an American citizen was murdered on board and callously tossed into the sea, the sea-jackers retired to Port Said where they were arraigned, but President Mubarak denied that he had any knowledge of the mastermind of that terrorist act, at the same time that he gave him shelter in his country. The affair of the ship Karine A, which in early 2002 was seized by the Israeli Navy in the Red Sea, illicitly carrying weapons to the Palestinians, under the command of one of Arafat's associates, was totally denied by Arafat and the Palestinian Authority as an "Israeli plot." Then when presented by the facts and when he shipment of weapons was exposed to world media, Arafat said that he "had no knowledge of it personally," and only when he was confronted with the documents he had personally signed, did he have no choice but apologize to President Bush.

In the aftermath of September 11, similar patterns of behavior were detected in the Muslim world. In spite of their joy that they could not contain, Muslims from Pakistan to America, from Egypt to Afghanistan, denied that any Muslim could "commit such horror," because it was patently against "the compassion and tolerance of Islam," and verses were cited in support of that contention, such as that Islam "was opposed to compulsion in faith," or to the execution of "innocent civilians," unless they challenged Islam or "humiliated it." (Since the perpetrators claimed that they were humiliated by America, their acts were then justified). They also contended that an act of terror of such proportions could not possibly have been planned, let alone executed, by any Muslim state or organization, thus exonerating themselves in advance, even if that implied their admitting their incompetence in carrying out operations of such a scale. Even as the evidence was being gathered and divulged of the Qai'da involvement, and demands were mounting for its indictment, they continued to insist that "unless America provided decisive and undisputed evidence for Muslim involvement," it was wrong on the part of the West to "smear the entire Muslim world," (which was "opposed to terrorism", as we know, in any case), on account of the "yet unproven" deeds of the few. And so, the roles were again reversed: the Muslims, who needed no evidence for their delusions, and never stop to reflect on the irrationality of their accusations against the West and Israel, suddenly became scrupulous about "evidence," when the accusations are laid at their door. And so they found themselves pledging that should any evidence emerge of Muslim involvement, the culprits ought to be pursued to "Muslim justice," and dealt with according to Muslim legal procedures, which meant in effect exonerating Muslims altogether. But the facts kept pressing at the door, and when the Muslim claims of "innocence" became ludicrous in the eyes of world opinion, the stage of projection and laying the blame on others began. As in the cases where Israelis were accused by Palestinians of "provocations" in mounting terrorism against their own citizens in order to blame the "innocent and peace-loving Palestinians," or of concocting the Karine A arm smuggling in order to smear the Palestinian "impeccable reputation" of "law-abiding" and of "respect for its commitments," the Muslim world orchestrated a campaign of projection on others of the evils of September 11. First, it was claimed by Muslims in Egypt and Pakistan, America and Saudi Arabia, that the Jews, the CIA or the Israeli Mossad "did it," with countless "indications" indicting, successively or simultaneously, either or all of them. Again, becoming suddenly meticulous about "data gathering" and the provision of "conclusive evidence," they began to fabricate piecemeal fantastic stories about Israelis or Jews who "had been pre-warned and evacuated the premises of the Twin Towers prior to the blast," or the takeover of control towers by "suspect elements," also presumably Jewish, who "collaborated with the hijackers," or other hoaxes that never cease to raise our admiration for the boundless imagination of their inventers. Indeed, even though the reality of Muslim day dreaming is not itself limited by imagination, it proves to us to be more fantastic than their fantasies. From the concept of imagination we often use the positive derivative of the "imaginative," but they are bent on the "imaginary," which seems to fill their world and satisfy their emotions. In this Kafkaesque world of the unreal, only non-Muslims are supposed to be sin, and therefore anything projected on them is either true, or could be true even if it is not proven.

This is the foundation of the vicious and sustained campaigns of denigration and diminishment of the West and the Jews in Muslim circles, countries, and societies, that we commonly call incitement and that is the prerequisite for terrorism against them. Incitement often means delegitimation of the enemy, making them look corrupt, decadent, an inherent enemy of Islam and Allah, and therefore deserving of annihilation through terror. To that end, any means is suitable, even inventing lies, making up false quotations from non existent sources, like the "citations" by Palestinians in their text books of "passages" that never were, which "prove" the Jewish conspiracy, its "evil," and its ill-intentions against Islam and the rest of humanity; or the ritual repetition of the blood libel as a fact of history, or liberal quotations from the forged *Protocols of the Sages of Zion* as true documents, etc. It seems amazing to us that they care little not only for the truth as long as it serves their goals of libeling Israel and the West, but even less about educating their children on falsehoods and training them to consider imaginary texts as "citations."[108] In May 2002, when the Israeli armed forces launched their Defensive Shield Operation against terrorist bases in Jenin, which was led extremely carefully and sparingly with regard to civilians, the Palestinians immediately shouted: "Foul Game!" They had conducted a series of murderous attacks against Israeli civilians, and blown up one hundred of them within one week, including during the Passover Seder in April 2002, where entire families were wiped out (29 killed in all), and that passed in the Palestinian public as a matter of routine; but when Israel decided to root out the bases of terror in the West Bank, immediate accusations of "aggression" and "massacres" began, echoed by the Arab and Muslim press, (and also by the European press, and the numbers of "massacred" people kept increasing, reaching the peak of 5,000 according to Saeb Arekat, the Chief Palestinian negotiator. Then it turned out that "only" 50 Palestinians were killed in that center of terror, and for the most part amid very heavy fighting where 22 Israeli fighters lost their lives. There was no massacre, in short.

Similarly, when the Americans opened their counterattack against the Taliban, and thoughtfully attempted not to harm civilians, to the extent possible, in the process, and even dropped

---

[108] e.g., Raphael Israeli "Identity and State-building: Educating Palestinian Children after Oslo," *Journal of Terrorism and Political Violence,* Spring 2002.

significant quantities of food to sustain them during the fighting, it was the stories of "massacres" of "innocent civilians," "poisoning of the dropped food parcels," the "intentional bombing of schools and food depots," the "cruel arrest of Taliban POW's" and their transport to Guantanamo where they were treated "inhumanly" like "the Nazis would," that dominated the Arab and Muslim reporting of the operation, not the intentional atrocities committed by the Taliban themselves and their supporters. Like in the "Jenin massacre" that never was, in the second Lebanese war of 2006 and the Gaza war of 2008-9, never were the acts which the Hamas and the Hizbullah did to trigger the fighting mentioned. For the Arab and Muslim audiences in all these cases, the story was not about reporting a balanced truth, where the evils, intentional or incidental, and motivations of both parties were recounted, and where the cause and effect sequence had to be explained, of horrendous terrorist attacks against civilians which had to be retaliated against and rooted out, but only about the "callous and senseless American and Israeli aggressive attacks against civilians," without reason or cause, just to satisfy the evil instincts of Bush and Sharon. For them, vilifying, debasing, calumniating, and libeling their enemies was the only way to delegitimize them as inhuman predators, so as to pave the way for future additional terrorist attacks against them. Projecting on the enemy, by heaping lies and pipe-dreams against him, by the way of pure and primitively simple incitement, however, does not only permit his delegitimation and encourages more attacks against him, but also, more significantly, belies and exposes the hidden dreams of what the Muslims would do to the Americans and the Israelis, if they could. Projection-cum-incitement, therefore, reveal to the West what fate is awaiting him, should the Muslim world win this confrontation. Wasn't it the Secretary General of the Arab League, 'Azzam Pasha, who declared on the day the Arab armies invaded nascent Israel in 1948 in order to eliminate it, that a "massacre would ensue that the world had never seen since the

Mongols"? He meant a massacre of the Jews, exactly as the Muslim terrorists mean and implement today, but instead of piecemeal by terrorism—in one big stroke.

Thus, while Americans and Israelis, in their reprisals in self-defense, have espoused the strategy of saving civilian lives to the extent possible, and would rather fight surgically, at the risk of their own casualties, to minimize the enemy's civilian losses, rather than blanket-bomb entire cities or population centers, Muslim terrorists act differently. Their stated aim is to maximize civilian casualties in the enemy's ranks, as evidenced in the Twin Towers and in the massive explosions in crowded civilian places in Israel, where nails and bolts are added to the bombs for maximal effect, and sometimes poisonous substances are tucked on to the bombs for added damage. In other words, while the West operates with a considerable restraint of its forces, for fear of their devastating impact, Muslim terrorists act with the maximum unleashing of their power, something that leads to the fear in the West that they would not hesitate to use unconventional weapons if they laid their hands on them. That is exactly the soft-belly of the West, which ties in with its concern for human life, for due process of law and restraint in using power, which the Muslim terrorists who are not shackled by those limitations seek to exploit and strike at. To make that happen, roles are once again reversed: "We are not the terrorists!!!, You are!!!," they shout at the West. For, what Muslim martyrs do in terms of wanton killing, is not only justified, because it is in the Path of Allah, but by delegitimizing the West as terrorist itself, the fight against it is called for, and to be fought by all means available to the Muslims, precisely those that the West has restrained itself from using.

Sheikh Qaradawi has made some stunning statements not only about politics but also about social issues that hardly qualify him or his followers as moderate. He said, for example,

> [John] Kerry, who ran against Bush in the 2004

> elections, was supported by homosexuals and nudists. But it was Bush who won, because he is Christian, right wing, tenacious and unyielding. In other words, the religious overcame the pervert. So we cannot blame all Americans and westerners. But unfortunately, because the westerners… want to flatter these people on account of the elections, disaster strikes. In order to succeed and win the elections, he flatters these people, rather than saying to them:" No you are sinning against yourselves, against society, and against humanity. This is forbidden. … Lesbians and homosexuals should be punished the same punishment as any sexual pervert, the same as any fornicator. The schools of thought disagree about the punishment. Some say they should be punished like fornicators, and then we distinguish between married and unmarried men, and between married and unmarried women. Some say both should be punished the same way. Some say we should throw them from a high place, like God did to the people of Sodom. Some say we should burn them, and so on,. There is disagreement. The important thing is to treat this act as a crime… Lesbianism is not as bad as homosexuality, in practical terms.[109]

If these are the envisaged punishments to be meted out to Muslim sinners, how much more so for Unbelievers who were deemed as sinning towards Muslims! One of the most respected Deobandi scholars believes that aggressive military Jihad should be waged by Muslims "to establish the supremacy of Islam " worldwide. Justice Muhammed Taqi Usmani argues that Muslims should live peacefully in countries such as Britain, where they have the freedom to

[109] Interviews with Sheikh Qaradawi,:"Homosexuals Should be Punished like Fornicators, but their Harm is less when not done in Public", *Al-Jazseera,* 5 June, 2005. Taped on video by Memri 1170, 5 June, 2006.

practice Islam, only until they gain enough power to engage in battle. His views explode the myth that the creed of offensive, expansionist Jihad represents a distortion of traditional Islamic thinking. Usmani sat for 20 years as a *shari'a* judge in Pakistan's Supreme Court, and has been an adviser to several global financial institutions. Polite and soft spoken, he revealed to *The Times* a detailed knowledge of world events and his words, for the most part, were balanced and considered. He agreed that it was wrong to suggest that the entire non-Muslim world was intent on destroying Islam. Yet, this is a man who, in his published work, argues the case for Muslims to wage an expansionist war against non-Muslim lands. Usmani's justification for aggressive military Jihad as a means of establishing global Muslim supremacy is the climax of his book, *Islam and Modernism.* The work is a polemic against Islamic modernists who seek to convert the entire Qur'an into "a poetic and metaphorical book", because, says he, "they have been bewitched by western culture and ideology". The final chapter delivers a rebuke to those who believe that only defensive Jihad is permissible in Islam. He refutes the suggestion that Jihad is unlawful against a non-Muslim state that freely permits the preaching of Islam. For Usmani, the question is whether aggressive battle is by itself commendable or not. If it is, he contends, then "why should the Muslims stop simply because territorial expansion is considered there days as bad? And if it is not commendable, but deplorable, why did Islam not stop it in the past". He answers his own question thus: "Even in those days, aggressive Jihads were waged... because they were truly commendable to establish the grandeur of the religion of Allah". These words are not the product of a radical fanatic, they come from the pen of one of the most acclaimed modern scholars of Islam.[110]

---

[110] .Andrew Norfolk, "Our Followers must live in Peace until Strong enough to wage Jihad", *The Times,* 8 September, 2007.

There is no prospect of resisting and surviving this wave of renewed Muslim proclivity for confrontation and triumphalism unless one defines facts and events unequivocally and sets one's mind on facing them without recoiling. No other groups of people, no adherents of any other faith have so relentlessly vowed to destroy western culture in general, and Israel in particular, as modern Muslims have. The repeated pledges of Iran's Ahmadinejad, who has nothing to do with the Arab-Israeli conflict, to "wipe Israel off the map" for purely Islamic reasons, have perhaps blunted the sensitivity of world peace and human rights champions, who beyond the ritual statement that this is "unacceptable", have done nothing to oust the culprit from the international community of civilized nations or to discontinue their business with him. There are plenty of poor and frustrated people in the *favelas* of South America,, the shack cities of Asia and the jungles of Africa. But in none of them is this unstoppable desire to kill westerners and Jews as evident and manifest as in the case of Muslims and their Islamikaze vanguards. Western countries have tried in vain to skirt the issue of Islamic terrorism in the hope that it might disappear. But it did not. Only a clear western definition of what constitutes terrorism, which has to be announced, not negotiated, can indicate the decision of civilized nations to stand fast against this aggressive mood which nurtures Jihad. In Muslim eyes, terrorism is what is done to them, like the US in Iraq, NATO in Afghanistan, Israel in Palestine and Lebanon, and India in Kashmir. What Muslims do is only self-defense, therefore they can never be accused of terrorism, meaning that any violent act committed by Muslims is justified by definition, because they are oppressed, humiliated and frustrated by the western rivals. While the west pursues the means-oriented criterion to define terrorism, namely that regardless of the goals or motives of terrorists, noble as they may be to them, innocent civilians cannot be harmed intentionally and indiscriminately, Muslim countries systematically reject this concept. For them, in the "struggle against tyranny and injustice", all means are acceptable and none of them is deemed illicit. For the citizens of western countries and Israel, who share the "unjust and tyrannical" regimes of their countries, cannot be deemed "innocent", and are in their thinking "permissible".

For many Muslims there is even a Qur'anic justification for terrorism *(irhab)* against Unbelievers, since the Holy text prescribes to Muslims to sow *irhab* in the hearts of the enemy. And since the enemy is identified as Israel or the west in general, that in itself provides a doctrinal rationalization of terrorism. Iran, Pakistan, Syria, the Palestinian Authority and others continue to give shelter to terrorists, but they are rather proud of doing that, and no longer embarrassed. For the Iranians, al-Qa'ida, the Hizbullah, the Hamas and such, encouraging terrorism is simply a practical manifestation of their doctrinal convictions and commitments. One should not be fooled by this double talk which reflects the Muslim state of mind. Even when they dispatch or *post-factum* approve of, acts of obvious terrorism which they call "martyrdom", i.e. praiseworthy and religiously sanctioned deeds (like Islamikaze), for the sake of Allah, that cannot be, by definition called "terrorism", which is a downgraded and damnable mode of action in the West. That is the reason why whenever a major terrorist attack by Muslims is perpetrated against the west or Israel, there is jubilation in the Muslim street, regardless of the numbers of innocent civilian victims. That is also the reason that UN attempts to come to a unified definition of terror in order to optimize the world battle against it has fallen on death ears, as long as all Muslim countries insist that "resistance" against "occupiers" is not terrorism, and when they admit it is, then it is of the worthy martyrdom kind. Muslims reserve to themselves the right to define who is an occupier, be it Israel in Palestine, India in Kashmir, Russia in Chechnya, the US in Iraq, NATO in Afghanistan. In a Muslim conference in Stockholm, Qaradawi made his differentiations, specifying that Islamikaze attacks (what we erroneously call "suicide bombings, and consider the epitome of terrorism) are not only permitted in Islamic law, but condoned and recommended. His main arguments were summed up in a major Arabic medium published in London[111]

In view of their understanding of the present state of affairs, Muslim militants have drawn several lessons and they prepared a blueprint for the confrontation with the west, which in its gradually emerging details is proving quite popular with the masses of Muslims in general, who are in no mood of compromise and accommodation. The sense that Allah has been blessing their venture is so deeply rooted in their hearts that they fear no fatigue, and they do not recoil from implementing their plan even if, or precisely because, there seem to be obstacles and difficulties on the way to realization. For Allah had tested in the past many of his followers and he ultimately ensured their victory, as one of his many names (*al-Nasser* – the Victorious) connotes. Victory is sought and nothing less. The Muslims who wish to confront the West and Israel are equipped with the requisite faith, zeal and enthusiasm, as the acronym of *Hamas (*the Islamic Resistance Movement) indicates; they are boundlessly devoted to Allah, as their various Hizbullah (Party of God) groups profess; are determined to pursue their *da'wa (*Mission, Call) the world over, as many of their organizations mention; are intent to wage a merciless Jihad in their "peaceful" messages demanding surrender are not heeded by their enemies, as many of their associations ("Islamic Jihad") remind us; and lastly, many of of them are coordinated by the main base (*al-Qa'ida),* physical and spiritual, which used to train candidates for Islamikaze, finance their operations, plan their schemes and initiate the time and place of their spectacular strikes. Admittedly, after the temporary defeat of the Taliban in Afghanistan, al-Qa'ida is no longer what it was, and its activities have been largely decentralized, but the flame was not extinguished as evidenced by the spectacular comeback of the

---

111 *Al-Sharq al-Awsat,,* 19 July, 2003. These passages are translated and summarized in R. Israeli, *Muslim Minorities,in the Modern States,* Transaction, N.J., 2009, pp. 101-103.

Mujahideen in the fields of Qandahar, Helmand and Jalalabad during the US and NATO 20 year struggle there.

While Muslim ambitions and desires are expressed and fought for by a handful of radical Muslims, who defy the superiority of the West and are not deterred from a long war of attrition, whatever it takes, surrounded and encouraged by the sympathy of most Muslims who sit on the sidelines and applaud on occasion the victories of their coreligionists, the components of the Muslim blueprint, which are shared by most Muslims can be summarized as follows:

1. The west must be defeated, or at least weakened, frightened and put on the defensive. For not only does the West corrupt the Muslim world with its debauchery, permissiveness, alliance with certain Muslim countries and its value-less societies, but by its posing a luring alternative to young Muslims, with its immodest dress, co-ed education, pop music, pornography, mixed partying and frolicking, alcohol, and western movies, it threatens the next generation of Muslims. Naturally, militant Muslims, with the acquiescent silent support of conservatives, dread the prospect of their societies slipping from under their grip and supervision. Therefore they enlist for their endeavor any Allah-fearing Muslim, who though not necessarily of their affiliation, is concerned, like them, about the rapid drift of the young towards modernity and the West. This matter is particularly acute in the Palestinian territories, where they daily frictions with the Israelis make them more prone to such a deviation from traditional Muslim norms.

2. A first step towards the goal of defeating the west is to cultivate the rift between pro-Arab, pro- Muslim Europe, on the one hand, and "Zionist-controlled America" on the other. Thus, while both belong to the evil west, it is imperative to go easy on Europe for now, due to its assistance, both directly to

the Muslim world, and indirectly by diminishing America's power and somehow keeping it in check. This policy has proven a success for the time being, inasmuch as the European Council has been openly favoring the Palestinians over the Israelis despite American misgivings, while the Muslims have succeeded in enlisting the European to their side in the Balkans (in Bosnia, Kosovo, Macedonia). The Muslims have even managed to engage the US in implementing jointly with NATO those European-Muslim designs. The change of government in the US, with the seemingly more engaging policy of Obama on the one hand, and the schism within the Palestinian people between the western-supported PLO and Muslim-supported Hamas, seem to dictate new adaptations of this policy orientation.

3. Europe's turn will come after America is driven out of its hegemonic status in the world and Israel is eliminated. Muslim radicals speak about their own *reconquista* in Europe, first of the territories that used to be under Muslim rule (Andalusia, southern France, Sicily) and then the rest of the continent. A special awareness of this turn of events has been evident among North African immigrants into Europe who are conscious of the historical reversal that has been under way. Indications of such a scheme dawned on the Europeans on the morrow of September 11, after which several major Islamic terrorist strikes were foiled in Paris, Strasbourg and Brussels. Al-Qa'ida bases and undercover lodges exist in practically all European capitals and can be activated when time comes, as has been the case with the many terrorist attacks in Spain, England and Germany since. Part and parcel of preparing for the showdown in Europe has been both testing the ground for the eventual Muslim takeover, first of the vestiges of Spanish colonial rule (Ceuta and Melilla) and some islands in the Mediterranean, and increasing the numbers of

Muslim migrants to Europe. The upward of 30 million Muslims in Europe of the 27 today, who constitute between 5 and 10% of the population in virtually all European countries, hasten to take up political rights individually, and then will begin to demand cultural and group rights. Only the reversal, of late, of the liberal multi-cultural policies in countries like Holland and England, may begin to check that trend.

4. And above all the US, which by its military and economic power not only dominates the west and leads it but also attempts to battle Islam into submission (at least until Obama's advent to power), protects Israel and serves its purposes, and produces and disseminates the decadent sub-culture which arouses the wrath of Islam. The US is deemed to be the first model of emulation for youth all over the world, including Muslims, and this circumstance is purported to be the reason for all the ills of the world. If America cannot be reduced to submission, then at least it can be battered, threatened, humiliated and weakened, to the extend that it would no longer be able to protect its citizens and its interests around the world. The rationale and purpose behind this outlook is so that its many allies, primarily Europe, Israel and the illegitimate Muslim regimes it sustains, would no longer trust the UN and rely on it. America is also singled out by the militants for being the only power that can, and is willing, to block effectively the fulfillment of their schemes. Hence the hatred of America, first and foremost, which is decried by the slogans and the propaganda statements of the militants, and also by the massive acts of terror committed against it.

5. Pending the anticipated Muslim victory, much long term groundwork is required, which the Muslim radicals wholeheartedly support and initiate, and even push Muslim governments

and Muslim individuals to fund. The list is long: recruiting new converts in the West, lending financial support to families of martyred Islamikaze, raising money, either through bogus charitable organizations in the West, to be used against it, or from donor states or individuals (Saudi Arabia and wealthy sheikhs in the Gulf), erecting mosques and Islamic centers and *madrasas* in world capitals and significant concentrations of Muslims worldwide, ostensibly for Muslim populations in the west, but diverting their use to conversion programs, indoctrination, and the diffusion of hatred and propaganda, and recruitment of Islamikaze for martyrdom operations. They also use the funds to strengthen already Muslim countries of the periphery, like Central Asia, Indonesia, and raising Muslim consciousness among the Muslim minorities of Nepal, Thailand, India, Israel, Europe and America. It is the fruit of such endeavors which supports the Taliban in the *madrasas* of Pakistan, the Shi'ite fanatics in the religious schools of Qum in Iran, the Hizbullah in the Lebanese fields of opium, the Islamikaze terrorists in Afghanistan, and the mosques of Europe and America, from whence emerged the planners and executors of September 11.

6. Jews, and by inference Israel and Zionism, have to be eliminated, according to this conviction, as Bin-Laden, Iran, Hamas, Hizbullah and ISIS have vowed. They are accused of having invaded the lands of Islam in Palestine, established the Zionist state, which in effect tore off a valuable piece of *dar-al-Islam* and turned it into *dar- al Harb,* which requires Jihad for retrieval. The Jews constitute a western salient in the midst of Islamic society which they intend to corrupt and undermine from within. The Jews stand accused of desecrating the holy places of Islam in Jerusalem with a view to insulting Muslims. And, most dangerous of all, they act as the American agent in the Middle East, hence their close links to Washington, to the extent that

makes it hard to determine who is subservient to whom. For all these reason, Jews are targets not only in their Israeli state, but worldwide, as the frequent attacks against them, throughout their world diasporas, have demonstrated.

Andre Malraux, the great French luminary of the first half of the 20th Century, saw before most others the coming of the aggressive wave of Islam in the contemporary world. It is worthwhile citing his immortal words:

> The violence of the Muslim rise is the great phenomenon of our era. Underestimated by most of our contemporaries, it can be compared to the beginnings of Communism under Lenin, and the full extent of its impact is still impossible to predict. At the beginning of the Marxist Revolution, the belief was prevalent that problems could be patched up by improvised solutions. But neither Christianity nor organizations of employers of employees could find the answers. Similarly, the world does not seem today able to face the problem of Islam, which seems to be even more difficult to confront. Maybe the limited French aspect thereof could be tackled if there were a real statesman around to deal with it. The impression is that various forms of Muslim dictatorship will prevail in the Arab world. When I say "Muslim" I do not think necessarily of religious, but of civil structures emanating from Mohammed's doctrine. Already now, the Moroccan Sultan, as well as President Bourguiba [of Tunisia], are acting as dictators of sorts. It may be that current problems could have been patched up if they had been undertaken in time... But its is already too late. "*Les miserables* " have nothing to lose any more, they will prefer to preserve their misery

within their Muslim communities, and their lot will probably remain unchanged. We regard them from a Western angle, but they will probably prefer their own future to the welfare that we pretend we are able to bring them. Black Africa will not stay for long indifferent to this process, and all we can do is to become cognizant of the gravity of this phenomenon and try to postpone its breaking point[112].

[112] Andre Malraux, 3 June, 1956, cited in *Valeurs Actuelles,* Paris, December 2001.

# Bibliography

## *Foundational Documents, Written and Electronic Media, Books and Articles*


**Foundational Documents**

The Holy Book of the Qur'an

The Holy Bible

UN Document-.HR/IP/SEM/1999/1 (Part I), 15 March, 1999

The Charter of the Hamas

**Written and Electronic Media**

*Actualites Juives Hebdo.*

*Akhbar al-Yaum (Kuwait),*

*Al-Ahram Weekly*

*Al- Ayyam (*Yemen*)*

*Al-Gumhuriyya,* 7 October, 2001. See MEMRI 289, 19 October, 2001.

*al-Islam wa-Filastin*

*Al-Istiqlal (*the Weekly of Islamic Jihad in Gaza)

*Al-Jazseera*

*Al-Masri al-Yaum*

*Al Quds al-Arabi* (London.

*Al-Sharq al-Awsat*

*Al-Risalah,* (Gaza

*China Reform Monitor*

*Christian Science Monitor*

*City Journal*
*Daily Telegraph*
*Executive Intelligence Review*
*French News Agency* (AFP)
*haaretz.com*
*Inquiry & Analysis Series*
*Jerusalem Issue Brief*
*Jerusalem Letter*
*Le Figaro*
*MEMRI (*Middle East Media Report)
*Middle East Times, issue 13, 1999*
*National Post*
Official PA daily *Al-Hayat Al-Jadida,*
*Online Journalism Review, November 15, 1999*
PMW (Palestinian Media Watch)
*Post Holocaust and Antisemitism,*
*RSA Journal*
*Sawt al-Haq wa-l-Hurriya*
*Special Report of INSS* (Israeli Institute of Strategic Studies)
*Terrorism and Political Violence*
*The Times*
*Valeurs Actuelles*

**Books**

Alexander, Y. (ed.) *The 1988-89 Annual of Terrorism*, Martinus Nijhoff, 1990, The Netherlands, pp. 99-134.

Bartal, Dr. *The Fedayeen Emerge, The Palestine-Israel Conflict, 1949–1956* (Bloomington,Authorhouse, 2011.

Bat Ye'or *The Dhimmi,* Fairleigh Dickinson, 1985.

Bat Ye'or, *the Decline of Eastern Christianity under Islam,* as above 1996.

Bat Ye'or, *Islam and Dhimmitude,* as above, 2002.

Bat Ye'or, *Eurabia,,* as above, 2006.

Green, D.F, *Arab Theologians on Jews and Israel: The Fourth Conference of the Academy of Islamic Research*, Editions de l'Avenir, Geneva, 1974.

Israeli, Raphael, *Peace is in the Eye of the Beholder,* Mouton, Berlin and NY, 1985.

Israeli, Raphael *Islam and Israel,* University Press of America, ch. 7, pp. 123-170.

Israeli, Raphael, *Islamikaze: Manifestations of Islamic Martyrology*, Frank Cass, London, 2003, pp. 443-447.

Israeli, Raphael, *Green Crescent Over Nazarerth: The Displacement of Christians by Muslims in the Holy Land,* Frank Cass, London, 2004.

Israeli, Raphael, *Muslim Minorities in Modern States,* Transaction, NJ 2003.

Israeli, Raphael. *Muslim anti-Semitism in Christian Europe: Elemental and Residual anti-Semitism,* Transaction, New Jersey, 2009.

Israeli, Raphael, *Itinerant Jihadis:Arab and Muslim War Volunteers,* Strategic Books, TX, 2011.

Israeli, Raphael, *Hatred, Lies and Violence in the Islamic World,* Transaction, NJ, 2013

Israeli, Raphael, *The Death Camps of Croatia:Visions and Revisions: 1941-5*, Transaction, NJ, 2013.

Israeli, Raphael, *Years of Upheaval: Axial Changes in Islam in 1989,* Transaction, NJ, 2016

Israeli, Raphael, *Paranoia, Inferiority Complex and Fanaticism: The Case of Islamic Attitudes Towards Jews,* Strategic Books, TX, 2018

Israeli, Raphael, *Black Upon White: American Racism and Black Dignity,* Strategic Books, Tx, 2020.

Israeli, Raphael, *Glittering Stars in a Dark Landscape,* Strategic Books, TX, 2020.

Israeli, Raphael, *The Rebellion of the Dhimmis,* Strategic Books, 2022.

Israeli, Raphael, *Human Rights and Human Development in Arab and Islamic Lands,* Strategic Books, TX, 2022.

Israeli,Raphael, *Duplicitous Constitutions in Arab and Islamic Lands,* Lambert Academic Press, Dusseldorf, 2022-3.

Khadduri, Majid, *War and Peace in Islam.* Johns Hopkins, 1969.

Kuntzel, Matthias *Jihad and Jew-hatred:Islamism, Nazism and the Roots of 9/11, T*elos Press, 2007.

Lively, Scott and Kevin Abrams: *The Pink Swastika:Homosexuality in the Nazi Party*, The Founders Corporation, Oregon, 1995.

*Qira'a fi Fiqh al-Shahada, (*Readings in Islamic Martyrology) was published on 5 June 1988, as a special addendum to *al-Islam wa-Filastin* (Islam and Palestine) that appeared in Nocosia, Cyprus, and has been the ideological supporter of the Palestinian Islamikaze operations against Israel.

Salsal, Boualem, *Gouverner au nom d'Allah:Islamization et Soif de Pouvoir dans le Monde Arabe,* Gallimard, Paris, 2013.

Waite, Robert, *Vanguard of Nazism:: The Free Corps Movement in Post[W W I] War Germany, 1918-23,* Norton and Company, NY, 1969.

Waite, Robert, *The Psychopathic God Adolf Hitler*, Signet Books NY, 1977

**Articles**

Ayman, Poet, "Poem against Israel", *Al-Istiqlal (*the Weekly of Islamic Jihad in Gaza), 13 December, 2001.

Barkan,. "The Islamic Movement in Israel: Switching Focus from Jerusalem to the Palestinian Cause," Inquiry & Analysis Series, report no. 628, Middle East Media Research Institute, Washington, DC, July 30, 2010.

"Beyond the Vacuum," *Al-Ahram Weekly*, April 13–16, 2006.

Eisenman, Dr. (ed.), *China Reform Monitor* 1496, February 23, 2022, Washington DC.

Gerstenfeld, Manfred, "Antisemitism: Integral to European Culture", in *Post Holocaust and Antisemitism,* No 19, 1 April, 2004,

p. 4, published by the Jerusalem Center of Public Affairs.

Ginat, Gitit " Freedom fighter", *www.haaretz.com* – 18 May, 2006

Hirsch, Maurice "When you lack any History, just Invent one", PMW, Sep 4, 2022.

Israeli, Raphael, "The Charter of Allah: The Platform of the Islamic Resistance Movement" in Y. Alexander (ed.) *The 1988-89 Annual of Terrorism*, Martinus Nijhoff, 1990, The Netherlands, pp. 99-134.

Israeli, Raphael, "Islamikaze and their Significance", in *Terrorism and Political Violence*, Frank Cass, London, Fall 1997, pp. 96-121.

Israeli, Raphael "The Islamic Movement in Israel," *Jerusalem Letter*, Jerusalem Center for Public Affairs, Oct. 15, 1999.

Israeli, Raphael, "Identity and State-building: Educating Palestinian Children after Oslo," *Journal of Terrorism and Political Violence*, Spring 2002.

Kawach, Nadim, "Arab food gap crosses $180bn over past decade,"*Emirates 24/7*, June 27, 2010. http://www.emirates247.com/eb247/.

economy/uae-economy/arab-food-gap-crosses-180bn-over-pastdecade-2010-06-27-1.259717.

Kerry, Secretary John, "Press Conference at the State Dpt", 17 October, 2014, broadcast live worldwide.

Kuperwasser, Yossi *The Jerusalem Issue Brief, Vol. 22, No. 5, March 21, 2022,* the Jerusalem Center for Public Affairs.

Lavi, Galia, "Interview with Y. Schihor: American Interests Affect the Changes in Israel-China Relations", *Special Report of INSS* (Israeli Institute of Strategic Studies), Tel-Aviv University, Aug.8, 2022.

Lewis, Bernard, "How did the Infidels Win?," *National Post*, June 1, 2002.

Macartney, Jane, "Rebiya Kadeer Accused of Being behind Uighur Violence in East Turkestan," *The Times,* July 7, 2009; and The

Times Online July 14, 2009.

Malraux, Andre, 3 June, 1956, cited in *Valeurs Actuelles,* Paris, December 2001.

Meyer, Claude, "Interview with Jean-Claude Milner" the author of *The Criminal Inclinations of Democratic Europe), in Actualites Juives Hebdo, No 823, No 823,* 11 December, 2003. Cited by Manfred Gerstenfeld, "Antisemitism: Integral to European Culture", in *Post Holocaust and Antisemitism,* No 19, 1 April, 2004, p. 4, published by the Jerusalem Center of Public Affairs.

Moore, Malcolm, "The Uighur Issue", *Daily Telegraph,* July 14, 2009.

Norfolk, Andrew, "Our Followers must live in Peace until Strong enough to wage Jihad", *The Times,* 8 September, 2007.

Pipes, Daniel, "Fighting Militant Islam, Without Bias," *City Journal,* Autumn 2001. http://www.city-journal.org/htm/41/fightingmilitant.html.

Qaradawi, Sheikh Yussuf (interviews with):"Homosexuals Should be Punished like Fornicators, but their Harm is less when not done in Public", *Al-Jazseera,* 5 June, 2005. Taped on video by Memri 1170, 5 June, 2006.

Salsal, Boualem, "La fatwa de l'Iran contre Salman Rushdie attente à toute l'humanité" (Iran's fatwa against Salman Rushdie amounts to a life attempt against all humanity) *Le Figaro*, 20 August, 2022.

Sharon, Moshe, "*Hudna* and *Sulh* in Islam" (Hebrew), *Nativ,* Summer 2002.

Turabi, Hassan, "Islam and a Pan-National Movement", *RSA Journal,* August-September, 1992, pp. 608-19.

# Analytical Index

## *Names, Places, Events and Terms*

**G-H-I-J**

Review Requested:
If you loved this book, would you please provide a review at Amazon.com?

CPSIA information can be obtained
at www.ICGtesting.com
Printed in the USA
LVHW100343011222
734242LV00009B/56